THE NEW TRIPLE CONSTRAINTS FOR SUSTAINABLE PROJECTS, PROGRAMS, AND PORTFOLIOS

THE NEW TRIPLE CONSTRAINTS FOR SUSTAINABLE PROJECTS, PROGRAMS, AND PORTFOLIOS

GREGORY T. HAUGAN

CRC Press
Taylor & Francis Group
Boca Raton   London   New York

CRC Press is an imprint of the
Taylor & Francis Group, an **informa** business
AN AUERBACH BOOK

CRC Press
Taylor & Francis Group
6000 Broken Sound Parkway NW, Suite 300
Boca Raton, FL 33487-2742

First issued in paperback 2019

© 2013 by Taylor & Francis Group, LLC
CRC Press is an imprint of Taylor & Francis Group, an Informa business

No claim to original U.S. Government works

ISBN-13: 978-1-4665-0518-6 (hbk)
ISBN-13: 978-0-367-38105-9 (pbk)

Visit the Taylor & Francis Web site at
http://www.taylorandfrancis.com

and the CRC Press Web site at
http://www.crcpress.com

To my grandchildren and great-grandchildren,

who will have to help make this world a better place despite population,

climate change, and energy problems.

Seth, Jessica, Katie, Jason, Buckey, Mike, Alexandra,

Nicholas, Erika, Jonathon, Jeffrey, and Alia

Contents

SECTION III Energy Overlay

SECTION IV   Supporting Appendices

Preface

For several years, in addition to extensive work in project management, I have been active as an instructor in adult education programs for a local community college and making presentations to local churches and civic groups on the topics addressed in this book. I have been teaching short courses exploring issues in oil and energy, global warming, and climate change. It has been illuminating to see how poorly informed people are on these major issues, considering the current and potential impacts on their lives.

I am active in volunteer work for my local county government where I led the development of the current county Comprehensive Plan and was active in the revision of the current zoning ordinances. Some of my activities were the development of zoning overlays for the historic district, the protection of land for reservoirs, for highway traffic flow, and other special purposes. The concept of a set of sustainability overlays addressing the new triple constraints of population, climate change, and energy applied to the existing project management triple constraints of cost, schedule, and quality/performance arose from that experience.

This book is geared toward two segments of the professional population: first, the 350,000 members of the Project Management Institute (PMI®) and hundreds of thousands of other project, program, and portfolio managers who are just beginning to realize that the historic planning paradigm has changed, but don't have a reliable source or the time to track down the facts:* and second, the many managers who are responsible for organization strategic plans who normally would use extrapolations of historic data as their bases for projecting into the future. This book provides a series of overlays of major changes occurring in population, climate, and energy areas that are not indexed to history but to changes currently occurring that collectively represent a major turning point in world use of resources and the necessity to seek sustainability. This book is also geared toward the grandchildren and great-grandchildren of these managers who will be living in a world that depends significantly upon decisions made or not made now. The question is: How well informed are managers on the

---

* PMI® has also awarded the PMP© Credential to nearly 420,000 persons and there are nearly 680,000 copies of their *Project Management Book of Knowledge*, PMBOK© Guide, in circulation.

three topics of population, climate change, and energy?* And, how are they incorporating the current major departures from historical trends into their planning? Sound bites on the topics are broadcast every day, but they seem contradictory, and for most people are just treated as noise. It is apparent from discussions at the PMI meetings and with managers that their horizons need intelligent expansion if they are to make decisions that depend on assumptions as to the stability of the assumed and current life-cycle environment.

The papers on "sustainability" in the PMI publications primarily address the use of renewable resources on projects and "green" projects and do not often address the significance of finite limits of key resources or the changes in consumption that must occur. The decades of the 2010s and especially the 2020s and beyond are potentially periods of great opportunity as well as great stress and threat due to unique and dramatic changes in population, climate, availability of oil and natural gas, and sources of energy. The demographic, economic, and geopolitical impacts are expected to be considerable and variable. Current scientific data and projections indicate the coming two to three decades will be a period of transition to even greater changes later this century.

These issues are important to managers since most life cycles of programs are 5–10 years or longer, and portfolio and strategic planning managers must look beyond that horizon to a world we hope is sustainable. Infrastructure projects commonly have 50-year life expectancies. The new triple constraints will become more consequential and will have an increasingly significant impact on programs in decades to come. Government and industry responses, as the likely scenarios play out, will create opportunities for portfolio managers that will be implemented through the actions of project and program managers.

The aim of this book is to provide a rational basis for approaching the problems that program and portfolio managers are facing and will face in the future from the three issues of population, climate change, and energy. This is simply risk management where the planner evaluates the likely impact of these issues and thereby makes a more rational decision. This should enable them to take advantage of the coming and ongoing changes in their life-cycle planning and portfolio selection.

---

* Some people believe a fourth major constraint is fresh water. Certainly Fred Pearce's book *When the Rivers Run Dry* would support this; however, this is beyond the scope of this book at this time.

Acknowledgments

In the preparation of this book I wish to express my appreciation and acknowledge the support received from Allan R. Kostreba, senior principal, acquisition and software economics, Noblis, Falls Church, Virginia; from William Kirby, a retired National Science Foundation senior manager; from Gregory T. Haugan Jr., a senior manager in the Department of Homeland Security; from Lee Allain, systems engineer and retired CEO of MicroNetworks Corp. of Worcester, Massachusetts; and Dr. Lynton S. Land, professor emeritus, Department of Geological Sciences, University of Texas; and from my wife, Susan, who helped with the editing and research.

All provided comments and recommendations to my draft and most of their comments were incorporated. I should point out that if there are any errors, they are mine.

In addition, I appreciate the assistance provided by John Wyzalek, Robin Lloyd-Starkes and Joselyn Banks-Kyle of Taylor & Francis Group; and I wish to thank John Cook of SkepticScience.com for the use of several of his graphics.

About the Author

Gregory T. Haugan, PhD, PMP, is the owner of GLH Incorporated, specializing in project management support for both U.S. and international organizations, and an instructor in areas of energy, population, and climate change. He has more than 40 years of experience as a consultant and as a government and private-sector official in the planning, scheduling, management, and operation of projects of all sizes; and in the development and implementation of program management information systems.

Dr. Haugan has been active in the field of resources and sustainability for many years. He has led courses for the Rappahannock Institute for Lifelong Learning (RILL), including *Development of Human Societies: Lessons for the Northern Neck of Virginia* with major emphasis on current problems with potential shortages in energy and water resources. This was followed by *Oil, Energy and Global Warming*. It recognized the indivisibility of the topics, presented current theories, and discussed the relationship to the Northern Neck of Virginia and what actions were warranted. In addition, he has presented two courses on climate change and global warming, addressing the issues of the science, the impact, and the mitigation actions, and presenting the various claims and theories with regard to global warming phenomena and their current and projected impact on our lives. His interest and knowledge in these areas led to this book.

He has written five project management books published by Management Concepts, Inc. of Vienna, Virginia, including *Effective Work Breakdown Structures*, published in 2002; *Project Planning and Scheduling*, also published in 2002; *The Work Breakdown Structure in Government Contracting*, published in 2003. *Project Management Fundamentals* was published in 2006 and the second edition was published in late 2010. Two of the books have been translated into Japanese and Chinese.

He and his wife reside in Heathsville, Virginia. For recreation, he hiked the 100-mile West Highland Way trail in Scotland in 2006. The year before, he climbed Mt. Whitney in California. He also hiked the Lolo Trail in Idaho after hiking the Inca Trail in Peru and the Chilkoot Trail in Alaska. In 2010, he hiked trails in Tuscany between mountain villages. He is a former member of the U.S. Triathlon Team and competed in the world championships in Wellington, New Zealand, in 1994.

Dr. Haugan received his PhD from the American University, his MBA from St. Louis University, and his BSME from the Illinois Institute of Technology. Further information is available on the web at www.pmhaugan.com.

Prologue

It ain't what you don't know that gets you in trouble. It's what you know for sure that just ain't so.

—Mark Twain

In Jared Diamond's book *Guns, Germs and Steel*, the protagonist, the New Guinea chieftain Yali, asks a question regarding the relative inequity in the distribution of "cargo" around the world. How come Europe and the Americas had so much "cargo" and the New Guineans so little? We all originated from the tribes that survived the ice ages some 11,000 years ago. Diamond's book attempted to answer that question. In a sense, this book builds on *Guns, Germs and Steel* or maybe even the subsequent book by Diamond titled *Collapse*. We are setting the stage for a selfish question: What changes are coming down the pike that we as project/program/portfolio managers need to be aware of so that we can adjust, adapt, and take advantage? How do we construct a sustainable future? It is selfish because the focus of many other books on these topics is to identify and propose mitigation policies, or to declare the sky is falling and tell us why, while I am simply looking at it from a point of view of identifying and recognizing the current and projected circumstances in order to help adapt, judge risk, and take advantage of an environment that is overwhelmingly complex. The problems include a rapidly growing and changing world population, environmental threats from emissions and depleting natural resources—all components of a collapse of civilizations. However, with respect to our civilization, Jared Diamond is an optimist and he ends his book *Collapse* with several reasons why he does not expect our civilization to follow in the footsteps of Easter Islanders, the Incas, Mayans, and others. He believes we have learned our lessons from history. We recognize the need for sustainability. Time will tell.

Some of the material in this book may be considered controversial; it really is not if you believe facts. However, the reader should look at the material presented from two perspectives: (1) as a set of normative statements or standards of what you ought to do considering the body of scientific data, and (2) as input to a large risk management analysis that considers options and alternatives and probable impacts. It is not an issue

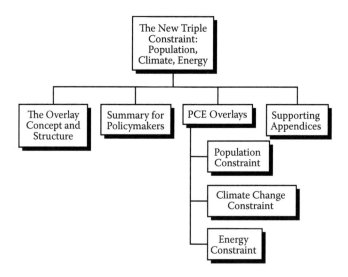

FIGURE 0.1
Book organization.

of belief in when the population will reach 10 billion, or whether global warming and climate change exist, or whether or not there are oil supply problems; they are easily evaluated by looking at facts and are aspects of program or enterprise risk management. What should be your position as a program manager or enterprise manager or strategic planner when facing decisions regarding the likelihood of specific future events? Should you buy insurance or self-insure? What if the scientists are wrong? What if they are correct? What if (insert your source of data) is wrong? What if (insert your source of data) is correct? You must look at the data—at the facts. In graduate school I was taught to go to original sources, see what the actual data say; do not let other people interpret the facts for you.

The book is organized as illustrated in Figure 0.1.

The first part of this book provides a description of the overlay concept and the major considerations in using an overlay for planning—whether at a project, program, portfolio, or strategic level. For those interested in getting right to the meat of the subject and the overlays, a summary for policymakers is included. This summary is followed by the major sections addressing population and climate change, which provide the current data and forecasts on those subjects and establish the overall new setting for planning. The last section, on the energy constraint, addresses fossil fuels and renewable energy solutions and opportunities in the form of a set of overlays based on a strengths, weaknesses, opportunities, and threats

(SWOT) analysis for the various resources and technologies that will be needed to accommodate the needs of a growing population faced with climate changes and problems with fossil fuels. How do we achieve a sustainable future?

> I have thus sketched the general outline of the argument, but I will examine it more particularly, and I think it will be found that experience, the true source and foundation of all knowledge, invariably confirms its truth.[*]

> **—T. R. Malthus, 1798**

---

[*] T. R. Malthus, *An Essay on the Principle of Population*, Originally published 7 June 1798, (Lexington, KY: Maestro Reprints, November 2010) Chapter 1, p. 7.

1

Sustainability Overlay Concept and Structure

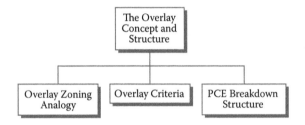

Chapter 1 outline.

OVERLAY ZONING ANALOGY

In land use planning, overlay zoning is a regulatory tool that creates a special zoning district, placed over an existing base zone(s), which includes special provisions in addition to those in the underlying base zone. The overlay district can share common boundaries with the base zone or cut across base zone boundaries. Regulations or incentives are attached to the overlay district to protect a specific resource or guide development within a special area.*

---

* University of Wisconsin Center for Land Use Education, *Planning and Implementation Tools, Overlay Zoning*, November 2005, http://www.uwsp.edu/cnr/landcenter/pdffiles/implementation/OverlayZoning.pdf (accessed April 18, 2011).

In land use and community planning, overlay districts are used for many different purposes:

- to manage development in or near environmentally sensitive areas,
- to protect historical areas, to guide development along transportation corridors,
- to protect special areas from development, and so forth.

The author has been involved in developing local government zoning overlays for all of these special considerations.

Overlay zoning districts are created following three basic steps:

1. Define the purpose of the district.
2. Identify the areas that comprise the district, including the scope and boundaries of the district.
3. Develop specific rules that apply to the identified district.

There are other general considerations that involve the implementation and administration of overlay zones that include consistency between the overlay and the basic zoning district involved and the review of the applicability and usage by higher levels of municipal management and the general public.

These concepts, purposes, and considerations can be transferred to the overlays of population impacts, climate changes, and energy constraints onto our project, program, and enterprise planning. For simplicity, in future descriptions I will simply refer to *program planning* rather than the complete *project, program, and enterprise planning*.

Figure 1.1 presents a graphic of the overlay concept and the major sections of this book.

OVERLAY CRITERIA

The application of the analogy of the zoning overlay to an overlay set of population, climate, and energy constraints for program life cycle planning is explained in the following text in terms of the three steps of the previous section used to define an overlay district.

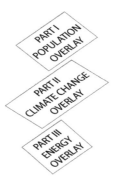

FIGURE 1.1
Overlay concept.

Purpose

Three major constraints exist that apply to future and ongoing multiyear projects and programs and apply to programs in portfolios of enterprises. These are changes in *population, climate change,* and the availability of *energy*—PCE constraints. Most managers have some familiarity with various aspects of these constraints and do consider them in their planning. We believe these have been *underrepresented* in many planning and programming activities for a variety of reasons. The intent of these overlays is to assist program managers in the consideration of and application of more robust PCE constraints in their planning and risk analyses.

Applicability

The PCE overlay set is applicable to all projects, programs, and portfolios whose planning horizon extends into the next decade. All programs are impacted to some degree by these constraints.

Population factors include any impacts or assumptions regarding changes in demand, demographics, racial composition, immigration, migration, birth rates, or death rates. Changes in these factors drastically impact workforces.

Climate factors include any impacts or assumptions regarding weather, sea levels, biota, ice, and glaciers that are involved in the performance of the project end items or in the development of the products, services, or results that are the purpose of the basic project. The forecast changes in climate are expected to result in conditions different from what the Earth has seen for over 10,000 years. It makes no difference whether one "believes" the scientists or not; a prudent businessman and planner will take these risks into account.

Energy factors include any impacts or assumptions regarding the availability or cost of energy in the management of the program or in the resulting product, service, or result. It is difficult to identify any program that doesn't rely on or involve use of energy in some form.

Indirect factors may, for example, include the impact of population aging affecting the economic strength of a country, which in turn may reduce (or increase) a military threat. A reduced military threat may indicate a change in the performance requirements of a new military aircraft. Or an arctic construction project may depend upon the continued existence of permafrost in an area where current data and climate models show significant increases in temperature are occurring and continuing to occur, threatening the stability of the ground. Or a school district is developing its capital budget for new school construction based on projections of historic population data in an area that scientists project to be adversely and seriously impacted by droughts exacerbated by climate change and impacted by immigration, for example, west Texas.

Specific Rules

The overlays provide specific information and guidance to both the program manager and the higher level of management charged with reviewing, approving, and implementing the plans.

When reviewing a project of any size where an overlay is applicable, it is important that the program be consistent not only with the content of the overlays, but with the long-term goals and the overall program/portfolio plan. That is, the basic schedule, cost, and performance criteria still apply; the overlay is just that—an overlay—as shown in Figure 1.1.

Consideration of the overlay should be incorporated into the existing program/portfolio review process for large-scale development programs and all multiyear life cycle programs. It should become the norm to consider these three new constraints in all planning and how they relate to a sustainable future.

A series of overlays should be an enterprise-wide requirement and be part of the criteria in addition to return on investment (ROI) or cost effectiveness or other standard metrics used to select programs and to guide the program manager. They complement budgeting, scheduling, and quality/performance activities. Many organizations are already doing this piecemeal for climate change impacts.

PCE BREAKDOWN STRUCTURE

One of the principal tools in project planning is the work breakdown structure (WBS), which is used to provide the framework for planning and to define the scope. This is part of Project Management 101. It is addressed in the *Project Management Book of Knowledge*, PMBOK® Guide, and in many other project management texts and courses. There are two roles of the work breakdown structure in project portfolio management: (1) displaying the projects or programs in a logical hierarchical format for presentation purposes, and (2) using a WBS to design a portfolio management system.* The first instance is not really a WBS; it is only using some of the WBS logic and familiar display techniques to organize the elements to facilitate communication. Figure 1.2 presents the PCE overlay and the outline of this book using this first type of WBS. This figure was developed using WBS ChartPro software.

The plan of this book is to follow a typical approach used in presenting the results of scientific or analytical data. Just as many major reports start with an abstract and provide a summary for policymakers, we will provide the content up front in this synthesis of the discussion and description of each PCE overlay. Since we are not able to predict the future any better than anyone else, we will also present and discuss scenarios and then some possible and probable solutions or outcomes that provide the basis for evaluating the risks involved.

Under or near the heading for each section, the applicable overlay statement is included in a box. These are also summaries of the material in the section.

---

* Gregory T. Haugan, *Work Breakdown Structures for Projects, Programs and Enterprises* (Vienna, VA: Management Concepts, 2008) p. 190.

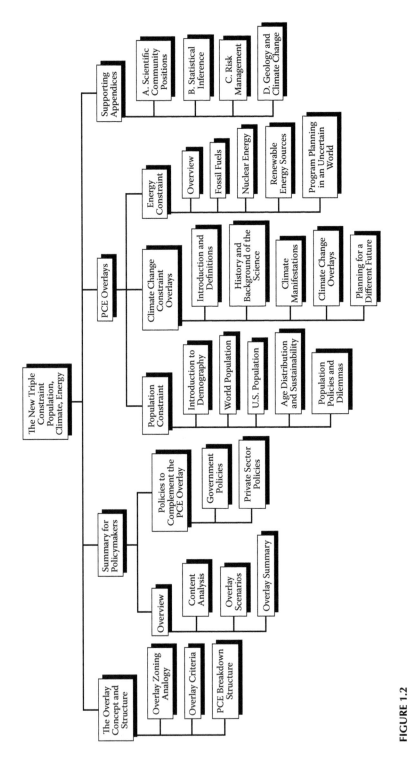

FIGURE 1.2
PCE overlay WBS.

2

Summary for Policymakers: PCE Overlay

All mankind is divided into three classes; those that are immovable, those that are movable, and those that move.

—Arabic Proverb

This summary for policymakers provides an overview of the overlays and their application to life cycle programs of the coming decades. It addresses the overlays in summary form with the bulk of the remainder of the book providing their detailed backup, supporting data and information, and lower level overlays. The diagram below presents an outline of this chapter.

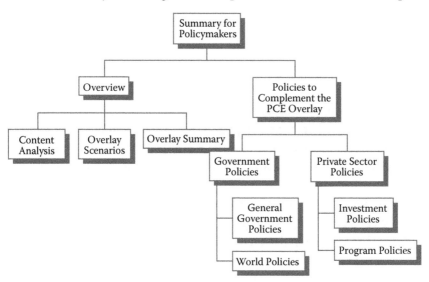

Chapter 2 outline.

OVERVIEW

This section contains a description of the content or base for the overlays, then a discussion that puts them in context in the form of scenarios of the future followed by a brief summary.

Content Analysis of the Population, Climate Change and Energy (PCE) Overlay*

> **Overlay:** The world has a significantly increasing population, which will demand more energy to maintain and/or increase its standard of living. Until public concern and action about carbon emissions rises, the energy will come primarily from coal and natural gas. Their prices will probably remain fairly stable because of the large supply, while the cost of oil increases considerably as the demand continues to increase in the face of a supply constraint and increasing extraction costs. Climate change resulting from human emissions will slowly and surely cause increasing problems as storms and droughts become more intense, temperatures and moisture content in the atmosphere continue to rise, glaciers and ice shelves continue to melt, sea water levels continue to rise, and the world biota continue to be impacted.

This is the future in a single overlay. Timing, however, is not addressed.

The changes will be driven by population growth and population redistribution, climate changes, and energy constraints; all will impact as a package in the coming decades. An overview of these changes follows:

1. The Population Constraint Overlay has several messages that must be considered in planning:
   a. The world population is growing and will continue to grow from the current 7 billion to approximately 10 billion by 2080, and is very likely to level off or grow slowly at a sustainable level from

---

* A content analysis is a systematic analysis of the content rather than the structure of the concept to determine the objective or meaning of the concept (*American Heritage Dictionary of the English Language,* Houghton Mifflin, 4th Ed., Boston, MA: 397).

that point onward. The projections of population up to 2050 are virtually certain because they are based on people already in the pipeline and their birth and mortality rates are not likely to change significantly in the next decade.

b. For projections beyond 2050 there is a reasonable confidence in the numbers because of the completeness and accuracy of the data and knowledge bases used; therefore it is very likely that the projections are accurate to the end of the century.[*]

c. These same databases show the U.S. population will increase by approximately 100 million people between today and 2050 based on present birth and death rates, assuming no significant change in immigration policies or immigration rates.

d. The demographic changes accompanying these population changes will have a significant impact on social structures, workforces, political composition, and immigration and migration patterns of the world's peoples.

e. Countries such as those in the European Union, Japan, Russia, and China are expected to undergo major demographic changes and perhaps disruptions due to an aging workforce and low birth rates that will impact the ability of their economies to continue to grow at current rates.

Population, immigration, and related demographic changes cannot be ignored in program/portfolio long-range planning.

2. The Climate Change Constraint Overlay contains five basic dimensions that must be considered in planning:

a. Avoiding risk is a standard principle of management; like a tornado or robbery or fire or piracy at sea, you do not have to believe it will happen, but a responsible manager will review the data, evaluate the risk, and (1) plan accordingly or (2) hedge, (3) buy insurance, or (4) self-insure. The latter is similar to taking no action; sometimes it is deliberate and other times not. Climate change presents a set of unique risks that must be evaluated and

---

[*] Forecasts are generally probabilistic and have ranges depending upon the assumptions or on the statistical standard deviations derived from the basic data. In this book we keep to the midrange forecasts wherever possible.

decisions must be made. Doing nothing is a decision. This overlay will help in the evaluation.

b. Climate change is being caused by human emissions of greenhouse gases, particularly by combustion of the fossil fuels coal, oil, and natural gas. There is no natural cycle that explains the current set of temperature increases. The climate is a global system; therefore, to mitigate global climate change, total human emissions need to be significantly reduced. Reducing emissions on a global scale requires a global solution. Efforts to reduce emissions on a global scale will have global costs and benefits; both sides of the equation are involved in the overlay.

c. Temperatures will continue to rise as CO_2, methane, and other emissions rise and these increasing temperatures, no matter how slowly they rise, will cause far more adverse effects than favorable effects, including more moisture in the atmosphere, melting of ice sheets and glaciers, and warmer oceans. There will be net adverse consequences on almost all sectors of the economy and all regions of the world from the warming climate, including stronger storms, more heavy precipitation events, more floods, and rising seas, and these adverse consequences will compound as warming increases.

d. World biota are all impacted, some positively, some negatively, but on balance most severely; this includes species extinction where adaptation does not occur swiftly enough. Invasive species will move northward from lower latitudes and shifting climate zones; all programs that depend on the natural environment, such as bee pollination and farming, will be subject to this constraint. Warmer climates in the subarctic, however, may reduce some climate constraints as growing seasons lengthen and viable farmland becomes unfrozen.

e. Increased carbon dioxide, CO_2, in the atmosphere is causing the oceans to absorb more CO_2, thereby becoming more acidic and impacting sea life, especially shellfish. CO_2 will initially stimulate growth in some plants, but has been shown to eventually cause stunting as the CO_2 level increases and temperature rises.

Just near-term population growth is preordained by actions previously taken, near-term climate change due to temperature increases is preordained by current and previous CO_2 and other emissions. There is an approximate decadal lag in the system caused by the slow release of heat by the oceans, which has a moderating effect. The Earth has not yet stabilized from the CO_2 currently in the system. Continued emissions at the current rates will seriously impact future generations and must be a factor in near- and long-term planning if a sustainable future is to be attained. Both the population and global temperatures are increasing with inexorable certainty; the results are predictable and need to be overlaid on decadal planning. The nature of this constraint is such that many of the opportunities created exist in two areas: carbon emissions reductions and climate change adaptation schemes; both are important and the overlay considers these elements.

3. The Energy Constraint Overlay involves three major elements: fossil fuels, nuclear energy, and renewable energy sources, including the new technologies that provide clean energy. This overlay addresses changes in the energy sector that are occurring and projected and changes that will seriously constrain future and existing long-term programs and portfolios. The Energy Constraint Overlay is where most of the opportunities exist and the Chapter 5 Energy Constraint Overlay section includes a SWOT* analysis of each energy source to assist in focusing the issues and in applying the overlay to your programs. The technologies and policies related to increasing efficiencies, providing alternate energy sources, and reducing carbon emissions impacts from fossil fuels are extremely important. The messages that form the basis of this overlay are as follows:

   a. There is abundant coal and natural gas available for energy well into the next century but not beyond, although not without serious side effects that may impact supply.

   b. The world is probably past or at "peak oil" and this has several consequences:[†]

      1. Discovery of new sources of oil has not kept pace with demand for nearly a generation, and extraction costs of the

---

* Strength-Weakness-Opportunity-Threat.

† Peak oil occurs when it is estimated that only half of the total God-given recoverable supply is still left in the ground.

remaining oil are rising since all the "easy" oil has been discovered and extracted.

2. World oil production rates are very likely at or close to their maximum and the rates will *decrease* as the years go on as wells and oil fields are depleted. The production rate reduction will depend upon (1) the willingness of the consumers to pay high prices consistent with extraction costs in remote areas, (2) the validity of the reserve estimates in the Middle East, and any OPEC policies to conserve reserves and control the market, and (3) the amount of oil that is really available in oil sands, shale, the Arctic, and offshore.

3. There will be instability in oil prices, with high peaks and then drops because prices will be sensitive to small perturbations in the remaining world supply and refinery capacity.

4. There will be significant and continuing increases in prices of products that depend on oil, such as fertilizers, pharmaceuticals, plastics, and transportation.

5. The overall trend of oil prices will go in only one direction, *up*—with an increasing slope.

c. Up to one-third of the U.S. current electric power plants are 40 years old and need modernization or replacing. Climate concerns related to carbon emissions and other pollutants will provide pressure for closing older coal power plants and for substitutions with natural gas, which will be the principal replacement fuel at least in the interim. It is cost competitive and has half the emissions of coal.

d. Nuclear energy was given a setback with the Japanese power plant earthquake/tsunami problem resulting in a slowdown in the planning in the United States and Europe. China is expected to continue the increase in nuclear plants since they do provide clean energy, although not without some cost and disposal problems.

e. Renewable energy technologies to provide alternatives to coal and natural gas for generation of energy are expensive and not cost competitive in most markets at present, but that may change as research and development (R&D) efforts pay off and as fossil fuel shortages and supply disturbances increase.

f. There must and will be serious investments in clean technologies to provide alternatives to fossil fuels, especially coal and oil, to provide energy to run the world's economies. Opportunities exist in this area.

So as a program manager who has a basic job of balancing cost, schedule and performance/quality, or a balanced portfolio of programs, you now have an overlay set of three other major constraints or opportunities: growing population with its increased demand for energy and products that depend upon cheap energy, the climate change and necessary adaptations and mitigations that also impact the energy sector, and a changing energy mix to meet a strong and rising demand while reducing carbon emissions and accommodating oil shortages.

In the next section on scenarios we will address the integration and interrelation of these constraints to provide a discussion of the overlay elements. The scenarios are just another way of explaining the role of the overlays and presenting the conclusions for executive consideration.

Overlay Scenarios

A tool for planning is to establish multiple sets of alternatives and assumptions in the form of scenarios and then perform projections and analyze the results. Following are two scenarios to provide a basis for discussing options for program and portfolio managers. These are different from policymakers since policymakers are expected to solve these problems on a broad scale while our program managers are expected to live with the problems, solve them for their program, and take advantage of the opportunities that present themselves (or hedge the risks).

In both scenarios presented, the population forecasts are the same and are based on credible and accepted U.N. data as discussed in Chapter 3 on the Population Constraint Overlay. The substantive sections of this book address these issues in more detail.

Each scenario is a possible overlay in itself because it can provide the framework for your planning.

Scenario 1: Business as Usual (BAU) Baseline. This scenario assumes that population growth will continue as expected, there is no near-term attempt to mitigate climate change, and that energy users are slowly shifting away from coal into more natural gas and even nuclear fuels, but nothing dramatic. In fact, in China, for example, a large number of coal-fired power plants are being planned and built to meet immediate needs. This assumption is the basis for the energy figures and graphics and the Energy Information Agency projections. Technology and political mandates will provide an increasing percentage of energy from alternative sources such as wind and solar, but *no global concerted action on climate change or reducing emissions occurs.* The United Nations continues talking but there is no action—business as usual. Improved and new technology and an increasing use of coal overseas are sufficient to accommodate a significant portion of the increased demand while the basic current levels of demand are supported by fossil fuels. In other words, increases in demand will be met by a combination of new technologies and coal with natural gas as a backup.

So this BAU scenario is the default position and the most likely for the short term at least. It is where we are starting. There is no overlay for this since it is business as usual and the overlays all recommend changes to business as usual.

Scenario 2: Oil prices increase constantly and actions are taken worldwide to reduce emissions. Population growth continues per the projections. New technology in renewable energy is sufficient to accommodate a significant portion of the increased demand while the basic current levels of energy usage continue to be supported by fossil fuels. Technology improvements enable more energy to be provided from alternative sources such as wind and solar. Carbon taxes and cap-and-trade mechanisms are utilized to dampen demand for fossil fuels and the funds used for energy alternatives and efficiencies.*

The overlay scenario consists of six layers as follows:

A. The world population data are pretty solid to 2050, so this can be part of the basic assumptions; beyond 2050 it is likely the population will increase to approximately 9 billion and then the growth will slow significantly, taking until 2083 to reach 10 billion. This assumes that there will not be severe disruptions caused by war or climate change.

B. The probability of an oil supply problem and rapidly increasing prices and all the secondary impacts are very likely, as discussed in Chapter 18 in the sections on reserves and peak oil. The timing is somewhat uncertain in the very near term but some ups and downs in price are anticipated. The impact of speculation is unknown. But by 2020 there will probably be at least one big spike in price and then a serious continued increase in oil prices as the production cannot

---

* Regardless of some political rhetoric, cap-and-trade programs have been effective. *Cap-and-trade* is a methodology, a tool, like cost–benefit analysis or discounting and it is the application to the problem at hand that is important.

keep up with demand due to supply problems. It is also not clear exactly how large the remaining reserves of oil really are and therefore how quickly the world economy is going to consume them. The U.S. reserves of natural gas appear to be adequate to the end of the century, but there is some degree of uncertainty in the secondary effects of the new fracking process of extracting the gas from shale, which could impact the price.

C. Concern over oil and energy shortages will have at least these four impacts:

    a. Increased investment in alternative energies such as solar and wind and nuclear to replace diminishing fossil fuel resources

    b. Increased investment in nontraditional oil sources such as oil sands, biofuels, shale, and the more difficult sources such as off-shore and Arctic to complement current oil sources

    c. Continued investment in technologies to increase energy efficiency and to decrease carbon intensity

    d. Increased concern by the military of oil shortages since the military machine runs on oil

D. Any worldwide emissions reduction in the near term is unlikely. It also appears unlikely that the U.S. government would take any action since it is focused on the near term: always the next election and secondarily on governance. Political emphasis is on costs, not benefits. For a politician, the prudent paths are usually business as usual, oppose any change, or talk change but don't do it. The current economic growth of the Chinese, Indian, Brazilian, and other developing economies is based on increasing energy usage and this will continue. Until the general populations are convinced that the benefits of taking action to preclude additional significant adverse events from climate change outweigh the perceived costs of near-term slowdown of growth, it is unlikely that any emissions reduction will take place. Cynically, it is unlikely any serious emission reduction effort will occur until there is a massive tragedy that is clearly linked to climate change or until a series of major weather events around the world are all linked. Aggressive emissions reduction, if it occurs, will have little near-term (2030) impact on global warming and climate change, although some costs would be incurred. Acceptance of and adaptation to the effects is the most likely short-term outcome. The bomb shelters of the Cold War are being replaced by storm shelters to protect from weather events.

E. Detailed predictions of the impacts of climate change on specific locations over the rest of this century are subject to wide variations, especially after 2050. Continued burning of fossil fuels will continue to increase the CO_2 in the atmosphere, but the full range of impacts this will produce cannot be precisely determined due to the complexity of the problem. There is a long list of macro effects that are being forecast reasonably accurately: sea level rise, glacier melt, increased precipitation, increased drought, shifting seasons, and the like. Data are available on each and these need to be considered in the detailed planning.

F. Even if carbon emissions are controlled and held to current limits, we are committed to an increasing temperature rise due to the lag in the system. The planet has already warmed 1.4°F and there is another 1.0°F in the pipeline.[*]

What is likely to happen is a continued climate change with weather becoming increasingly severe, peak oil, and no action on emissions until sometime later. This is not the preferred scenario, nor the one that should be encouraged.

The scenario analysis needs to be recast as an overlay implemented through risk analysis. In this general case we are using the classic definition of risk as cost of the *consequence* versus the *probability* that it will occur. A methodology is discussed in Appendix C: Risk Management.

It is suggested that the risk items, if you prepare a risk matrix, be categorized by the timing of the impacts. The results are different if you are looking at melting of the Greenland Ice Cap or the change in an Asian monsoon because of the timing of the consequences. The monsoon is immediate and the melting takes many years before there is a noticeable effect on shorelines. The risk analysis should be based on observed data and the likely impact on future activities. There are many charlatans who are serving special interests that are using deliberate misinformation to distort climate change realism. Base your risk analyses on solid data such as that referenced herein.

The slow change in most climate events makes most policymakers reluctant to make long-term investments beyond their expected terms of office.[†] But, as the person involved in making investment decisions and managing

[*] Skeptical Science, http://www.skepticalscience.com/prudent-risk.html (accessed March 3, 2011).
[†] Stephen Schneider, "Confidence, Consensus and the Uncertainty Cops: Tackling Risk Management in Climate Change" in Bill Bryson, ed., *Seeing Further: The Story of Science, Discovery & the Genius of the Royal Society* (London: the Royal Society and Harper Collins, 2010) pp. 424–443.

life cycle programs, program and portfolio managers are obliged to perform risk analyses of options and take into account the consequences and probability of impacts of the three constraints occurring in the identification of consequences.

The succeeding sections of this book present the supporting data regarding population, climate, and energy with credible projections by experts of the current trends out to about 2050 and beyond.

> "The theory on which the truth of this position depends appears to me so extremely clear that I feel at a loss to conjecture what part of it can be denied."*
>
> —**T. R. Malthus, 1798**

Overlay Summary

There are only five talking points or major overlays:

1. The population is growing and the characteristics of the nature of the growth, i.e., demographics, will be different in the coming decades from the past decades.
2. Severe resource shortages such as oil and water will occur and are being predicted.
3. Technology is important and needs to be sponsored in the areas of alternate fuels and carbon-free sources of energy, but these may not arrive in time to compensate for the resource shortages.
4. Climate CO_2-mitigation efforts are critical and their total costs are significantly lower than the costs resulting from business as usual, and the benefits from mitigation have been shown to be much higher than the costs.
5. Adaptation to resource shortages and adverse climate impacts will create many opportunities as well as problems.

Sustainability depends on the recognition of these drivers as situations that need to be addressed.

One resource I have not addressed that needs further exploration is the looming global fresh water shortage. Not everywhere, Scotland will do fine, but all current desert climates are at risk; many regions that rely on snow or glacier melt are at risk, and all regions that rely on aquifers are at

---

* Malthus, Chapter 2 in Bryson, *Seeing Further*, p. 12.

risk. The general pattern of climate change is that areas of the world that are dry will get even drier and areas that are wet will get even wetter.

Malthus said: "That the difficulties of life contribute to generate talents, every day's experience must convince us. The exertions that men find it necessary to make, in order to support themselves or families, frequently awaken faculties that might otherwise have lain forever dormant, and it has been commonly remarked that new and extraordinary situations generally create minds adequate to grapple with the difficulties in which they are involved."[*]

POLICIES TO COMPLEMENT THE PCE OVERLAY

We properly revere our forefathers for making material and mortal sacrifices for our benefit. One only hopes that our descendants will hold us in similar regard.[†]

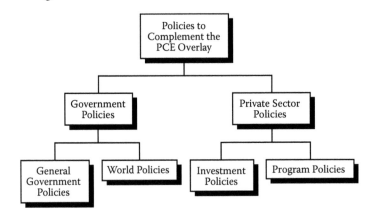

Government Policies

Overlay: Encourage government policies that consider population, climate change, and energy as a package. Influence the initiation of processes for adaptation and for mitigation of problems.

---

[*] Malthus, Chapter 19 in Bryson, *Seeing Further*, p. 102.

[†] Climate Scientist Kerry Emanuel from MIT at the U.S. House of Representatives Committee on Science Space and Technology hearing on Climate Change: Examining the Processes Used to Create Science and Policy, March 31, 2011.

General Government Policies

To my knowledge, there have been no scientific or scholarly analyses or assessments of the triple constraints of population, climate change, and energy as a package. One of the early writers, Paul Ehrlich (1971), with his book, *The Population Bomb*, introduced the idea that our patterns of consumption of resources and population were on a collision course with sustainability. One popular book by Thomas Friedman addresses two of these in easy-to-read prose focusing on population and climate change.[*] Another is Laurence Smith's book on *The World in 2050*, which focuses on the northern latitudes and addresses demographic trends, resource shortages, and climate change.[†] For most others, the focus is usually on one or the other with simplifying assumptions made regarding the other two.

A partial exception is a study published in the *Proceedings of the National Academy of Sciences* that considered the substantial changes in population size, age structure, and urbanization that are expected in many parts of the world this century.[‡] Although such changes can affect energy use and greenhouse gas emissions, emissions scenario analyses have either left them out or treated them in a fragmentary or overly simplified manner. In their analysis that accounts for a range of demographic dynamics, they show, for example, that slowing population growth could provide 16–29% of the emissions reductions suggested as being necessary by 2050 to avoid dangerous climate change. On the other hand, you can interpret their results and conclude that a business-as-usual growth would result in significantly increased emissions from today's levels. They also find that aging and urbanization reduce emissions in particular world regions because of reduced energy usage per capita. This is a step toward generating detailed data so that intelligent decision making can proceed.

Many sources that are referenced address government policies or recommendations concerning population, energy and fossil fuels, and climate changes. Some are easy to read like Mann and Kump, or Gore, or Flannery, or Krupp and Horn, or Craven (see bibliography for complete references) but the most comprehensive is the 2007 International Panel on

---

[*] Thomas L Friedman, *Hot, Flat, and Crowded: Why We Need a Green Revolution and How It Can Renew America* (New York: Farrar, Straus and Giroux, 2008).

[†] Laurence C. Smith, *The World in 2050: Four Forces Shaping Civilization's Northern Future* (New York: Dutton, Penguin Group, 2010).

[‡] Brian C. O'Neill, et al., "Global Demographic Trends and Future Carbon Emissions," *Proceedings of the National Academy of Sciences of the USA* 107, no. 41 (October 12, 2010): 17521–17526. http://www.pnas.org/content/107/41/17521.full (accessed February 16, 2011).

Climate Change (IPCC), Report from Working Group III, *Mitigation of Climate Change*, which has nearly a thousand pages of analysis and recommendations, including technical explanations and rationale. A new special IPCC report has updated findings on the status and application of renewable energy sources.[*] Dr. James Hansen has strong recommendations in his book (see bibliography). Other typical references are narrowly defined reports such as *Chesapeake Futures*,[†] which looks at the Chesapeake Bay watershed, and "Choices for the 21st Century" or *Global Climate Change Impacts in the United States*,[‡] or *America's Climate Choices*,[§] recently prepared by the National Research Council of the National Academy of Sciences at the request of Congress.

World Policies

Overlay: The basic policy that should be followed is fairly simple: the governments of the world should immediately take dual actions to mitigate and adapt to climate change, take actions to accommodate expected reductions in the availability of cheap oil and do both in the context of a rapidly increasing and aging world population.

We are the first generation facing the evidence of global change. It therefore falls upon us to change our relationship with the planet, in order to tip the scales towards a sustainable world for future generations.[¶]

Energy Information Agency (EIA) data[**] show that if there are no new climate policies, worldwide increases in output per capita and relatively moderate population growth overwhelm projected improvements in

---

[*] IPCC Working Group III, *Special Report on Renewable Energy Sources and Climate Change Mitigation (SRREN)* (New York: Cambridge University Press, May 2011).

[†] Donald F. Boesch and Jack Greer, eds., *Chesapeake Futures: Choices for the 21st Century* (Edgewater, MD: Chesapeake Bay Program, Scientific and Technical Advisory Committee, 2003).

[‡] Thomas R. Karl, Jerry M. Melillo, and Thomas C. Peterson, eds., *Global Climate Change Impacts in the United States* (New York: Cambridge University Press, US Global Change Research Program, 2009).

[§] National Research Council, *America's Climate Choices* (Washington, DC: National Academies Press, 2011).

[¶] 3rd Nobel Laureate Symposium on Global Sustainability, Stockholm Sweden 16–19 May 2011, *The Stockholm Memorandum*, p. 5, http://globalsymposium2011.org/wp-content/uploads/2011/05/The-Stockholm-Memorandum.pdf (accessed May 24, 2011).

[**] U.S. Energy Information Administration, International Energy Outlook 2011, Report DOE/EIA-0484 (2011), September 2011, Page 144. http://205.254.135.24/forecasts/ieo/pdf/0484(2011).pdf. Last accessed March 3, 2011.

the amounts of energy and carbon used per person; meanwhile CO_2 keeps rising.

Emphasis on increasing efficiency by reducing energy intensity (energy usage per capita) appears to have been relatively effective worldwide. However, rising standards of living, as shown by the increasing output per capita and an increasing population, are generating increasing emissions. It is apparent that the current business-as-usual path will result in increasing total emissions even as the energy intensity and carbon intensity (CO_2 per person) decrease. The world is increasing its efficiency and reducing carbon usage per capita, but with the increasing population the total emissions are increasing.

Policies need to encourage innovation in alternate energy sources since technology is needed to replace most of the energy currently provided by fossil fuels with carbon-neutral sources. The concern about reliance on foreign oil has been improperly cast as only a concern about unfriendly sources. It will soon be replaced by concern about having enough foreign and domestic oil to last until we have developed alternatives to meet the demands of an increasing population.

Population increases and demographic changes need to be incorporated into decision making and policies of both government and private sector institutions. Increasing from 7 to 10 billion persons in the world between now and 2080 is not a trivial event. Increasing from 300 million to 400 million persons by 2050 in the United States is also not a trivial event. Joel Kotkin's book (*The Next Hundred Million*) addresses nicely his opinions and analyses of how we will absorb them, and where they will live and work, and Laurence Smith's book (*The World in 2050*) looking at the northern latitudes in 2050 also contains implied necessary policies as he looks at demographic trends, natural resources demand, climate change, and globalization.

As mentioned earlier, a one-sentence summary from the climate science world: "[U]nmitigated climate change would, in the long term, be likely to exceed the capacity of natural, managed and human systems to adapt."*

Private Sector Policies

> It is not the strongest of the species that survives, nor the most intelligent, but the one most responsive to change.
>
> —Charles Darwin

---

* IPCC Working Group II, *Special Report*, p. 71.

Overlay: Encourage private sector organizations to consider the New Triple Constraint Overlays in their strategic planning. The major current shortfall is accounting for climate change. Insurance companies and some major corporations are beginning to focus on all three since they have to set rates based on probabilities of these occurring.

Most of the readers of this book will be either in the private sector or working managing government projects and programs. As program managers you are involved in life cycle management of programs and as a portfolio manager you are selecting new programs for investment. The world is already seeing dramatic evidence of climate change and the New Triple Constraint at work. Wind and solar energy sources are becoming ubiquitous on the landscape as a small step away from fossil fuels. The United States just finished its 10-year census illustrating the demographic changes in the country since the year 2000. They are dramatic in the movement of people and the change in ethnic mix and implications for the future.

The energy industry and related associations regularly provide estimates of oil, coal, and natural gas reserves and the data and analyses are published by the Energy Information Administration and are available to all.

The following section addresses specific policies of some segments of the world economy.

Investment Policies Considering Climate Change

Investment policies considering population and energy are easily established and rather straightforward. However, apparently few major companies are thinking about the impacts of climate change and adaptation, according to a survey discussed in a National Research Council report.[*] Only about 25% were providing information requested by investors regarding efforts to plan for the effects of climate change. This is not the case in the financial community, especially in Europe. In February 2008, Citigroup, JP Morgan, Chase, and Morgan Stanley launched

---

[*] National Research Council, *Informing an Effective Response to Climate Change* (Washington, DC: National Academies Press, 2010) p. 67.

the Carbon Principles, a voluntary framework aimed at addressing climate risks associated with financing carbon-intensive projects in the U.S. power sector. The Bank of America, Credit Suisse, and Wells Fargo also endorsed the principles later that year. In December 2008 a second group of global financial institutions, including Credit Agricole, HSBC, Munich Re, Standard Chartered, and Swiss Re, announced their adoption of the principles to thereby expand beyond the United States. Others include F&C Asset Management and BNP Paribas. These principles provide a good planning and overlay guide for the private sector. According to The Climate Group, which monitors the activities related to the principles:

> Every organization that adopts the Climate Principles is actively managing climate change across the full range of financial products and services, including: research activities; asset management; retail banking; insurance and re-insurance; corporate banking; investment banking and markets; and project finance.[*]

An iterative risk management framework is the recommended approach for evaluating projects and programs.[†] For many of us in the program management profession, an iterative risk management process is a given for decision making on major programs (see Appendix C). The import is that it is recognized by a broader community as important to make explicit the assumptions regarding climate change and to incorporate climate change risk items in our risk and decision matrices. The iterative process is also important because of the status of climate change. Every year the data change and the government response changes, which impacts private sector programs.

Climate-related decisions are particularly difficult to make because of their long-term nature and fiscal implications. In many cases they are in the nature of avoiding a Type II error, as discussed in the section on statistical inference in Appendix B. (A Type II error is not taking action which later proves necessary.)

There are many climate-dependent decisions that need to be made by private sector organizations or even by government organizations considering programs and projects for investment.

---

[*] The Climate Group, http://www.theclimategroup.org/programs/the-climate-principles/.
[†] National Research Council, *Informing an Effective Response*, p. 122.

Some of the relevant types of decisions an organization or company will have to make, sooner or later, due to climate change are as follows[*]

- How to reduce CO_2 emissions from operations and supply chains, and whether or not to participate in regional and global carbon markets and offsetting
- How to develop good information for consumers and stakeholders about carbon in products
- Whether and how to influence government and international policy through best practice demonstration, lobbying, business networks, etc.
- Whether and how to insure climate risks
- How to adapt to climate risks and respond to climate impacts in a globalized market
- Whether to invest in businesses and technologies that are vulnerable to climate risks or are not limiting their emissions
- Whether to start up a new business focused on solutions to climate change
- How to respond to pressure from nongovernmental organizations, shareholders, and investors regarding climate change
- How and what to communicate about climate change (especially from media and the cultural sector)
- Funding for research and development projects and the selection of those projects

All of the above are dependent upon the conclusion that climate change creates risks.

There are many decisions that need to be made as individuals and these are identified in many other books in the bibliography. One that needs consideration and is not always specifically identified is the degree to which personal investments (including pensions) are in portfolios with low climate risk or in climate-responsible businesses.

Studies are increasingly being developed that provide analyses or assessments of the impact of climate change on private sector organizations and their decision making. A study released in February 2011 by Mercer (a subsidiary of Marsh & McLennan Companies, Inc.) indicated that a continued delay in climate change policy action by national governments and lack of international coordination could cost institutional investors

---

[*] National Research Council, *Informing an Effective Response*, pp. 26–27.

trillions of dollars over the coming decades.* This study was sponsored by the International Finance Corporation of the World Bank and study participants included representatives from such major investment organizations as the California Public Employees Retirement System (CalPERS), Maryland State Retirement Agency, Government of Singapore Investment Corporation, and others from around the world. All these organizations are involved in making investment decisions for large portfolios. These are the heavy hitters weighing in on the real concern about climate change from those organizations whose future economic welfare is based on evaluating the data and reaching conclusions.

The report analyzes the potential financial impacts of alternate climate change scenarios on investors' portfolios. Andrew Kirton, Chief Investment Officer at Mercer, commented:

> Climate change brings fundamental implications for investment patterns, risks and rewards. Institutional investors should be factoring long-term considerations, such as climate change, into their strategic planning. Mercer is pleased to have had the opportunity to kick start such strategic discussions with a group of leading global investors.[†]

While the report identifies a series of pragmatic steps for institutional investors to consider in their strategic asset allocation process, these also apply to individual organizations, portfolio managers, and program managers that have 10-to-20-years or more planning horizons.

Some of the key findings of this international private sector study show that by 2030[‡]

- Climate change increases uncertainty for long term institutional investors and, as such, needs to be proactively managed.
- Investment opportunities in low carbon technologies could reach $5 trillion.
- The cost of impacts on the physical environment, health, and food security could exceed $4 trillion.

---

* Mercer, *Climate Change Scenarios: Implications for Strategic Asset Allocation,* February 15, 2011, http://www.mercer.com/articles/1406410.

† Quoted in Click Green, http://www.clickgreen.org.uk/analysis/business-analysis/121903-trillions-of-dollars-at-stake-from-climate-change-over-next-20-years.html, February 15, 2011.

‡ Click Green, http://www.clickgreen.org.uk/analysis/business-analysis/121903-trillions-of-dollars-at-stake-from-climate-change-over-next-20-years.html, February 15, 2011.

- Climate change related policy changes could increase the cost of carbon emissions by as much as $8 trillion.
- Increasing funds allocation to "climate sensitive" assets will help to mitigate risks and capture new opportunities. Engagement with policy makers is crucial for institutional investors to proactively manage the potential costs of delayed and poorly coordinated climate policy action. Policy developments at the country level will produce new investment opportunities as well as risks that need to be constantly monitored.

Program Policies

> The barriers are not erected which can say to aspiring talents and industry: thus far and no farther.
>
> **—Ludwig van Beethoven**

Awareness of the New Triple Constraint issues is important to assuring positive outcomes from longer-term life cycle programs. Actions involve being prepared to either implement risk management or direct planning action whenever any aspects of the Triple Constraint impinge upon your program. Understanding population and demographic changes is important in staffing plans and resource availability for programs in the United States as well as internationally. As time goes on, in some countries, such as those in the European Union and Japan and Russia, there will be serious labor shortages and program planning will need to accommodate that situation. In the United States, the labor mixes, both skilled and unskilled, will be changing as more diversity results from increasing Hispanic and Asian percentages in the population. However, the biggest problems will be overseas, especially in Africa and parts of Asia and South America, as the population continues to increase, energy costs increase, and the impacts of climate change become more widespread and severe, especially on the food supply. This is currently coming to pass as has been forecast for many years.

Costs of long-term programs will be increasingly difficult to estimate as the oil supply problem relentlessly drives up the price of oil and gasoline and all derivative products. This is virtually the entire economy since not only gasoline but fertilizers, plastics, pharmaceuticals, beauty products, and the like are all dependent upon oil. Food prices are already rising significantly due to a combination of increased transportation and fertilizer costs and shortages due to the increased number of extreme climate events. The latter can only be explained by climate changes affecting weather patterns and the increased moisture in the air due to warming.

As indicated in the Section 3 Energy Constraint section, there are many opportunities for new and expanded programs, which are needed to provide alternate sources of energy and alternatives that reduce carbon emissions. Because of the agreement that the Western world needs to "reduce the reliance on foreign oil," programs to provide alternatives are welcomed and encouraged around the world. Although the recognition of "peak oil" is camouflaged by suppliers of oil, limits in supply and increasing costs of exploration and extraction of oil will drive the prices up. Air transportation is particularly vulnerable to declining oil supply and increased prices because of the current lack of reasonable economic alternatives to jet fuel.

The rapidity of climate change, driven by increasing carbon emissions from an increasing population and the ability to adapt or mitigate it is the big unknown. Regardless of the current ability of special interests to impede any attempts at mitigation, the climate will continue to warm, storms will get more severe, oceans will rise, droughts will get more serious, and eventually the U.S. government will join the rest of the world in attempts to mitigate the causes of climate change. You cannot legislate climate change away as was proposed in Montana[*]— CO_2 will continue to rise as long as carbon emissions from humans continue to be released into the atmosphere—and the climate will change. This has been known since the time of Tyndall and Arrhenius in the late 1800s. Opportunities for programs related to mitigation currently exist and are encouraged almost universally in the world where the populations "get it." The amount of CO_2 in the atmosphere will continue relentlessly upward with time and the related temperature increases will follow because of the simple physics involved in the necessity for the Earth to move toward a heat balance.

Programs, therefore, should be planned to use less energy, and use renewable and sustainable energy sources like the solar-thermal generators that are now providing energy in Europe at competitive prices.

When faced with a problem or uncertainty with possible costly outcomes, the conservative businessman will do things such as buy insurance, hedge the risk, reduce downside exposure, and protect assets. This is basic

---

[*] Brad Johnson, "Montana Legislator Introduces Bill to Declare Global Warming 'Natural' and 'Beneficial,'" February 17, 2011, Think Progress, http://thinkprogress.org/2011/02/17/montana-global-warming-bill/ (accessed March 24, 2011).

to running a business. Students are taught this in basic business classes. It is also common sense. However, many businesses are not looking at population-driven climate change as a risk item and are assuming or hoping that the scientific consensus on global warming will turn out to be wrong or too far in the future to be concerned. According to Bracken Hendricks, "This is bad risk management and an irresponsible way to run anything, whether a business, an economy or a planet."* In statistical inference, this is a Type II error: not taking action when the null hypothesis is true—carbon emissions from humans are causing dangerous global warming.

Remember, upon the conduct of each depends the fate of all.

—Alexander the Great

---

* Bracken Hendricks, "Why Fighting Global Warming Should Be a Conservative Cause," *Washington Post*, November 7, 2010, p. B2.

Section I

Population Overlay

3

Population Constraint Overlay: Introduction

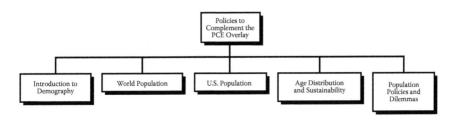

Chapter 3 outline.

Overlay: *The Stockholm Memorandum*: "Priorities for Coherent Global Action: Greatly increase access to reproductive health services, education and credit, aiming at empowering women all over the world. Such measures are important in their own right but will also reduce birth rates."[*]

The first of the three forces driving changes in our world that need to be accommodated in program and portfolio management is the changing population and related demographics. It is the fundamental driver that impacts the other two of the new triple constraints as well as our personal lives and projects. Change due to population growth and demographics are factors that need to be considered in a business plans and program plans. The problem is not that planners and programmers are not aware of population changes; it is just that the magnitude and nature of the changes are really dramatic and exceed what the world has seen before. Figure 3.1 presents the outline of this chapter.

---

[*] 17 Nobel Laureates and other representatives, Royal Swedish Academy of Sciences, 3rd Nobel Laureates Symposium on Global Sustainability, *The Stockholm Memorandum*, Published by the Secretariat, reference Item 6, p. 5, http://globalsymposium2011.org/wp-content/uploads/2011/05/The-Stockholm-Memorandum.pdf.

The world population is changing rapidly, which impacts the basic assumptions behind virtually all long-term analyses and any life cycle cost activities that are related in any way to population, consumers, demand, economic growth, and the like. Our planning baseline is changing fast—it is moving and it is a variable. With the completion of the 2010 census, there has been a spate of articles on the changes and they have made the headlines. At the same time there have been many world events that have also dominated the headlines, so while most people are aware that there have been changes in the last decade, the impacts on the future have gotten lost. There are two primary facts that you need to know: First, the current world population of 6.8 billion is expected to grow to 9.3 billion by 2050. We have added 2 billion persons since 1975 and will add another 3 billion between 2010 and 2050*. These are big numbers. Although we are projecting a little less than 40 years into the future to 2050, these numbers for population are mostly already set. Demographers know the birth and death rates of the populations of every country in the world and their trends. They have good data on the migration of people between countries and regions. Yes, there may be factors that occur to change the numbers within a country, but the volatile ones are not that numerous. There will be changes, but the totals will not change much.

The second fact is you need to know about the expected population changes in your own country and region or state. How do you relate to the 3 billion world increase? In the United States we are at approximately 300 million (308,745,538 according to the 2010 census) and will progress to over 400 million by 2050. So, how will we accommodate an additional 100 million? This also is a big number. Where will they live? Where will they work? Where will the energy come from that they will need to survive and that we will need to maintain or improve our current standard of living? What will be their environmental impact? What will be their emissions? Just think, 100/300 = 33% more traffic on the roads on average compared to today. They will not be spread evenly around the country but will be mostly in the cities, those trends are clear. (I am glad I live in a low-density rural area.)

So why is this useful to me? From the point of view of portfolio management, almost everything is related either directly or indirectly to population and demography. Marketing programs are dependent on population and demographic data as are transportation and other economic sector programs.

---

* See tables in Chapter 5.

The author was responsible for the economic studies of the Northeast Rail Corridor to determine the economic viability of the proposed upgrade to the Amtrak service. Demand for transportation between the various cities was a key determinant of many of the engineering upgrades. How many riders was the system designed for? The actual demand analysis was very complex and we used a variation of Sir Isaac Newton's Law of Gravitation to predict the ridership between all stations and in total. The gravity model is driven by demographics: the population size of two places and the square of their distances apart. In general, larger places attract more people than smaller places, and places closer together have a greater attraction than places farther away. Just like gravity, this is the principle of the model.

$$Ridership_{ij} = K\left(\frac{Population_i \times Population_j}{Distance^2} \right)$$

In this grossly oversimplified version of the model, the ridership between two cities i and j is equal to a constant K multiplied by the ratio of the product of the two populations divided by the distance between the two cities squared. The factor K is determined empirically (by previous observation).

Now, this wasn't today's populations that were important it was the populations several years hence. We wanted to estimate the likely ridership when the project was finished—after 5 years of construction and rebuilding, and then after another 25 years, the design life of the project.

In addition, the demographics of each city with a station were important. The distances that people lived from the stations were an important determinant in the overall analysis and for this aspect very detailed demographic data were used in the analysis, similar to that used to determine legislative districts within a county. The analysis had to consider the likelihood that people would and could travel to the rail station so income data were also integrated into the mix. Several other determinants of ridership went into the final analysis, including ticket price and service frequency and express versus local service.[*]

The very simple model above assumes the people in the population are all likely train riders and only population and distance are the determi-

---

[*] Although I was the program manager, I personally developed a sophisticated return on investment (ROI) cost model and ran a series of sensitivity studies to analyze the impact of various cost variables such as number of passengers per rail car or the cost of the rail car or use of concrete ties versus wood ties.

nants. The many projects that were a part of the system upgrade were all dependent upon the estimates of travel demand—from the station platform design to the roadbed design and electrification system power requirements. The important message is that understanding changes in populations and demographics is important.

4

Introduction to Demography

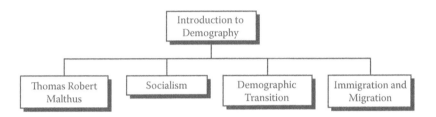

Chapter 4 outline.

Overlay: Projected demographic changes must be considered in planning. Demographic analysis has many dimensions and significant changes are driven by birth rates in countries and by immigration. Some awareness of population theories is useful to put current practices in perspective.

The scientific study of human populations is called *demography*. We are interested, in this first leg of the new triple constraints, in several aspects of demographic analysis as follows:

1. How large is the population? How many live in a given place? What are their program needs and how do they impact our program or portfolio?
2. What is the growth or decline in population in total, by region or country? How do they change over time? How does that impact our planning?
3. What are the various demographic processes? What are the levels and trends in fertility, mortality, and migration? How does this impact our program assumptions and risks?

4. Where are the people located? How are they distributed around the world or country? Why did the distribution occur and what are the implications for our programs? What is the impact of globalization?*

5. How many are males and females? How many are of each cohort? What does the age distribution look like? What is the composition of the workforce? Is the workforce aging?

6. What are the overall characteristics of the segment of population that is of interest to our program or our portfolio or enterprise—education, income, occupation, immigrant status, and so on?

Based on the data, we are able to make defensible projections and assumptions in our analysis.

We are not going to get into all of these in any detail. We will identify the major trends so the reader can use these to put the other constraints—climate change and energy—into context. For over 10,000 years, since the end of the last Ice Age, humans have been the driving force on this planet and the demographics and demographic changes not only explain much of our history but provide a forecast of our future.

In this section we will discuss relevant aspects of selected demographic theories, starting with Malthus and the Socialists.

THOMAS ROBERT MALTHUS

The modern theories of demographics and demographic analysis start with Thomas Robert Malthus's *An Essay on the Principle of Population*, published in 1798.[†] His essay was based on the belief that population grew geometrically while food supply grows arithmetically. The end result would be poverty and misery as the population outgrew the food supply. His answer to the dilemma was moral restraint in having children to slow down population growth. Later writers building on his theory proposed birth control as the solution rather than restraint.

---

[*] *Globalization* essentially means ignoring country boundaries and using the most efficient sources for goods, services, and materials considering total costs, including transportation. It is built on the concept of comparative advantage where each entity in the process is chosen based on its inherent capability to produce the most competitive product.

[†] Thomas Robert Malthus, *An Essay on the Principle of Population, 1798* (Lexington, Kentucky: Maestro Reprints, 2010).

We are all aware that we are not yet all living in misery due to short-age of food. On a worldwide basis there is a surplus after 213 or so years of *geometric growth*. Malthus[*] was unable to predict the green revolution, which dramatically increased the productivity and yields of farmers, especially in the last half of the twentieth century. For many years, Malthus has been identified as one of many seers whose dramatic warnings failed to materialize. However, the reader should not give up on Malthus. Authors such as Julian Cribb write about current food crises that exist in many parts of the world and warn of coming famines.[†] There is a question about the carrying capacity of the world—how many people the Earth can sustain—is Malthus right but the timing wrong? That we will discuss later.

SOCIALISM

Marx and Engels had a different perspective from Malthus. They believed that capitalism would result in overpopulation and resulting poverty; but with socialism, population growth would be readily absorbed by the economy with no side effects. They saw no reason to suspect that science and technology could increase the availability of food and other goods at least as quickly as the population grew.[‡] Whatever population pressure existed in society was really pressure against the means of employment rather than the means of subsistence. Poverty is the result of a poorly organized society (i.e., capitalism) and cannot be blamed on the poor. Implicit in their writings is the idea that the normal consequence of population growth should be a significant increase in production. Each worker was producing more than he or she required; therefore, in an orderly socialistic society, there would be more wealth, not more poverty. Conclusion: the more workers, the wealthier the society.

We all know that the Marxian concept is far from ideal. The Soviet experiment showed that all the assumed evils of capitalist societies and

---

[*] Malthus's *Essay* is 108 pages long. This brief summary does not do him justice regarding the elegance of his writings or eloquence nor the flood of criticisms that follow to this day.

[†] Julian Cribb, *The Coming Famine: The Global Food Crisis and What We Can Do to Avoid It* (Berkeley: University of California Press, 2010).

[‡] John R. Weeks, *Population: An Introduction to Concepts and Issues, Tenth Edition* (Belmont CA: Wadsworth Cengage Learning, 2008, p. 84).

free markets existed behind the Iron Curtain. Besides the collapse of the Soviet Union, China has had to stray far from Marxian principles in order to control its runaway population with the one child rule. (It also strayed for economic reasons.) Nevertheless, the policy of encouraging larger and larger populations exists within some cultures throughout the world. Plans to inhibit population growth get strong resistance. Increasing populations provide more members of an ethnic or religious group and result in more political power.

DEMOGRAPHIC TRANSITION STAGES

The composition of the current world population is heterogeneous and analysis of trends is a complex undertaking. The current concept of demography is not based on Malthus or Marx but on the concept of rates of changes in births and deaths in homogenous segments. Since these are constantly changing, we evaluate the *demographic transition*. This is really a set of transitions as follows:[*]

- *Stage I: The starting baseline* where a community has high and similar rates of birth and death. This occurs typically in a preindustrial state with a small and relatively stable total population cohort.[†]
- *Transition Stage II: Health and mortality transition* where there are falling death rates but no change in birth rate, resulting in a rapid increase in population. This is typically initiated by improved medical and health care in a developing country.
- *Transition Stage III: Fertility transition* where births are falling but overall population is still rising swiftly but at a decelerating rate due to falling death rates.
- *End Stage IV: Population stable* but at a new higher level; low and similar rates of birth and death.

---

[*] The presented stages are a composite from Weeks, *Population*, pp. 98, 99; Laurence C. Smith, *The World in 2050: Four Forces Shaping Civilization's Northern Future* (New York: Dutton, Penguin Group, 2010), p. 45; and David Yaukey, Douglas L. Anderton, and Jennifer Hickes Lundquist, *Demography: The Study of Human Population, Third Edition* (Long Grove, IL: Waveland Press, Inc., 2007), pp. 46–49.

[†] A *cohort* is an age group used in demographics; "men age 30–39" could be a cohort.

These theoretical stages are based on the European demographic transition. Each society in the world did not or is not going through these stages simultaneously and various societies take longer or shorter periods to go through each of the transition stages.

Some demographers include additional stages between Stages III and IV, such as an *age transition* where society accommodates an increasing age of the population due to longer life spans and lower birth rates; *migration transition* where there is movement toward urban areas due to increased opportunity; and a *family and household transition* where accommodations are made to adjust to longer lives, lower fertility, older age structure, and urban versus rural residence.* In any event, these are descriptions of observed conditions, not political theory.

IMMIGRATION AND MIGRATION

The other important demographic variables are immigration and migration. People move toward opportunity for a better life. Some governments encourage immigration to acquire important labor components and experienced and skilled persons to enhance and complement their workforces. Other governments put constraints on immigration to control population growth and to protect the existing workforce from low-cost competition. The population of the United States in particular has been significantly modified by immigration, which has significantly changed the Stages III and IV transition with large infusions of classes of workers who themselves were in earlier stages. Migration is often driven by climatic factors such as continuing drought, floods, and hurricanes. We saw the migration out of New Orleans after Hurricane Katrina, with many moving permanently to Houston and other cities in Texas and Louisiana.

---

* Weeks, *Population*, 98.

5

World Population

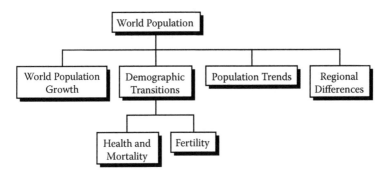

Chapter 5 outline.

World population growth is dependent on many factors, but the primary ones are the demographic transition status of the individual societies. Inexpensive oil and high agricultural productivity go hand in hand and encourage population growth. They improve economic conditions so young people are more likely to start families or increase families knowing that they will be able to support them. Immigration policies and local economic factors affect movements of peoples in evaluating demographic changes. Education and poverty are important metrics to program and portfolio planning managers. Birth rates in first and third world countries—Organization for Economic Cooperation and Development (OECD)* and non-OECD countries are determining the shape and location of the workforce and both are changing, but at different rates. Migration and immigration policies strongly influence population demographics.

---

* See the Glossary for listings of the countries in the OECD.

WORLD POPULATION GROWTH

Summary Overlay: Strategic planning needs to reflect the population of the world increasing to more than 9 billion people in 2050, then slower growth and peaking at 10 billion in 2080. This is up from the current 6.9 billion. The additional 2–3 or more billion people will be almost entirely from the countries in the developing world. Planning and policies should continue to encourage education of women since the current and projected growth of total population is caused primarily by changes occurring in fertility rates in the developing countries as women choose to take control of their lives.

Table 5.1* presents the world population growth to date and as estimated to 2050 by the United Nations Population Division.

The population growth of the world has been amazing. From the end of the ice ages 10,000 years ago it took until approximately AD 1500 for

TABLE 5.1

World Population Growth

Year	Population in Millions	Year	Population in Millions
10,000 BC	4	AD 1970	3,685
5,000 BC	5	AD 1975	4,061
1,000 BC	50	AD 1985	4,846
AD 1	300	AD 1990	5,290
AD 500	200	AD 2000	6,115
AD 1000	310	AD 2005	6,512
AD 1500	500	AD 2010	6,896
AD 1700	650	AD 2015	7,284
AD 1800	1,000	AD 2020	7,857
AD 1850	1,260	AD 2025	8,002
AD 1900	1,650	AD 2030	8,321
AD 1930	2,070	AD 2040	8,874
AD 1950	2,520	AD 2045	9,106
AD 1960	3,023	AD 2050	9,306

---

* U.S. Census Historical Estimates of World Population (BC to 1950 AD), http://www.census. gov/ipc/www/worldhis.html; data for 1950 and beyond from the Population Division of the Department of Economic and Social Affairs of the United Nations Secretariat, *World Population Prospects: The 2010 Revision*, http://esa.un.org/unpp/wpp (accessed March 3, 2011).

the world to reach a population of a half billion; then it took only another 300 years to reach 1 billion. From the premodern age up until about 1650 and the start of the Industrial Revolution, harsh living conditions, epidemics, infectious diseases, famines, and floods all resulted in high mortality and slow growth in population.

Part of the Industrial Revolution included breakthroughs in medicines and vaccines that extended lives as well as reduced infant mortality. This resulted in high population growth rates that continued until about 1960. Table 5.1 shows that the world's population reached 2 billion by 1930, only 430 years after reaching 1 billion, then 3 billion by 1959 after only approximately 30 years.

According to the U.N. Population Division, following are the specific dates to reach more "billion marks"*:

3 Billion: 20 October 1959
4 Billion: 27 June 1974
5 Billion: 21 January 1987
6 Billion: 5 December 1998
7 Billion: 31 October 2011
8 Billion: 15 June 2025
9 Billion: 18 February 2043
10 Billion: 18 June 2083

Regardless of the total numbers, we really live in two very different demographic worlds on this planet. One of these worlds is poor and growing rapidly, the Less Developed Regions (LDRs). It contains the vast majority of people who live in the countries of Africa, Asia, and Latin America. Eighty percent of the world population is present in these countries. The More Developed Regions (MDRs), include the Western world—the OECD nations of North America, Europe, Japan, Australia, and New Zealand. These countries are relatively rich and are growing slowly if at all.†

Demographic Transitions

The changes in population depend upon three factors, which are defined as follows:

---

* See United Nations, Department of Economic and Social Affairs, http://esa.un.org/unpd/wpp/ other-information/faq.htm (updated 3 April 2011; accessed May 6, 2011).
† See Glossary for complete list of OECD countries.

Fertility and fertility rate: The number of live births to women ages 15 to 49; the ratio of live births in an area of the population, usually expressed per 1,000 persons per year. This is very important since it is currently the primary variable in forecasting future population size.

> *Replacement level* of fertility. The level of fertility that would, if maintained indefinitely in the absence of migration, ensure a stationary population in the long run. This is the level at which women, on the average, have enough daughters to "replace" themselves in the population. Replacement level fertility rates have to be above 2.0 since at least one son is born for every daughter and some potential mothers die early. The replacement level is generally associated with a total fertility rate of about 2.1 for first world countries and 2.3 for third world countries where mortality rates are higher.[*]

Mortality and mortality rate: the annual number of deaths in a population; the ratio of deaths in an area to the population, usually expressed per 1,000 persons. The mortality rate is dependent upon the availability of health services.

Migration and migration rate: the number of persons that change residence, including social affiliation, across geopolitical boundaries; the numbers of migrants per 1,000 persons. While the migration rate has a limited impact on the total numbers, it is significant when it comes to population changes in specific countries.

Health and Mortality Transition

> **Overlay:** The continuing increase in life spans throughout the world will primarily impact the developing world where improving medical services and increased standards of living are occurring. The net result is a larger and older population.

Referring back to the demographic transition stages, the Stage II Health and Mortality Transition began for the Western world at the end of the eighteenth century coincident with the Industrial Revolution. Doctors

---

[*] Yaukey et al., *Demography*, 205.

discovered medicines and improved procedures and vaccines and eventually antibiotics and more powerful drugs. Insecticides were developed to control insects and diseases. An understanding of the methods of transmission of diseases evolved as did the mitigating actions. Improved methods of food production were developed that reduced famines and provided improved nourishment, which also added years to the life expectancy. At first, these improvements were primarily limited to the Western world or the MDRs. In about 1950, they spread rapidly to the LDR, where 80% of the world population resides, with explosive results. This transition, which is resulting in longer life spans and has mostly run its course in the MDRs, is continuing today in the LDRs. The trajectory of improvements in infant mortality and overall life expectancy in each country can be estimated with a relatively high level of confidence for another generation to 2050 or so.

Neither Transition Stage II nor Transition Stage III is really ever completed, only mostly. Although the United States has basically completed Transition Stage II, there are still areas of the country, such as Appalachia and in some Southern areas, where poverty is the rule and the transition is a work in progress.

World War II is considered a modern turning point in worldwide decreases in mortality. In order to protect their soldiers, each side in the war spent millions of dollars figuring out how to prevent the spread of disease among troops, including ways to clean up water supplies and deal with human waste. At the same time they were working on new ways to cure disease and heal sick and wounded soldiers. All of this knowledge was transferred to the rest of the world at the war's end, leading immediately to significant declines in the death rates.[*]

Historically, socioeconomic development was a necessary precursor to improving health in a country; it needed economic resources and experience and training and facilities. However, after the war, public health services and international nongovernmental organizations (NGOs), and the U.N. World Health Organization (WHO), were able to move into the poorest of the LDR countries and have a significant impact by bringing these techniques and tools and medicines to them. My daughter is a registered nurse (RN) and she goes biannually with her church group to work with an orphanage in Honduras to teach health and nutrition principles and bring donated medical and school supplies.

---

[*] Weeks, *Population*, 153.

In general, however, lower mortality rates are associated with higher incomes and the life expectancy tables clearly show the longer lives are in the countries with the higher standards of living.

Lower infant mortality and longer life expectancy translate into two obvious population impacts. One is that the population will get larger if more people live to adulthood and if fewer people die; the second is that the population will get older. See Chapter 7 for a further discussion of aging in the population.

Fertility Transition

The Stage III Fertility Transition accompanies the mortality transition but lags by several years because in the case of mortality, people readily adopt technology and respect medical doctors and their recommendations that extend life; but fertility reductions are different. They are constrained by culture and depend upon education and the empowerment of women, an urban lifestyle away from the farm, access to contraception, and down-sized family expectations, all of which take more time.[*]

The fertility transition usually starts after the mortality transition has started. The greater survival of children starts women thinking about limiting the number of children they have because of the probability of more surviving. Similarly, because women start to live longer, they recognize they can delay childbearing, have fewer children because their children will survive to adulthood, and also they will survive beyond childbearing years. This gives them many more opportunities to do something beyond simply childbearing and rearing and raising children. Demographers believe this awareness becomes a tipping point in societies, which leads to an almost

Overlay: Fertility rates of approximately 2.1 per woman are required to maintain a constant population; rates below that result in shrinking populations. The worldwide trend is moving toward less than 2.1 by 2050, which would result in a peaking then shrinking world population. The economic model of all countries currently relies on increasing populations to increase growth and gross domestic product (GDP); therefore, population changes are precursors of economic growth patterns within the individual countries or regions.

---

[*] Smith, *The World in 2050*, 12.

irreversible decline in birthrate.* On a worldwide basis, this tipping point was reached in about 1965 shortly after China started recovering from The Great Leap Forward.

In addition, as the probability of children surviving increases, there are also more resources available for their support if there are fewer children. The resources of a society get partially redirected from raising children to raising the standard of living of the family and taking advantage of the longer lives. It is all a positive feedback situation.

Some countries in the LDRs that are in Transition Stage II have experienced amazing growth rates and are expected to reach enormous population sizes by the middle of the twenty-first century. Table 5.2, shown later in this chapter, illustrates this situation.

The population growth rate is less than 1% in the United States and France, and nearly 0% in Sweden, Germany, and Austria. The reasons for the low rate of population growth in Transition Stage III MDRs are population education and women in schools and the following:

1. Higher marriageable age (25 years or more)—delayed marriage translates into fewer births (this was one of the tools recommended by Malthus)
2. Ready acceptability of small family norms and family planning techniques
3. Fewer religious taboos on birth control
4. Economic well-being and a liking for high living standards, and recognizing that a smaller family means more discretionary income

The U.N. data indicate that the world will most likely peak at a population of approximately 10 billion people about 2080 and then level off. It assumes the average woman will move toward 1.85 children, which is slightly below replacement rate. At present it is difficult to predict the birth rate in the Muslim countries since it depends upon the education of the women and this has not been progressing as rapidly as expected. Recent unrest in the Arab world may change this situation. Figure 5.1 presents the world population by region and graphically illustrates the changes to date and how they are expected to continue to 2100.

The shape of the total population curve after 2050 is strongly dependent upon fertility rates. The Population Division of the Department of Economic and Social Affairs of the UN has prepared a set of population

---

* Weeks, *Population*, 100.

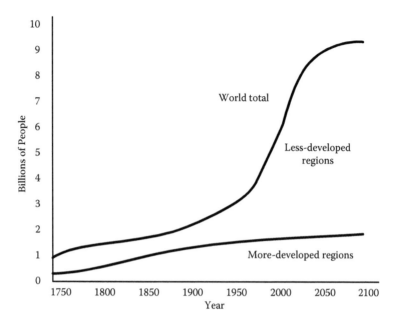

FIGURE 5.1
World populations by region.

projections to the year 2300 for each country of the world.[*] In terms of fertility, the medium scenario assumes that the total fertility of each country will fall below replacement levels and remain at those levels for about 100 years, after which it will return to replacement level and remain there until 2300.

So, the most likely scenario has a decline due to reduced fertility, then a return to replacement level, and a plateau at about 10 billion people into the next century. This is a reasonable target for sustainability planning. The increase between now and the 10 billion stability level is virtually all within the LDRs—the less developed regions and countries. Regardless of the forecast to 2100 and beyond, it seems clear that we will have approximately 3 billion more persons on this planet by 2080 and they will require resources.

Population Trends

Figure 5.2 is the current estimate of world population to 2050 and Figure 5.3 is a graph of the associated world population growth rates.

---

[*] United Nations, Population Division, *World Population in 2300 Highlights* (New York: Department of Economic and Social Affairs, Report ESA/P/WP.187, December 9, 2003, http://www.un.org/esa/population/publications/longrange2/Long_range_report.pdf).

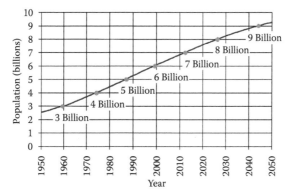

Source: U.S. Census Bureau. International Data Base. June 2010 Update.

FIGURE 5.2
World population 1950–2050.

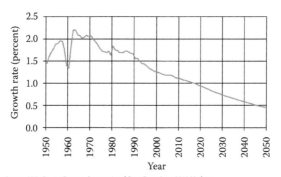

Source: U.S. Census Bureau. International Data Base. June 2010 Update.

FIGURE 5.3
World population growth rates.

Figure 5.3 is an interesting chart. The world population growth rate rose from about 1.5% per year from 1950 to 1951 to a peak of over 2% in the early 1960s due to reductions in mortality. Growth rates thereafter started to decline due to rising age at marriage as well as increasing availability and use of effective contraceptive methods. Note that changes in world population growth have not always been steady. A dip in the growth rate from 1959 to 1960, for instance, was due to the Great Leap Forward in China. During that time, both natural disasters and decreased agricultural output in the wake of massive social reorganization caused China's death rate to rise sharply and its fertility rate to fall by almost half.

In addition to growth rates, another way to look at population growth is to consider annual changes in the total population, as presented in Figure 5.4.

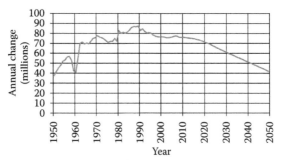

Source: U.S. Census Bureau. International Data Base. June 2010 Update.

FIGURE 5.4
Annual world population change.

The annual increase in world population peaked at about 87 million in the late 1980s. The peak occurred then, even though annual growth rates were past their peak in the late 1960s, because the world population was higher in the 1980s than in the 1960s.

If you look at a combination of Figures 5.2, 5.3, and 5.4, you can see how the world has changed with regard to population growth and what is likely to occur. If you were a member of the birth class of 1930 when the Earth's population reached 2 billion, you are now living in a world with over three times as many people. It is obvious that this is a different world if only for the number of people, but all of them need food and water, want education, housing with heat and air conditioning, clothing, transportation, and so forth. All consume resources and create emissions. And as shown in the figures, a lot more are on the way: another 3 billion by 2050. In fact, a net of approximately 2 more mouths per second.[*]

Figure 5.3 presents the average annual growth rate. Even though the growth rate has been dropping since 1960, the total population has increased from 3 billion to today's 6.8 billion. The reason is explained by simple arithmetic. Although the recent rate is small, the base has grown to be very large. The 1.2% growth rate in 2010 still adds 78 million net people in 2010 to the 6.8 billion base. Even in 2050, with a projected 0.4% growth rate, this translates into 35 million net additional people that year. While the annual change is decreasing, we are still adding a lot of people each year. These charts illustrate that although death rates or health rates are important, it is fertility rates that are driving the world's population machine.

---

[*] Weeks, *Population*, Table 2.2, 37.

Regional Differences

> **Overlay:** There are major changes in process as the world popula-
> tion continues to grow and its composition evolves. A much older
> population will increasingly depend on a decreasing workforce.
> Planning needs to recognize the rapidly growing third world with
> large unemployment; and a Western world with a stable or decreas-
> ing populations and potential labor shortages will provide many
> challenges and opportunities.

Table 5.2[*] contains projected population growth between 2010 and 2050
in several selected countries. They are not random selections, but were
chosen depending upon their individual anomalies and the curiosity of
the author.

Table 5.2 has many dimensions and provides a basis for planning overlays. Some of them are as follows:

- Looking toward the bottom of the table, the population of the world
  is projected to increase by 35% between 2010 and 2050; as mentioned
  before, this is a lot of people.
- Most of the population increase will be in the Less Developed
  Regions with 44% being the LDRs and 4% the MDRs. If you look at
  the top lines of the table, African nations lead the pack. The countries chosen are roughly representative of the rest of Africa. Again,
  these are big numbers. Since there is a correlation between population growth and economic growth, at least in the more developed
  nations, the countries with the low population growth will need
  labor from the high population growth regions. For the LDRs, slower
  population growth is believed to be necessary to increase the standards of living, with energy directed to more than just keeping large
  families alive. Smaller families mean fewer resources directed to the
  raising of children and more to making the lives more productive
  and meaningful. The immigration and growth policies of nearly all
  the countries in the world will need to be reviewed by each country
  to see if its current trajectory is viable.

---

[*] U.S. Census Bureau http://www.census.gov/ipc/www/idb/informationGateway.php. Accessed Dec 2010.
Plus http://www.globalhealthfacts.org/topic.jsp?i=86 for land area.

TABLE 5.2

Selected Country Population Growth 2010–2050

Country	Area Sq. Mi.	Density Pop./ Sq. Mi.	Population 2010 (000)	Population 2050 (000)	% Change
Zimbabwe	151,000	77	11,652	25,198	116
Central African Republic	241,000	20	4,845	10,339	113
Nigeria	357,000	427	152,217	264,262	74
Bangladesh	56,000	2808	156,118	250,155	60
Pakistan	307,000	600	184,405	290,848	58
United States	3,718,000	83	308,745	439,010	42
India	3,288,000	357	1,173,000	1,657,000	41
Mexico	761,000	148	112,469	147,908	32
Indonesia	741,000	328	242,968	313,021	29
Canada	3,854,000	9	33,760	41,136	22
France	213,000	304	64,768	69,768	8
China	3,704,000	359	1,330,141	1,303,723	−2
Germany	138,000	597	82,283	73,607	−11
Italy	116,000	499	58,091	50,390	−13
Russia	6,591,000	21	139,390	109,187	−22
Japan	146,000	869	126,804	93,674	−26
World	57,309,000	120	6,853,019	9,284,107	35
Less Developed Countries			5,621,913	8,114,829	44
More Developed Countries			1,231,105	1,279,277	4

Source: U.S. Census Bureau, International Data Base (IDB), http://www.census.gov/population/international/.

- The populations of the more developed nations are projected to only grow at a very low rate. If the United States were excluded from the grouping, the growth rate would be below zero. Look at Japan; it has a low birth rate and the longest life expectancy of any nation, so its population is not only shrinking but is growing much older at the same time.* This does not support continued economic growth. The countries with negative growth are undershooting the Transition IV status of neutral growth. They are countries that would be expected

---

* Japan is another special case with special problems and a very low birth rate combined with a highly restrictive immigration policy to keep Japan Japanese. It will be interesting to see how it solves its problems.

to go into decline as they are unable to continue to increase their GDP and standard of living. This would please Malthus, but Socialists would be appalled. China is another special case resulting from its population control mechanism of limiting families to one child. As a result, the growth rate is in decline and the population is getting much older. It will get worse because of the preference for sons; there is now a major mismatch in quantities of young females, which will exacerbate the situation. India will surpass China as the most populous nation and with a more balanced workforce.

- The population density column is also informative. It gives some rough indication of how crowded each country is and the amount of land available to support future generations. Of course, there is not much vacant land just sitting around waiting to be plowed like America in the seventeenth century. Low-density areas usually mean hot desert climates or cold northern areas. Climate change may bring some benefits to subarctic countries and likely will worsen conditions in LDRs.
- The United States and Canada are both expected to grow and prosper. The numbers look good, actually. The United States is discussed in more detail in the next chapter.

There are some studies that predict large migration due to droughts caused by climate change and other studies that predict people will not migrate due to climate change but will try to "make do" and stay near friends and family. I believe movement will occur to improve economic opportunity, and only indirectly be climate driven between now and 2050; after that it may be a different story if it becomes visually and environmentally apparent that serious climate changes are occurring. Over the next 40 years, the global labor force will grow rapidly and nearly exclusively in developing countries. These countries will potentially accrue the economic benefits of population growth as their working-age population rises, while that of industrialized countries falls. But as is happening in many developing countries, the economic development is lagging and much of the working-age population is unemployed and restless. Some countries discourage immigration. It is difficult to imagine Japan changing policies to allow large numbers of immigrants from the less-developed nations. It has a basic culture that favors homogeneity. It is also not clear how the currently restless young people in the Arab countries will find useful employment.

6

United States Population

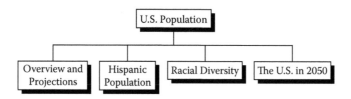

Chapter 6 outline.

The U.S. population is changing in total and in demographic composition. It is expected to grow by 130 million persons by year 2050. They will need jobs, housing, food, clothing, transportation, iPads, and the other things necessary to live in the United States.

OVERVIEW OF U.S. POPULATION AND PROJECTIONS

Overlay: The base population of the United States is expected to remain constant for the foreseeable future, and growth will come from immigration and an increasing Hispanic segment. Planners must closely watch changes in federal immigration policies since they may be a principal determinant of economic growth in the United States over the next 40-plus years. The United States needs young workers to replace an aging workforce.

The U.S. population is expected to grow from 308.7 million in 2010 to 439 million in 2050, as illustrated in Figure 6.1. This is a 42% increase overall, which appears to be a large number but reflects a population

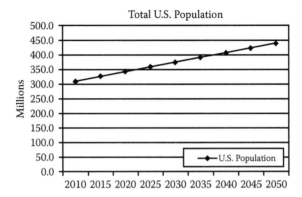

FIGURE 6.1

Total U.S. population. (Source, Annual Energy Outlook 2010, Table 20, U.S. Energy Information Administration)

average growth rate of only 0.9% per year. This forecast is consistent with that used in the Energy Information Agency (EIA) Annual Energy Outlook discussed in Chapter 5. For comparison, the growth in U.S. gross domestic product is expected to be in the 2.5% to 3% per year range between now and 2020. This bodes well for our current unemployment numbers to decrease.

The EIA uses four different sets of assumptions or scenarios regarding the future as the basis for their projections.* The U.S. population is projected to increase over the next four decades in all of the projection assumptions. The size of the increase is mostly dependent on the assumed level of *net international migration* to the United States (i.e., immigration). Naturally, a greater number of immigrants arriving in the United States will correspond to a larger increase in the size of the total population.

The level of immigration also impacts the rate at which the U.S. economy is projected to grow. The trends in the growth rate indicate that the highest levels of immigration correspond to the highest rates of economic growth, while lower levels or no immigration produces the lowest rates of economic growth. Notably, without immigration, the rate of population growth is low and expected to decline in all scenarios. This is attributed to projected fertility rates, which are assumed to remain fairly constant at or near the rate of replacement for the population. This is in contrast

---

* See, U.S. Energy Information Administration, International Energy Outlook 2011, Report DOE/ EIA-0484 (2011), September 2011, Page 144. http://205.254.135.24/forecasts/ieo/pdf/0484(2011).pdf. Last accessed March 3, 2011.

to Europe and some other advanced countries where the fertility rate is significantly lower than the replacement level. A caveat is necessary. Immigration occurs because of opportunities and jobs. Continuing recession slowed immigration.

HISPANIC POPULATION

Overlay: The fastest growing component of the U.S. population is the Hispanic segment, with the majority having Mexican ancestry. The Hispanic population also has a considerably lower median age than other ethnic groups and brings youth and vibrancy to the nation. International migration alone is not driving growth for the Hispanic population. Such growth is also attributed to fertility rates and a younger population. The Hispanic population of the United States has a higher level of fertility relative to all other racial and ethnic groups.

The Hispanic population is the key to continued economic growth in the United States. The terms *Hispanic* and *Latino* refer to persons who trace their origin or descent to Mexico, Puerto Rico, Cuba, Spanish-speaking Central and South American countries, and other Spanish cultures. Origin can be considered as the heritage, nationality group, lineage, or country of the person or the person's parents or ancestors before their arrival in the United States. People who identify their origin as Hispanic or Latino may be of any race. Notice this last statement: *people who identify their origin as Hispanic or Latino may be of any race.* This means that the Hispanic population cuts across normal race categories.

In 2010, the total population of the U.S. was 308.7 million and the White alone segment of the 196.8 million represented 64%. In 2010 with 50.5 million persons the Hispanic or Latino population accounted for 16.3% of the total population as also shown in Figure 6.2.

Of the 50.5 million Hispanic or Latino persons in the 2010 census, 26.7 million or 53 % were classified as White alone, 1.24 (2.5%) as African American alone, 0.68 million (1.3%) as American Indian or Alaska Native alone, 0.21 million (0.4%) or Asian alone, 0.06 (0.01%) Hawaiian or

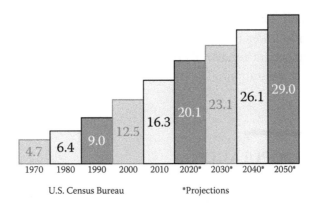

FIGURE 6.2
Percent Hispanic in the total population of the United States. (Source: U.S. Census Bureau. http://www.census.gov/population/www/socdemo/hispanic/hispanic_pop_presentation. html)

TABLE 6.1

Hispanic Origin in Total Population

Type of Origin	Number	Percent
Total	44,252,278	100.0
Mexican	18,339,354	64.0
Puerto Rican	3,987,947	9.0
Cuban	1,520,276	3.4
Dominican	1,217,225	2.8
Central American	3,372,090	7.6
South American	2,421,297	5.5
Other Hispanic	3,394,089	7.7

Source: U.S. Census Bureau, 2010, *American Community Survey.*
Table QT-P3.

Pacific Islander alone, 18.5 million (37%) as Some Other Race alone, and 3.0 million (6.0%) as Two or More Races.*

Table 6.1 presents the countries of origin of the Hispanic population who are mostly immigrants from Mexico. Table 6.2 shows that most resettle to areas where they already have friends and relatives who can assist with housing and employment.

---

* U.S. Census Bureau, 2010 Table P5. Census Data are accessed through the American FactFinder web page at http://factfinder2census.gov and inserting desired search parameters.
† Note within Table 6.1, this category is comprised of people whose origins are from the Dominican Republic, Spain, and Spanish-Speaking Central or South American countries. It also includes general origin responses such as "Latino" or "Hispanic."

TABLE 6.2

Top Five Counties by Hispanic Population Size: 2010

Rank	County	Population Size
1	Los Angeles County, CA	4,687,889
2	Harris County, TX	1,671,540
3	Miami-Dade County, FL	1,623,859
4	Cook County, IL	1,244,762
5	Maricopa County, AZ	1,128,741

Source: Pew Hispanic Center.

Michael Oppenheimer of Princeton and two coauthors forecast that as much as 10% of the Mexican population could migrate north to the United States in the next 70 years—as many as 6.7 million people—because of the crop declines and failures.[*] There is also a history of migration north that facilitates this migration.

The Hispanic population is important because it is the only ethnic group projected to maintain fertility above replacement level. Thus, the level of immigration, a large percentage of which is Hispanic, and ultimately the size of the Hispanic population affect the speed at which the total U.S. population growth rate changes and is also one of the factors that affects economic growth.

RACIAL DIVERSITY IN THE UNITED STATES

Overlay: The "white-alone" population share is expected to drop below 50% between 2040 and 2050.

The United States is expected to experience significant increases in racial and ethnic diversity over the next four decades as the percentages of the various ethnic groups move toward parity.[†] The highest levels of net

---

[*] Christopher Stolz, "Scientists See Hotter, Drier 21st Century with More Immigrants," *Ventura County Star*, http://www.vcstar.com/news/2010/dec/17/scientists-see-hotter-drier-21st-century-with/ #ixzz18Todf6U7- vcstar.com (accessed December 18, 2010).

[†] Jennifer M Ortman and Christine E. Guarneri, U.S. Census Bureau, *United States Population Projections: 2000 to 2050*, Analytical Document, http://www.census.gov/population/www/projections/ analytical-document09.pdf.

international migration correspond to the largest amount of growth for the Asian and Hispanic populations, which are the primary immigrant groups into the United States. These populations are projected to more than double in size between 2000 and 2050. Even if net international migration is maintained at a constant level of nearly 1 million, the Hispanic population is still projected to more than double between 2000 and 2050, while the size of the Asian population is projected to increase by 79%.

Most racial groups are projected to experience a moderate increase in size over the next four decades. One important exception to this is the non-Hispanic white-alone population, which is projected to experience a decline as a percentage of the total population. Without replacement by immigration from Europe, this population will decrease by about 6% from 2000 to 2050.

The black, American Indian and Alaskan Native, and Native Hawaiian and other Pacific Islander populations are expected to maintain their shares of the population. The Asian population is expected to experience an increase in its share of the population. As discussed earlier, the percentage of Hispanics in the U.S. population is projected to increase substantially in all projections.

For the non-Hispanic white-alone population, immigration has minimal impact on the pace of aging. For this group, the median age is projected to rise to approximately 45 years by 2050. The racial and ethnic diversity of the U.S. population is expected to increase as the proportion of the population that is non-Hispanic white-alone decreases. The amount of immigration that occurs during the next four decades could affect how quickly the non-Hispanic white-alone share of the population shrinks. Assuming migration continues at the current rate, the size of the non-Hispanic white-alone population is expected to decrease to the point that they represent a numeric minority between 2040 and 2050, the majority–minority crossover point. Based on simple arithmetic, higher levels of immigration cause the crossover to occur sooner, while less immigration causes the crossover to occur later.

UNITED STATES IN 2050

The current GDP of the United States is approximately $14 trillion and it is forecast to increase to $39 trillion by 2050. By that time, the four

Overlay: The United States will continue to be unique in the world as it will have a large economy as well as a very high standard of living, GDP per capita, compared to other countries in the world.

The country will continue to grow as it has in the past, slowly and steadily and following trends that are based on geography and culture. The country will change in terms of demographics as the Hispanic population continues to assimilate into the broader population, but the goals and the economic strength to enable an increasing standard of living to all citizens will likely continue, contingent upon solutions to the problems posed in Sections 1 and 3. The goals and principles of the United States will not change. This overlay of the United States in 2050 is important for it to remain sustainable and become a self-fulfilling prophesy. This picture of sustainability must be the framework for program and portfolio planning.

largest economies are expected to be the United States, China, India, and the European Union.* China is expected to surpass the United States in economic strength as measured by GDP and India will come close. This assumes China overcomes its population and standard-of-living problems.

However, the United States will be unique as it will have a large economy as well as a very high standard of living, GDP per capita, compared to China and India, as shown in the next chapter in Figure 7.5. Also it will have a growing working class population that will help it to maintain this growing standard of living. The biggest challenge and opportunity is the "creation of entrepreneurial and workforce opportunities for an ever-expanding population"†; in other words good jobs. Compared to the rest of the developed world and much of the developing world, we are projected to have a younger population, largely made up of Hispanics, which can provide the workforce needed so that the rest of us, the older population, can maintain our standard of living (e.g., a sustainable economic model).

Many areas of problems and challenge the country and its program managers will face are outlined in the following text. Demographic changes, continued assimilation of immigrant populations, and finding room for another 100 million people on the surface appear to be big problems.

---

* Ortman and Guarneri, U.S. Census Bureau, *United States Population Projections*, 9.
† Joel Kotkin, *The Next Hundred Million: America in 2050* (New York: Penguin Press, 2010), 211.

However, Joel Kotkin provides a positive and favorable perspective: "The America of 2050 may not stride the world like a hegemonic giant, but it will evolve into the one truly transcendent superpower in terms of society, technology and culture. Its greatest power will be its identification with notions of personal liberty, constitutional protections, and universalism."[*]

The country will continue to grow as it has in the past, slowly and steadily, but following predetermined paths that are based on geography and culture. The country will change in terms of demographic mix as the Hispanic population continues to assimilate into the broader population, but the goals and the economic strength to enable an increasing standard of living to all citizens will likely continue. The goals and principles of the United States will not change. The major dark clouds on the horizon are caused by a changing climate and constraining energy supplies, as is discussed in later chapters of this book.

---

[*] Joel Kotkin, *The Next Hundred Million*, 239.

7

World Age Distribution and Sustainability

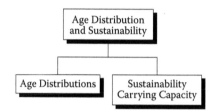

Overlay: Planners must recognize that the United States needs to have a strong immigrant population in order to provide the workforce necessary, which, when combined with technology, will maintain economic growth. The immigrant population should in total have a low median age.

Two additional aspects of population are of particular interest to program managers. The first aspect is age distribution within a country—if it has a slowing birth rate, where are the workers going to come from and how many will be available? Part of our basic economic model is somewhat of a Ponzi scheme. We require ever more young workers to supply the energy and productivity to keep our economic machine running and to support an ever-growing retired cohort. The other part of our economic model is the dependence on technology to constantly increase our productivity so that a proportionally smaller workforce is required. We still need young people, just not so many as in other countries. Second is the concept of sustainability. Remember that at the beginning of this book we discussed Malthus and his theories. If the geometric growth of the population and the arithmetic growth of the food supply are to bring catastrophe as he forecasted, for how long are we going to be able to increase our food supply? Fifty years? Indefinitely? Then the question arises as to how many people this planet can support: 6 billion? 9 billion? 18 billion? 72 billion? Maybe Malthus will be right in the end. We will return to this discussion later in this chapter in the section titled "Sustainability: Carrying Capacity."

AGE DISTRIBUTIONS

Analysis of age distributions is important since there are many significant changes occurring both in the United States and the world. Increasing median age is expected as the demographic transition Stage III progresses.

An age structure diagram, also called a *population pyramid*, is a graphic that shows the distribution of various age groups in a human population (typically that of a country or region of the world), which ideally forms the shape of a pyramid when the region is healthy. That is, a large number of workers support a much lower number of senior citizens.

It typically consists of two back-to-back bar graphs, with the population plotted on the horizontal *x* axis and age on the vertical *y* axis, one showing the number of males and one showing females in a particular population in 5-year age groups (also called *cohorts*). Males are conventionally shown on the left and females on the right, and they may be measured by raw number or as a percentage of the total population.

Population pyramids are often viewed as the most effective way to graphically depict the age and gender distribution of a population, because of the very clear image these pyramids present.

Figure 7.1 presents the current world age pyramid and Figure 7.2 the projected 2050 pyramid.*

While these can be analyzed individually, it is sometimes best to compare similar features. To begin with, look at the shapes. Figure 7.1 is much more like a pyramid, with more people at the lower ages and fewer at the top. Ideally it would look even more like a real pyramid with a large younger labor force and a smaller number of senior citizens. Figure 7.2 is more like a beehive, with similar percentages in all the lower age groups, indicating a smaller percentage of the total population is in productive

* Note: The reference for all the pyramid charts is http://www.census.gov/ipc/www/idb/groups.php, which is a gateway page where you can enter the data required and it is provided uniquely to your request.

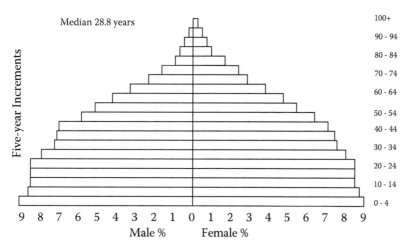

FIGURE 7.1
World 2010 age pyramid.

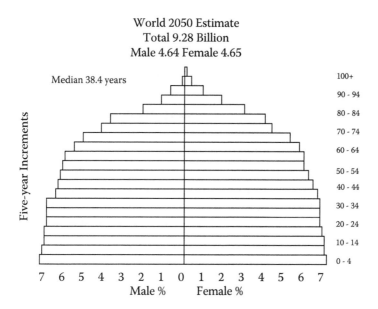

FIGURE 7.2
World 2050 age pyramid.

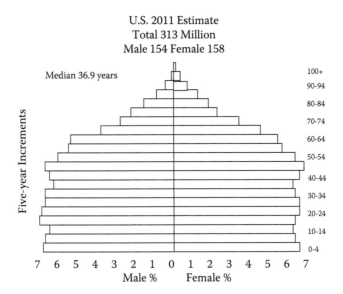

U.S. 2011 Estimate
Total 313 Million
Male 154 Female 158

FIGURE 7.3
U.S. age pyramid 2011.

ages. The lower two bars on each pyramid present the young children, cohorts 0–4 and 5–9. Look how the percentages are much lower in the 2050 pyramid, around 7% compared to 9%. Also look at the percentages above the 60–64 age cohort. This cohort is growing larger. This is also obvious from the median ages shown on the chart. So obviously, the world's population is projected to get older. This raises many questions regarding support for the older persons no longer in the workforce. Is this a threat or an opportunity?

Figures 7.3 and 7.4 present a set of age pyramids for the United States at present and forecast for 2050.

The U.S. age pyramid for 1970 shows why America's youth orientation was so strong at that time. Half of the population was under age 28, which explained why America was so youth oriented in that time period. But by 1990, the oldest baby boomers were in their mid-forties, and the U.S. age pyramid for that year shows a bulge in the middle. In 1990, baby boomers represented one out of three Americans, and the median age of the population was 32.8 years. Their concerns, from child care to health insurance and biological clocks, were America's most talked-about issues.

The 2011 age pyramid, Figure 7.3, moves away from the preferred triangular configuration, and for the United States looks more like a big bowl than a pyramid. That's because birth rates and mortality rates have both

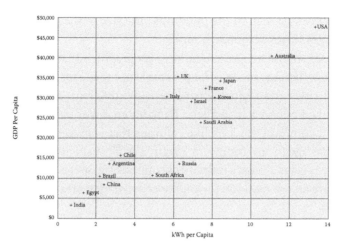

FIGURE 7.4
U.S. age pyramid 2050.

been low for many decades. The most noticeable feature of the American age pyramid is the bulge in the 50–60 year cohorts caused by the baby boom. Since 1946, this group has been working its way up the pyramid, providing a moving bulge as it progresses upward. By 2050 it has moved off the pyramid and the bowl changes into a lopsided beehive—lopsided because of the longer life spans of females.

In 2010 the baby boom generation was between the ages of 46 and 64 years and the U.S. population according to the 2010 census was 308,745,538. Approximately half of Americans were aged 39 or older. The abundance of aging Americans makes the U.S. pyramid start to look top-heavy. As baby boomers age, the situation becomes even more extreme, as illustrated in the 2050 pyramid and the median age increasing from 36.9 years to 39 years. The overall problem presented, of course, is a reduced workforce and an older population living off Social Security and other retirement income. Note that for 2050 the U.S. median age and shape of the pyramid matches the total world as shown in Figure 7.1. Based on the current world economic model, economic growth needs a growing workforce, not a growing grey retirement force.

By 2030, all of the baby boomers will have moved into the older population (those aged 65 years and older). The growth of this segment of the population can be seen in the pyramids. The size of the population at the younger ages varies across each series.

Businesses should be aware that local geographic situations don't necessarily follow the U.S. model. The pyramids are totals for the country, and individual cities and regions often look quite different. The age pyramids of youthful cities have a broad base. Baby-boom towns bulge in the middle. Retirement communities look like columns that lean to the woman's side. The median age in my county in Virginia is 52 years and the pyramid is upside down—it is almost a retirement community. So the recommendation is to prepare an age pyramid for your specific market area or service area.

SUSTAINABILITY: CARRYING CAPACITY

The simplest definition of sustainability is "To keep in existence, maintain."[*] Therefore, sustainability means that we will have figured out ways to generate a renewable supply of energy, water, and food for approximately 10 billion people. But to have these 10 billion people living healthier lives on the average than the current 6.5 billion means that the amount of energy and water and food per person will have to be higher than it is currently. To generate the wealth that will make that possible will almost certainly demand the use of vastly greater quantities of energy and of resources than we currently consume. More energy consumption

> **Overlay:** At present there is no good estimate of the carrying capacity of the Earth. The number of people that can be supported is unanswerable at the present state of knowledge due to the fact that there are too many variables, not the least of which is the evolving food technologies and the ability to turn barren land fertile. Typical of the unknowns is the rate at which the global warming that positively impacts land in the northern climes may open up new land for agriculture. Planners need to be aware that there will be strains in the food chains as population grows and to encourage R&D into ways of improving food productivity and the availability of fresh water.

---

[*] *American Heritage Dictionary of the English Language*, 4th ed. Houghton Mifflin. Boston MA, 2000. p. 1744.

will bring with it a greater amount of waste, including CO_2 contributions to the atmosphere. In the United States it will be difficult to minimize the impact of many more people using many more resources in a free-market economy. There will be increased impacts on where people live and how they manage their local environments.

The world will have to reconcile the huge inconsistencies in what we want to accomplish and what is possible. The desire to lower mortality leads to policies that promote population growth but add to the senior population. These have to be constantly countered by policies that promote fertility limitation. Our desire that more people should be able to live not only longer but also at a higher standard of living is probably doomed to failure if the birth rate does not drop more quickly than is currently projected or alternate forms of inexpensive energy do not become available. In any event, the requirement is clear—10 billion persons.

Figure 7.5 illustrates the problem. The world standard of living is far below what we in the United States would consider even a bare minimum

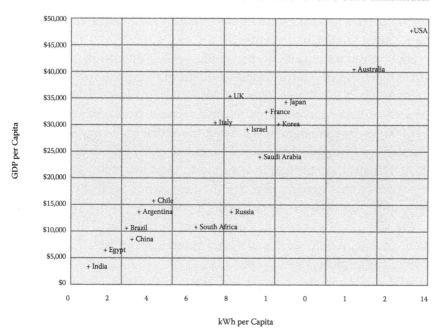

FIGURE 7.5
Per capita energy use versus wealth. (GDP per capita data from the CIA *The World Factbook*, 2011, https://www.cia.gov/library/publications/the-world-factbook/; kWh per capita data from The World Bank, Electric Power Consumption, World Bank Online Database, http://data.worldbank.org.)

to survive. Please note both scales are *per capita*. To increase the standards of living requires energy—energy to raise food, energy for transportation, energy for housing, energy for clothing, and so on. Look at the disparity. Look at the difference just to be equivalent to the United Kingdom. It is like a Catch-22 situation. As the population increases and lives longer, more energy is required. However, with a finite amount of energy available, it becomes apparent that the standards of living for most of the world population will not increase very fast. Faced with increasing storms and reduced crop productivity from a warmer world, the standards of living may decrease.

There has been much effort on trying to determine the number of people the world can accommodate and sustain. Grant recommends we look at the sustainable population by inverting current growth calculations.* If we take the current world gross national product (GNP) of $72 trillion and divide it by the average per capita GNP of the World Bank's top 50 countries (average = approximately $35,000/per person) we get a sustainable population of 2 billion. This assumes that the average is a good surrogate for a good standard of living. It also assumes the current GNP represents a sustainable level of GNP.

Look at the formula: GNP per capita = GNP divided by population. If GNP per capita = a reasonable standard of living = $35,000 per year, and we expect 9 billion persons in 2050, then the world GNP needs to be $315 trillion, or more than a fourfold increase from today to meet the $35,000 per year standard. It is difficult to see that occurring as the world standard of living probably will not increase much from today's level by 2050. But since people's aspirations are to improve, this will put strong pressures on many countries to reform internal policies that encourage a large difference between the rich and the poor.

The world needs economic development to increase GNP and at the same time see a decrease in population to increase the overall standard of living. The formula is very simple.

Or, for our current situation of a world population of 6 billion, the GNP per capita is about $10,000 per year—typical of the countries at the 80th rank in the table of GNP per capita of all the nations of the world.†

Joel Cohen, the author of *How Many People Can the Earth Support?*, concluded that the question is "unanswerable at the present state of

---

* Grant, Lindsey, *Too Many People* (Santa Ana, California: Seven Locks Press, 2000), 7.
† World Development Indicators database, World Bank, September 27, 2010, 1. http://sitesources-worldbank.org/datastatistics/resources/GNICP.pdf

knowledge."* His research found an enormous range of political numbers intended to persuade people one way or another.

It is suggested that the best answer may go back to Malthus, who indicated that when challenged, people find a way to a solution and we have not been really been challenged yet.

Malthus said rather elegantly: "That the difficulties of life contribute to generate talents, every day's experience must convince us. The exertions that men find it necessary to make, in order to support themselves or families, frequently awaken faculties that might otherwise have lain forever dormant, and it has been commonly remarked that new and extraordinary situations generally create minds adequate to grapple with the difficulties in which they are involved."†

---

* Op. cit. quoted in Kunzig, National Geographic, January 2011, 63.
† Malthus, *An Essay*, Chapter 19, 102.

8

Population Policies and Dilemmas

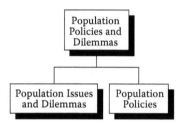

Chapter 8 outline.

This section will discuss the issues and dilemmas in population policies and their relevance to program managers.

POPULATION ISSUES AND DILEMMAS

Demographic transition theory seems to imply that, after a period of exceptional population growth resulting from the time lag between declines in mortality and fertility rates, every population and then eventually the whole world population will stabilize at Stage IV, and consequently no more acute population problems will appear.

On the contrary, it is not clear when the world might reach the end of the demographic transition and shift into Stage IV. Most projections have the populations leveling off after 2050. The major difficulty is that different countries are in different stages of their various transitions and so it is almost impossible to generalize about the global population situation except in the grossest terms. The fertility rate is the big driver now and local customs and cultures have an impact on the timing. Deliberate refusal to educate girls, such as in areas controlled by the Taliban, impact the number of children.

Overlay: The United States and the world will have significant increases in population between now and 2050, at which time it appears the world will stabilize at around 10 billion persons. Most of the countries of the world outside the United States and perhaps Canada will be suffering with either too many or too few people, although how this may play out overall is indeterminate. It is important for planners to anticipate serious strains between countries and regions simply due to population growth without comparable economic growth—climate change simply exacerbates the situation.

Overlay: The search for a better life will lead ever more people to move toward those economic environments where that better life seems like more than just a distant dream. Dealing with the globalization of migration will present an extraordinarily difficult set of policy dilemmas for virtually all of the wealthier countries of the world. However, in the midst of it all, we must not lose sight of the importance of maintaining every effort to keep bringing fertility levels down to manageable, sustainable levels in order to have resources to increase the standards of living—a dilemma.

Program and portfolio managers will need to include consideration of how global population changes impact the availability and distribution of the skilled resources their organization will require in the coming decades. Immigration policy becomes important in the competition for these resources with countries with serious declining birthrates.

The fact that the population is not growing fast in the United States does not mean that there are no population problems. The population of the middle states is scarcely growing at all and there are relatively few immigrants. On the two coasts, by contrast, there is much more rapid population growth, much of it fueled by immigrants.

Migration and immigration will be significant factors in the coming decades, resulting from people searching for better lives or to escape problems of war and hunger. There will be competition for the better-educated workers and resistance to those who are envisioned as drags on an economy. The United States has a built-in advantage due to its size and wealth and a history of welcoming immigration policies. It is important that this advantage is not lost.

The challenge of population, economic, and environmental policy is to continue to make sure infants grow to maturity and live longer, to assist them in increasing their standard of living, and "to encourage them to have as few children as is reasonable, and to have them living in places where they are able to contribute the most to the sustainability of human existence".[*]

POPULATION POLICIES

Overlay: There are two parts to population policies. One is limiting the total population due to the limited resources available for support. The other part of the equation is economic growth. The primary problem that needs solving is poverty, not overpopulation. The most effective population control mechanism is the most simple and is female education, which is occurring even in the most densely populated and repressive countries. Raising incomes is the key. With a stable total population and a continuing rise in GDP, the standards of living for the world's population would be increasing. Program planners should support and encourage programs that raise GDP and at the same time support and encourage education of women. The economic environment of programs in the coming decades will depend upon these two factors: population growth and per capita GDP growth.

Demographic science is used to shape the future, for trying to improve the conditions, both social and material, of human existence. It provides an understanding of how the causes of population change are related to the consequences:

- how and why mortality, fertility, and migration change;
- how they affect the age and sex structure of society and the urban environment;

---

[*] Weeks, *Population.* 53.3

- how households and families change as a consequence of demographic shifts;
- how population growth affects economic development, food resources, and
- environmental degradation.

Implicit in all those concepts is the idea that an understanding of what has happened in the past and what is happening now will provide insights about the future.

The four keys to stabilizing population all are based on women:[*]

1. *The widespread education of girls*; when girls are educated in large numbers they find ways when they grow up to be women to accelerate their own empowerment. They often delay the age at which they marry or begin having children. They participate in bringing about the next three keys;
2. *The social and political empowerment of women* to participate in the decisions of their families, communities, and nations;
3. *High child survival rates*, leading parents to feel confident that most or all of their children will survive to adulthood; empowerment of women enables them to demand increased health and nutrition and improved maternal health care; and,
4. *The ability of women to determine the number and spacing of their children.*

All four of these are required to be effective. The impact of declining fertility, which is the basis of these four items, is a common theme in population texts.[†] These are a key part of the Stage III demographic transition. Nearly all of the most developed nations have gone through the four transition stages and their populations have stabilized or are actually dropping or forecast to drop. A fortunate exception is the United States, which, because of its size and internal demography, is a special case.

The linkage between smaller populations and lower death rates historically has been a contradiction due to infant mortality. Experience has shown that when children survive into adulthood at very high rates, and

---

[*] Adapted from Gore, Al, *Our Choice, A Plan to Solve the Climate Crisis* (Emmaus, PA: Rodale Press, 2009), 228–229.
[†] Weeks, *Population*, 320–323.

when the first three factors from the previous list are present, the natural desire for most women worldwide is to have fewer children.

There is also a relationship between rapid population growth and socio-economic stability. Rapid population growth in the poorer nations results in an inability of the support services, health care, education, and the like to take care of the needs, resulting in a declining economy. Jobs cannot be developed fast enough, resulting in a very large and unstable unemployment situation and perhaps large out-migration or worse, such as happened in Rwanda and is happening in several Arab countries. Reducing population growth is one of the keys to developing a stable and sustainable planet.

Kunzig emphasizes that the problem that needs solving is poverty, not overpopulation.[*] Raising incomes is the key. The Carnegie Endowment for International Peace is forecasting gross domestic product (GDP) in the G20 nations to increase from $38 trillion in 2009 to $161 trillion in 2050.[†] Assuming 9 billion people, this would increase the GDP per person to $17,000 from the present $6,000. With a stable total population and a continuing rise in GDP, the standards of living for the world's population would be increasing.

The Carnegie report and the model upon which it is based do not address any possible resource shortages that may occur. Regarding climate change, it assumes that the carbon emissions commitments made by the 13 countries in the G20 are met. They will meet the 2020 goals of emissions and there-after they will remain constant. This will result in remaining close to the 2°C dangerous limit in global warming. The report admits this is "an extraordi-narily optimistic scenario."[‡] At present, there is little evidence that any of the major emitting countries are meeting their nonbinding commitments. The report indicates that the current business-as-usual scenario is likely to result in an increase of 5°C by 2050. They state: "Such an increase would likely have catastrophic consequences for many developing countries and low-lying areas of the world affected by rising sea levels and floods." This is discussed further in the next section of this book.

---

[*] Robert Kunzig, "Seven Billion—Special Series," *National Geographic*, January 2011, 61.

[†] Uri Dadush and Bennett Stancil, "The World Order in 2050," Carnegie Endowment for International Peace, Policy Outlook, April 2010 (a twenty-nine-page report downloaded January 1, 2011 from http://www.carnegieendowment.org/files/World_Order_in_2050.pdf).

[‡] Dadush and Stancil, "The World Order," 19.

Section II

Climate Change Overlay

9

Climate Change Constraint Overlay

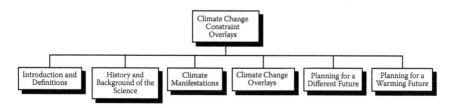

Section 2 outline.

Climate is what we expect, weather is what we get.

—Mark Twain

INTRODUCTION

This chapter addresses Constraint 2—climate change. It addresses three primary areas, some history and background, climate manifestations, the issues and overlays, and a discussion of the overlays for planning for a different and warmer, more turbulent future, or, as the National Academy stated, a future that is inherently uncertain, "but far from unknown."

Scientists using constantly improving methodologies and technology are collecting temperature and other data and publishing it in technical journals and on web pages on the Internet. There are approximately six major organizations like the National Aeronautics and Space Administration Goddard Institute for Space Studies (NASA GISS) that are collecting and publishing these data. They all tell the same story—exactly—since approximately 1980: the world has been warming and warming at an increasing rate. Each decade has been warmer than the previous decade up through

Summary Overlay: Scientists warn that anthropogenic* global warming is real and the resulting climate changes are real and need to be considered in program planning.

The following is the first paragraph of the response to the request from the White House on May 11, 2001, requesting the National Academy of Sciences to assist in a review of U.S. policy on climate change: "Greenhouse gases are accumulating in Earth's atmosphere as a result of human activities, causing surface air temperatures and subsurface ocean temperatures to rise. Temperatures are, in fact, rising. The changes observed over the last several decades are likely mostly due to human activities, but we cannot rule out that some significant part of these changes is also a reflection of natural variability. Human-induced warming and associated sea level rises are expected to continue through the 21st century. Secondary effects are suggested by computer model simulations and basic physical reasoning. These include increases in rainfall rates and increased susceptibility of semi-arid regions to drought. The impact of these changes will be critically dependent on the magnitude of the warming and the rate with which it occurs."

Appendix A provides a list of the world scientific organizations and their declarations on this topic.

The primary issue is not whether global warming is occurring, but what we do about it. What is our response to the probable risks?

---

* Anthropogenic is simply defined as "caused by humans."

2010, and there is no reason to expect that to change. The cause is the greenhouse effect from increasing levels of CO_2 emitted by mankind. The period is referred to as the *Anthropocene.* It is not caused by the sun or part of a normal cycle, and no scientific papers have been written providing any alternate explanation.

From the global perspective, the real issue is what should be done about it, not whether or not it is occurring or that man is the cause.

---

* Although we technically are in the Holocene Epoch, it has been recommended we rename the period starting about 1750 the "Anthropocene Epoch" or epoch of man. This was first proposed by Jan Zalasiewicz,, Mark Williams, Will Stefen, and Paul Crutzen, "The New World of the Anthropocene," *Environmental Science and Technology* 44, no. 7 (2010): 2228–2231.

How should you plan? What should you plan for? What is likely to happen? What are the probabilities? What is the risk of business as usual or doing nothing?

Currently in the United States the answers range from: "do nothing, it is a myth" to "immediately phase out every coal mine and coal-powered power station." This puts you—the program/portfolio manager—in the middle, but the solution is taught in basic management courses and is straightforward: look at it as a risk management situation for your programs and portfolio elements. It is obvious that we cannot afford to do nothing. That would be a serious error, as discussed in Appendix B. And we do not want to cause more harm than is on the horizon from climate change by overreacting (although cost–benefit studies show that the benefits far surpass the costs). Appendix A clearly puts the scientific community in the corner of recognizing that climate change caused by humans is real and ongoing and is serious. Program managers need to respond to the situation that continuing climate change will add some degree of risk to your programs. Do you take actions now that later prove unwarranted if the climate does not change dangerously or do you ignore it and when it proves true any mitigating actions are too little too late or very expensive? This section will assist you in your decision making by clarifying some of the major physical forces that impact the climate and also provide assistance in your risk analysis by providing overlays to your planning.

Program planning needs to consider three factors regarding the climate:

1. What are the actual, ongoing effects caused by climate changes and the likely consequences and timing?
2. What are the mitigation efforts of governments and major corporations and how do they impact your programs and portfolio?
3. What adaptation efforts of both the public and private sector are necessary and currently being done to reduce the adverse impacts of climate change events and what should you do to your program plan to mitigate or adapt?

Not everyone in the United States is convinced that humans are causing global warming or climate change. But regardless, in planning it is prudent to take into account the recommendations of the scientific world.

DEFINITIONS

A discussion of the climate needs to start with some clarifying definitions:*

> **Weather:** the state of the atmosphere at a given time and place with respect to the variables of moisture, temperature, wind velocity, and barometric pressure.
> **Climate:** the average of many years of weather for a certain time of year at a specific location.

These terms are often misused, sometimes deliberately, so it should be clear when we are talking about climate that it is a long-term event, not what appears out the window right now, which is part of a short-term event. The period used to evaluate whether climate is changing is usually at least 10 years, which approximates the current solar cycle.†

The climate has been predictable; it depends upon several physical characteristics:

- Roundness of the Earth: The Earth is an oblate spheroid—not truly round—so the amount of solar energy reaching the poles is somewhat different from that of a sphere.
- Shape of the orbit: The Earth is not always the same distance from the sun, so the amount of energy from the sun varies depending on the position of the Earth in its orbit.
- Tilt within the orbit: The poles of the Earth tilt with respect to the sun as it proceeds around its orbit and the seasons change as the Earth moves around the sun.
- Latitude: The distance along the surface of the Earth above and below the equator or below the poles; the climate varies with latitude. Latitude is measured in angular distance or degrees from zero at the equator to 90° at the poles.
- Oceans: A major moderating source due to proximity to land and source of various water currents that impact the weather.

---

* Roy W. Spencer, *Climate Confusion: How Global Warming Hysteria Leads to Bad Science, Pandering Politicians and Misguided Policies that Hurt the Poor* (New York: Encounter Books, 2008), 47.
† As discussed later, the sun's radiation increases and decreases by a small amount over an approximate 11-year cycle.

- Atmosphere composition: The mixture of chemicals and elements and water vapor, which varies with altitude.
- Atmospheric circulation: The regular and irregular annual and seasonal movement of the atmosphere, including several named atmospheric movements such as the Hadley Circulation, El Niño, La Niña, the Arctic Oscillation, the North Atlantic Oscillation, and others. These interact with ocean currents and the jet stream.

Global warming: The average increase in the temperature of the atmosphere and the troposphere,* which can contribute to changes in global climate patterns. (In common usage it refers to increases in temperature caused by increased emissions of greenhouse gases from human activities, or anthropogenic global warming [AGW]).†

Climate change: Any significant change in the measures of climate (temperature, precipitation, or wind) lasting for an extended period. Climate change may result from:

- Natural factors—changes in the sun's intensity or changes in Earth orbit
- Natural processes—changes in ocean circulation, monsoon cycles
- Human activities—changes in the composition of the atmosphere (e.g., from burning fossil fuels, deforestation and reforestation, urbanization, desertification)

---

* The troposphere is the lowest region of the atmosphere from the surface of the Earth to the point where temperature no longer decreases with altitude, called the tropopause. It varies from 7 to 10 miles above the Earth.
† Reference: EPA Climate Change web page. www.epa.gov/climatechange/downloads/climate_basics.pdf

10

History and Background of the Science

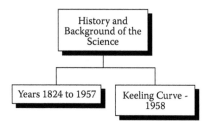

Chapter 10 outline.

Overlay: The increase in global temperatures resulting from increasing CO_2 in the atmosphere is not a new phenomenon and needs to be accommodated in planning. The amounts of CO_2 emissions into the atmosphere should be reduced to mitigate dangerous warming and climate change.

Arrhenius and other members of the scientific community of the nineteenth century developed the modern understanding of the impact of CO_2 on climate. The science of the significance of CO_2 and the relationship to global warming was actually settled in 1896. Although the amount of CO_2 in the atmosphere is only a few parts in ten thousand, Tyndall showed how it brings warming and Arrhenius showed the impact on temperatures from increasing the levels of CO_2.

In order to better understand the science of today, it is beneficial to review at least part of the path taken by the scientific community to develop today's scientific body of knowledge.

YEARS 1824 TO 1957

The history of the scientific efforts to understand the climate started in the time of the Industrial Revolution when in 1824 Joseph Fourier was wondering what determines the average temperature of the Earth. Why didn't the sun's heat just keep making it hotter and hotter? He concluded that the atmosphere must control the temperature of the Earth and also that it would become colder and colder if it weren't for the atmosphere that somehow holds in the heat. Fourier recognized that the atmosphere traps part of the radiation from heated surfaces and prevents it from escaping into space. Physicists of the time recognized that when the sun's radiation strikes a surface, it warms it and reradiates the heat as infrared radiation. The wavelength of the incoming radiation is changed when it is reradiated.

Fourier tried to explain why the Earth warmed by the analogy of a box covered with a pane of glass. The box's interior warms up when sunlight enters and the heat cannot escape. This was similar to the perception at that time of how a greenhouse works.[*]

Around 1859, Joseph Tyndall was trying to determine just how the atmosphere controlled the Earth's temperature. The scientists of that time thought all atmospheric gases were transparent to the outgoing infrared radiation that was a result of the surface of the earth heating, just as it was transparent to the incoming radiation from the sun.

Through a series of experiments and some good fortune, Tyndall discovered that while oxygen and nitrogen are truly transparent to the infrared radiation, carbon dioxide (CO_2) and other trace gases were not and would block it.

Weart quotes Tyndall: "Just as a sheet of paper will block more light than an entire pool of clear water, so the trace of CO_2 alters the balance of heat radiation through the entire atmosphere."[†] Much of the heat or infrared radiation rising from the surface of the Earth is blocked by the CO_2 in the atmosphere and the heat energy is retained in the atmosphere rather than getting lost in space. Not only is the air warmed, but some of the heat energy trapped in the atmosphere is re-reradiated back to Earth and warms it. Therefore, the surface is also warmer than it would be if no CO_2 were present. Tyndall also discovered that the most important warming

---

[*] Spencer R. Weart, *The Discovery of Global Warming* (Cambridge, MA: Harvard University Press, 2008), 3.

[†] Weart, *Discovery of Global Warming*, 4.

component in the air was water vapor (H_2O) since it readily blocks infra-red radiation. In 1862, Tyndall suggested as part of his ongoing study to determine the causes of the ice ages that changes in gases in the atmosphere could cause climate change. He was focusing on humidity and the interaction of volcanic eruptions and the related increases of CO_2.

Building on the work of Fourier and Tyndall, Swedish scientist Svante Arrhenius (who was also trying to discover the cause of the ice ages) investigated the impact on climate of significant increases or decreases in the CO_2 in the atmosphere. In April 1896, Svante Arrhenius published his famous paper "On the Influence of Carbonic Acid in the Air upon the Temperature of the Ground."[*] It was an abbreviated version of a longer paper (written in German) that was published in the *Proceedings of the Royal Swedish Academy of Sciences*, volume 22, at the same time.

In this paper he estimated the increase in global temperature that would occur with an increase in carbon dioxide in the atmosphere. Table VII on page 266 of his manuscript presents his estimate that there would be an increase of 3.52°C for an increase in CO_2 by a factor of 1.5 and he estimated an increase of 5.7°C for an increase by a factor of 2.0. (Multiply these centigrade temperatures by 1.8 to convert to Fahrenheit.) These estimates were for latitudes between 30 and 40 degrees north.

When converted to worldwide temperature increases, his estimates are high by only a little over half of a degree centigrade when compared to current estimates based on much more sophisticated techniques. To his further credit, on page 265 of his paper he indicates the 3.52°C increase may be high due to the nature of his calculations. On page 267 of his paper he concludes: "Thus, if the quantity of carbonic acid increases in geometric progression, the augmentation of the temperature will increase nearly in arithmetic progression."[†]

A summary of the verified science of that time follows[‡]

1. Greenhouse gases absorb infrared radiation in the atmosphere and re-emit much of it back toward the surface, thus warming the planet (less heat from the sun escapes; Fourier, 1824).

---

[*] *London, Edinburgh and Dublin Philosophical Magazine and Journal of Science* 41, no. 251 (April 1896): 237–276.

[†] Where he was in error was his estimate that an increase in CO_2 by 50% due to coal burning would take 3,000 years. In fact, it has increased over 30% in one century, 287 ppm to 390 ppm.

[‡] See Weart pages 205–212 for a complete list of milestones.

2. CO_2 has the property of a greenhouse gas and thus has the capacity to warm the planet (Tyndall, 1858).
3. By burning fossil fuels, human activities are increasing the greenhouse gas concentration of the atmosphere (Arrhenius, 1896).
4. Increased greenhouse gas concentrations lead to more heat being trapped, warming the planet further (Arrhenius, 1896).
5. Doubling the amount of CO_2 from 287 to 574 ppm (parts per million)[*] in the atmosphere will result in an increase in global temperature of approximately 3.5°C (Arrhenius, 1896).

The next major milestone occurred 42 years later in 1938 when Guy Stewart Callendar presented a paper to the Royal Meteorological Society in London that described how the burning of fossil fuels resulted in the emission of millions of tons of carbon dioxide gas, CO_2, and that this event was changing the climate.[†]

This was followed by more work, including an important paper by Gilbert Plass of the Office of Naval Research in 1956, who reported on how adding CO_2 to the atmosphere impacted the radiation balance.[‡] Other important research by Dr. Roger Revelle of the Scripps Institution of Oceanography in 1957 and others continued to demonstrate and elaborate on the critical role of CO_2 in changing the climate.

KEELING CURVE: 1958

One of the most important sets of data in the history of science is that collected by Dr. Charles Keeling starting in 1958 from Mauna Loa Observatory in Hawaii. These data are normally presented in the form of a curve, now called a Keeling Curve, and are the measurement of the current amounts of carbon dioxide in the atmosphere, measured in parts per million (ppm).

Figure 10.1[§] presents the current Keeling Curve from the National Oceanic and Atmospheric Administration (NOAA), which is a continuation of the

---

[*] The amount of CO_2 in the atmosphere is either measured in billions of tons or as a ratio in a typical sample such as parts per million.

[†] G. S. Callendar, "The Artificial Production of Carbon Dioxide and Its Influence on the Climate," *Quarterly Journal of the Royal Meteorological Society* 64 (1938): 223–240.

[‡] G. N. Plass, "Carbon Dioxide and the Climate," *American Scientist* 44 (1956): 304–316.

[§] Dr. Pieter Tans, NOAA/ESRL (http://www.esrl.noaa.gov/gmd/ccgg/trends/) and Dr. Ralph Keeling, Scripps Institution of Oceanography (http://scrippsco2.ucsd.edu/).

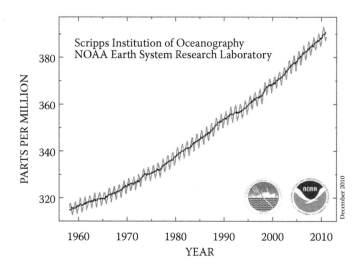

FIGURE 10.1
Atmospheric CO_2 at Mauna Loa Observatory.

data collection of Dr. Keeling, who died in 2005. The monthly mean in August 2011 was 390.02 ppm and in August 2010 it was 388.15 ppm.[*] The curve varies around the mean due to the seasonality of the data and is increasing at approximately 2 ppm per year.

The Keeling Curve is the clearest and most dramatic indication of the increases in carbon dioxide in the atmosphere that have been occurring. The reason for the zigzags is the changes caused by the seasons as the Earth "breathes."[†] The accuracy and validity of the data have been validated by other independent sources around the world. More discussion of CO_2 is included in the next chapter on the greenhouse effect.

There has been a phenomenal amount of scientific work performed on climate change. Much of this has been documented in the 996-page report of the Intergovernmental Panel on Climate Change (IPCC), which is "the standard scientific reference for all those concerned with climate change and its consequences."[‡] See Appendix A for a brief statement of the conclusions of this report.

---

[*] Available from http://www.esrl.noaa.gov/gmd/ccgg/trends/ (Accessed 26 May 2011)

[†] Monthly Keeling Curve data are available from NOAA at http://www.esrl.noaa.gov/gmd/ccgg/trends/.

[‡] Intergovernmental Panel on Climate Change (IPCC), Contribution of Working Group I to the *Fourth Assessment Report* of the IPCC, *Climate Change 2007—The Physical Science Basis* (New York: Cambridge University Press, 2007).

The IPCC has published four major reports: the *First Assessment Report* in 1990, the *Second Assessment Report* in 1996, the *Third Assessment Report* in 2001, and the current *Fourth Assessment Report* in 2007. We will refer to the fourth report as IPCC4 for simplicity.

While the IPCC has a small core staff, the bulk of the work is performed by hundreds of unpaid volunteers from the world's scientific community using peer-reviewed scientific studies for the basis for their findings.

Since Keeling started publishing his data, there has been a significant increase in the amount of research into the various aspects of climate change and global warming and many important discoveries. These are incorporated in the chapters that follow in this section.

> When I looked at what energy we had used over the past couple of centuries and what was in the atmosphere today, I knew there had to be a connection. I wasn't convinced by a person or any interest group—it was the data that got me. As I looked at it on my own, I couldn't come to any other conclusion. Once I got past that point, I was utterly convinced of this connection between the burning of fossil fuels and climate change. And I was convinced that if we didn't do something about this, we would be in deep trouble.
>
> **—Vice Admiral Richard H. Truly, USN (Ret.), former NASA administrator, shuttle astronaut, and the first commander of the Naval Space Command***

---

* Center for Naval Analyses, *National Security and the Threat of Climate Change* (Alexandria VA: CNA Corporation, April 2007), p. 14. Available at http://www.cna.org/reports/climate (accessed April 9, 2011).

11

Climate Manifestations

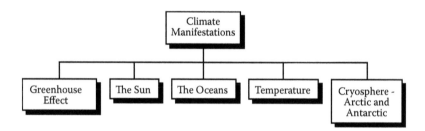

Chapter 11 outline.

This important section will address the current scientific data that relates to some of the major climate drivers and manifestations. Current evidence will be included such as the climate forcings from the sun, the impact of the oceans, and the documented changes to glaciers, the Arctic, and the Antarctic.

The Geological Society of London has prepared a brief that summarizes the geological evidence of previous climate change; it is included as Appendix D.

GREENHOUSE EFFECT

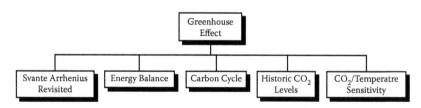

Greenhouse effect section outline.

Overlay: The existence of the greenhouse effect, the role of CO_2 and other greenhouse gases, and the understanding of the processes have been settled science for well over a hundred years. There is no dispute within the scientific community that CO_2 has been increasing and that the increase is due to human emissions of CO_2 and the burning of fossil fuels. Continuing carbon emissions will result in continuing increases in the Earth's temperature. This is an unsustainable situation.

The *greenhouse effect* enables life to live on this planet. This section delves into it in detail and addresses related items such as the energy balance of the Earth and historic levels of CO_2. Also covered are the relationships of CO_2 and temperature in more detail.

Svante Arrhenius Revisited

Overlay: The bulk of the scientific community expects changes to occur in the meteorological processes that are powered by temperature differences across the Earth's surface and throughout its atmosphere. These changes will, to some degree, be coupled with concomitant changes in oceanic circulation. It is absolutely clear that systematic meteorological changes can have profound effects on the incidence and strength of storms and thereby impact human activities.

Svante Arrhenius is my hero. As described earlier, in 1896 he published a paper based on physics that indicated there would be an increase in global temperature by approximately 3.6°C if the amount of CO_2 in the atmosphere doubled. The following quotation is from a 100-year anniversary commemorative book about Svante Arrhenius:[*]

We can only guess what Svante Arrhenius might think and say about the current increases in CO_2. These increases are larger and have occurred much more rapidly than he forecast. In 1896, he estimated that coal burning would cause a 50% increase in CO_2 in about 3000 years. In fact, it has increased almost 30% in one century, mainly due to the rapid increase in the use of fossil fuels.

---

[*] Henning Rodhe and Robert Charlson, eds., "In Commemoration of Svante Arrhenius: Scholar and Teacher with a Global Perspective," in *The Legacy of Svante Arrhenius: Understanding the Greenhouse Effect* (Stockholm: Royal Swedish Academy of Sciences, 1997), 10.

Arrhenius summarized the key features of the sun-atmosphere-Earth surface system that causes global warming.[*] Five factors are involved

1. The sun emits light at a temperature of about 5,800 K (Kelvin) (approximately 5,500 degrees centigrade); this includes light at many wavelengths ranging from ultraviolet to the infrared regions of the spectrum. The amount of energy is 174 petawatts. This incoming energy averaged over the globe *outside the atmosphere* is approximately 340 watts per square meter (W/sqM) (see Glossary).
2. Much of this light energy is transmitted through the atmosphere to the ground whereupon some of it is absorbed by the surface of the land or oceans.
3. The surface of the Earth reradiates this light or flux at a longer wavelength than the sun, generally in the infrared part of the spectrum. Without an atmosphere, the equilibrium temperature would be approximately 250 K (or −23°C, −9°F).
4. However, there is an atmosphere and the non-cloudy portion is very transparent to incoming sunlight, but less so to the infrared radiation from the Earth. As a result, the atmosphere is heated and the surface of the Earth is subsequently warmed to approximately 14°C (or 57°F or 287 K). See Figure 11.1.
5. The atmosphere contains several infrared (IR) absorbing gases that Arrhenius referred to as *selective absorbers* and which are now referred to collectively as *greenhouse gases*. These include water vapor, H_2O, as the dominant greenhouse gas, carbon dioxide, CO_2, nitrous oxide, NO_2, ozone, O_3, methane, NH_4, and others in trace amounts but which are still powerful IR light absorbers. All of these selective absorbers absorb IR radiation over one or more narrow ranges of wavelengths or absorption bands. Many of these bands are complex functions of wavelength, meaning that the amount of radiation absorbed varies widely over the IR spectrum. This makes the calculations of the amount of heating occurring in the atmosphere by a combination of the greenhouse gases a complex undertaking.

It is reported that it took Arrhenius a whole year to do his first set of calculations just using water vapor and carbon dioxide as the greenhouse

---

[*] Henning Rodhe, Robert Charlson, and Elisabeth Crawford, "Svante Arrhenius and the Greenhouse Effect," in Rodhe and Charlson, *The Legacy of Svante Arrhenius*, 15.

gases. Little was known of the other greenhouse gases and their impact on the conclusions was minimal—within the error of the basic computations. Today, the calculation process is much more rapid due to a better understanding of the various greenhouse gases and their physical characteristics, and also using a computer rather than hand calculations.

Energy Balance

Overlay: The continuing carbon emissions affect the Earth's energy balance. Heating of the atmosphere is the balancing response. Planning should be based on anticipation of continued heating of the atmosphere.

The evidence for the greenhouse effect, and the role CO_2 plays, can be seen in data from the surface and from satellites. By comparing the sun's heat reaching the Earth with the heat leaving it, the analysis shows that less long-wave radiation (heat) is leaving than arriving. Less and less radiation is leaving the Earth for space, as CO_2 and other greenhouse gases build up in the atmosphere. Since all radiation is measured by wavelength, the data show that the frequencies being trapped in the atmosphere are the same frequencies absorbed by greenhouse gases.

Figure 11.1 illustrates what occurs in the interactions among the sun, the atmosphere, and the Earth. The second law of thermodynamics indicates a balance must always exist between heat inflow and outflow. The primary variable is the composition of the atmosphere; as the amount of greenhouse gases increases, so does the temperature of the atmosphere in order to keep the physics in balance. As carbon emissions increase, the balancing temperature increases. Scientists, using basic physics, are able to calculate what the resulting stable system temperature will be for a given amount of CO_2 in the atmosphere. Since the system is dynamic and there is a lag in the system before it is in balance, the amount of CO_2 in the atmosphere today will continue to cause an increase in temperature for several years in the future—even if we stop emitting carbon dioxide completely. That is one of the reasons scientists are concerned. Today's emissions determine our grandchildren's temperatures and climate.

For the past 200 years or so, since the beginning of the Industrial Revolution (and before), there has been a regular increase in the type and amount of greenhouse gases emitted by humans, with a continuing

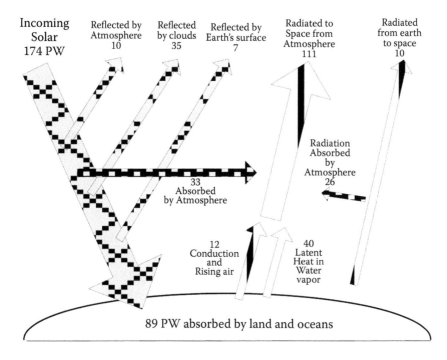

FIGURE 11.1
Global mean energy balance. (Graphic by Frank van Mierlo.)

change in the heat balance. This has accelerated since 1970. Scientific analysis from ice cores shows that during the most recent ice age, the CO_2 level was 160 ppm and other data show that prior to 1800 during the Industrial Revolution the level was 280 ppm. This was the level when Arrhenius performed his original analyses.

Figure 11.1[*] is a representation of the exchanges of energy between the source of the energy (the sun), the Earth's surface, the Earth's atmosphere, and the ultimate destination—outer space. The ability of the atmosphere to capture and recycle energy emitted by the Earth's surface is the defining characteristic of the greenhouse effect.

The total flux of energy entering the Earth's atmosphere is estimated at 174 petawatts. This flux consists primarily of solar radiation (99.97%, or nearly 173 petawatts or about 340 W m^{-2}).

---

[*] In the public domain, see http://commons.wikimedia.org/wiki/File:Breakdown_of_the_incoming_solar_energy.svg (accessed April 5, 2011).

We only have to look to our moon for evidence of what the Earth might be like without an atmosphere that sustained the greenhouse effect. While the moon's surface reaches 266°F in direct sunlight at the equator, when the sun "goes down" on the moon, the temperature drops almost immediately, and plunges in several hours down to −166°F.

When the sun goes down on the Earth at night, we are protected by the heat trapped overnight in the atmosphere (and in the ground and oceans). Without these, our nights would be so cold that few plants or animals could survive even a single night.

Carbon Cycle

The carbon cycle refers to the exchange of CO_2 between the Earth and the atmosphere. An example would be the absorption of CO_2 by trees and the subsequent release of CO_2 when burned or decaying. Climate change and a warmer climate would reduce the ability of the Earth's system (land and ocean) to absorb increases in emissions as they become increasingly saturated. As a result, an increasingly large fraction of human-generated CO_2 would stay airborne in the atmosphere. This is a long-term positive feedback that would increase the amount of CO_2 in the atmosphere above that otherwise occurring.

When carbon dioxide increases, and the atmosphere warms, more water vapor returns to the atmosphere and subsequently falls as increased precipitation. Today we are in uncharted territory regarding the total impact as carbon dioxide passes 390 parts per million. As shown in Figure 11.2, the carbon cycle is unbalanced by ~11 W/m sq, which can only be balanced by increasing temperatures.

Because of the current approximately 4 billion annual tons of carbon dioxide emissions,[*] the atmospheric carbon dioxide level continues to go up by about 2 ppm a year, as shown by the Keeling Curve. At this rate it would reach 400 by the year 2015 and 420 by the year 2025 and 450 by the year 2045. (And 550+ by 2100, a doubling of the figure at the start of the Industrial Revolution.)

Historic CO_2 Levels

At the beginning of the Industrial Revolution the concentration of carbon dioxide in the atmosphere was around 280 parts per million,

---

[*] EPA web page, http://www.epa.gov/climatechange/emissions/globalghg.html.

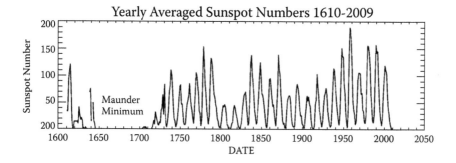

Yearly Averaged Sunspot Numbers 1610-2009

FIGURE 11.2

Complete carbon cycle. (From John Wood, Skeptical Science, http://www.skeptical-science.com/, with permission.)

> **Overlay:** The current levels of CO_2 in the atmosphere are significantly higher than at any time in the last 420 million years. This means that the entire list of impacts this will have is unknown, although we have a good idea based on what has happened to date and further scientific analysis. We are in the middle of a scientific experiment that is controlled by the CO_2 emission sources and this risk needs to be acknowledged.

or ppm (meaning 280 carbon dioxide molecules per million molecules of "dried air," or air with the water removed). It is thought to have fluctuated between about 180 and 280 ppm through the previous 600,000 years.* By 1900, as Europe and North America were industrializing, it had reached about 300 ppm and now the carbon dioxide concentration is at 390 ppm,

---

* Intergovernmental Panel on Climate Change (IPCC), Working Group 2, Fourth Assessment Report of the IPCC (IPCC4), *Climate Change 2007: The Physical Science Basis* (New York: Cambridge University Press, 2007), 443.

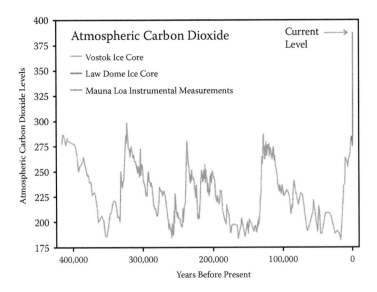

FIGURE 11.3

History from the Vostok ice cores. (From John Wood, Skeptical Science, http://www.skepticalscience.com/, with permission.)

which analyses of historic indicators show is probably the highest level in many millions of years.

To provide perspective to the nearly 1°C (1.8°F) increase in global temperature over the past century, it is estimated that the global mean temperature difference between the extremes of the ice age and interglacial periods is only about 5°C (9°F).

Figure 11.3 presents the history of CO_2 as taken from the Vostok cores and including the Keeling Curve data. These data from the Antarctic, indicates that the current CO_2 levels are significantly higher than at any time in the past 420,000 years. In fact, all the CO_2 peaks during the warm periods of the ice ages in the ice core record were less than 300 ppm CO_2.

CO_2/Temperature Sensitivity

Overlay: The U.N., in agreement with virtually all the governments of the world, has indicated that a 2°C increase in global temperature comparable to a CO_2 level of 450 ppm is the dangerous level for humanity and that actions need to be taken to stabilize the emissions so that that target is not exceeded. As of the date of this book, no serious, coordinated worldwide actions have been taken by the major polluting countries of the world to address this situation and achieve a stable, sustainable balance.

The bottom-line issue is specifically what happens to temperature as the CO_2 level increases, and what is the actual sensitivity of temperature to increasing CO_2? Table 11.1 presents the Most Likely, Very Likely Above, and Likely Ranges of the global mean equilibrium surface temperature increase above preindustrial temperatures for different levels of CO_2 equivalent concentration as projected by the International Panel on Climate Change (IPCC).[*] The IPCC Fourth Report (IPCC4), as discussed previously, has developed a set of alternate scenarios or assumptions of the future as a basis for its projections. For the next two decades, a warming of about 0.36°F per decade is to be expected for all its emissions scenarios.[†] The impacts of the CO_2 emissions are not felt immediately because there is a lag due to the slow release of heat by the ocean. This lag has been calculated to be approximately 10 years for most of the heat imbalances.[‡] This temperature increase is currently in the pipeline. There will be an increase in adverse weather and storm events, but the rate and intensity are difficult to predict. There are many variables that can impact them.

TABLE 11.1

Temperature versus CO_2 Estimates

Equivalent CO_2 (ppm)	Most Likely (°C)	Very Likely Above (°C)	Likely in the Range (°C)
350	1.0	0.5	0.6–1.4
450	2.1	1.0	1.4–3.1
550	2.9	1.5	1.9–4.4
650	3.6	1.8	2.4–5.5
750	4.3	2.1	2.8–6.4
1,000	5.5	2.8	3.7–8.3
1,200	6.3	3.1	4.2–9.4

Source: Intergovernmental Panel on Climate Change (IPCC), Contribution of Working Group I to the *Fourth Assessment Report, Climate Change 2007: The Physical Science Basis* (New York: Cambridge University Press, 2007).

---

[*] IPCC4, Table 10.8, p. 826.
[†] IPCC4, Summary for Policymakers, p. 12.
[‡] James Hansen, Makiko Sato, and Pushker Kharecha, *Earth's Energy Imbalance and Implications* (New York: NASA Goddard Institute for Space Studies, August 26, 2011), 29.

Note: *Equivalent CO_2*, sometimes written as CO_{2e}, means that the number includes the effects of the other greenhouse gases, including methane (NH_4), nitrous oxide (NO_2), and the halocarbons in terms of CO_2 impact. The Keeling Curve data therefore are somewhat lower than the CO_{2e} at a particular point in time, making the situation even more troublesome regarding temperature relationships.

Based on the extrapolations of the Keeling Curve data, and the best scientific estimate based on many factors that are discussed in detail in the referenced IPCC Fourth Assessment Report, it appears very likely that by approximately the year 2045 the Earth will be committed to a temperature increase of approximately 2.1 degrees centigrade (3.8 degrees Fahrenheit). The term *committed* is defined as the stabilization level for the Earth's heat/energy balance based on today's business-as-usual scenario.

This temperature is a worldwide average that means some places may average higher temperatures and some lower, as is the current situation.

There have been many scientific studies of the impacts of the changes in global temperature. In the note are three references out of many.[*] Discussion of the impacts is included in Chapter 13.

Appendix A documents the scientific community positions on the issue.

THE SUN

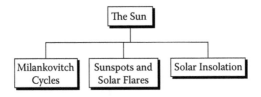

Sun section outline.

[*] IPCC4, Figure SPM.2 p. 16; and Thomas R. Karl, Editor, *Global Climate Change Impacts in the United States* (New York, Cambridge University Press, 2009). The full report (296 pages) can be found online at http://www.globalchange.gov/usimpacts; and Gerald C. Nelson, et al., *Climate Change, Impact on Agriculture and Costs of Adaptation* (Washington, DC: International Food Policy Research Institute, September 2009).

Overlay: The sun is not the cause of the current global warming. The data show that since approximately 1970, global temperatures have increased while the sun's irradiance has decreased. There is no credible science indicating that the sun is causing the observed increase in global temperatures; in fact, based on the historic 11-year solar cycle, the last 5 years should have been a cooling period. All scientific evidence indicates it is the known physical properties of CO_2 and other greenhouse gases that provide us with the only real and measurable explanation of the current global warming.

The sun supplies almost all the energy in the Earth's climate and therefore has a strong influence on climate. (Some small amount is provided by volcanic and related geothermal sources.) In this section we will discuss the three principal impacts of the sun on the climate. The first is the movement of the Earth around the sun, the second is sunspots and solar flares, and the third is solar insolation. Insolation is simply the amount of sunshine or solar radiation striking the Earth. (Actually, the term *solar insolation* is redundant since the "sol" in insolation refers to our sun.)

Milankovitch Cycles

Overlay: The sun played a major role in the onset and departure of the ice ages. However, this process took hundreds of thousands of years as it required a particular combination of the Earth's three orbital movements to occur. These *Milankovitch Cycles* have no impact on the present climate.

In the 1870s a British geologist named James Croll believed the cyclical nature of the ice ages had some relationship to the sun. After many years of effort, he published his laborious calculations of how the gravitational pulls of the sun, moon, and planets subtly affect the Earth's motions. The inclinations of the Earth's axis and the shape of its orbit around the sun oscillate slowly in cycles lasting tens of thousands of years. Over some thousands of years, the Northern Hemisphere would get slightly less sunlight during the winter than it would get other times. Snow would accumulate steadily, and Croll argued that could reflect away enough sunlight to keep the surface cold and bring on a self-sustaining ice age. He believed the timing of such changes could be calculated exactly using classical mechanics. His results did not match up with the data of the timing of the ice ages. The math was difficult and of course he did not have a calculator or computer available. Worse, the elite of the time did not recognize his credentials and so ignored his theories. A Serbian engineer, Milutin Milankovitch, took up his cause in 1941, but initially he also had troubles making the numbers and the physical data match but he eventually resolved the differences. It took until 1968, when Milankovitch's calculations got serious attention and the climate community recognized the validity of his data.* Starting with Fourier, it had been a goal of physicists to explain the ice ages in physical terms.

The Milankovitch cycles of the Earth's orbital changes include: (1) the tilt of the Earth's axis, (2) the changes in the eccentricity of the orbit, and (3) precession or changes in the direction of the axis tilt at a given point of the orbit. The tilt provides the seasons but inclination or changing tilt has a 41,000-year cycle. The eccentricity due to a slightly elliptical orbit has a 100,000-year cycle and the precession that changes in the direction of tilt has a 19,000- to 23,000-year cycle.† These have no impact on our present climate for two reasons. The first is that we are in an interglacial period and the next ice age would be 30,000 years in the future based on past history and the Milankovitch cycle periodicity. The second reason is the global warming from the human CO_2 emissions is far and away more powerful than the small incremental cooling from the alignment of the Milankovitch cycles that would precede any ice age. At present there is no reason to expect another ice age as long as we inhabit this Earth and release carbon emissions at the current rate.

Sunspots and Solar Flares

Overlay: Sunspots and solar inactivity have had a minor impact on climate in the past when there were long periods of solar inactivity. Currently there is no relationship between sunspot cycles and the world's climate. Data show reductions in solar activity have been occurring while temperatures have increased.

---

* Weart, *The Discovery of Global Warming*, 48.
† Fred Pearce, *With Speed and Violence*, 135.

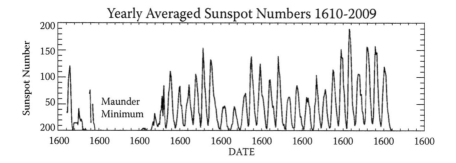

FIGURE 11.4

Sunspot cycles; temperature versus solar activity. (NASA image, http://solarscience.msfc. nasa.gov/images/ssn_yearly.jpg.)

Since man started inhabiting the Earth and developed curiosity, there has been interest in sunspots and solar flares. In 1843 Samuel Heinrich Schwabe, a German astronomer, discovered the existence of a regular solar cycle through a 17-year term of observations. The solar cycle is represented by the number of sunspots from year to year on the solar disk. Rudolf Wolf, a Swiss astronomer, carried out historical reconstruction back to the seventeenth century and established a numbering scheme for the cycles starting with the cycle of 1755–1766. The average duration of the cycles is just under 11 years, with some cycles as short as 9 years and others up to 14 years. We are now in Cycle 24, which started early in January 2008 when a reversed-polarity sunspot appeared. Figure 11.4 illustrates the sunspot cycles and the numbers of annual sunspots from about 1610 to the present.

Early records of sunspots indicate that the Sun went through a period of inactivity in the late seventeenth century. Very few sunspots were seen on the sun from about 1645 to 1715, as shown in Figure 11.4, and the period is called the Maunder Minimum. Although the observations were not as extensive as in later years, the sun was in fact well observed during this time and this lack of sunspots is well documented. This period of solar inactivity also corresponds to a climatic period called the Little Ice Age, when rivers that are normally ice-free froze and snow fields remained year-round at lower altitudes. There is evidence that the sun has had similar periods of inactivity in the more distant past. The Little Ice Age was apparently caused by a combination of factors that include cyclical lows in solar radiation, heightened volcanic activity, changes in ocean circulation, and inherent variability in global climate. Also contributing was reforestation and reduction of agriculture due to reduced populations from "black death" which reduced CO_2 levels. Also, the temperature anomalies noted for the Maunder Minimum and the Little Ice Age were not global but were regional, as evidenced in ice core data.

These incidences have led people to conclude (incorrectly) that the current period of warming may be due to activity of the sun. However, the sun has been in a less-active phase and if the sun were the main cause, the Earth should be getting cooler, not warmer.

Solar Insolation: Amount of Sunlight

Overlay: For the 1150 years prior to 1975 there has been a close match between a warming sun and a warming climate. Since then, the sun has been cooling while temperature has been increasing. The human influence on temperature increases is much more significant than solar insolation.

Until about 1960, measurements by scientists showed that the brightness and warmth of the sun, as seen from the Earth, were increasing. Over the same period, temperature measurements of the air and sea also showed that the Earth was gradually warming. It was not surprising, therefore, for many scientists to assume at that time that it was the warming sun that was increasing the temperature of our planet.

However, between the 1960s and the present day, the same solar measurements have shown that the energy from the sun is now decreasing. At the same time, temperature measurements of the air and sea have shown that the Earth has continued to become warmer and warmer. A more detailed comparison of sun and climate over the past 1150 years found that temperatures closely match solar activity until approximately 1975.[*] However, after 1975, temperatures rose while solar activity showed little to no long-term trend, which led the authors of the study to conclude: "During these last 30 years the solar total irradiance, solar UV irradiance and cosmic ray flux has not shown any significant secular trend, so that at least this most recent warming episode must have another source."[†]

---

[*] I. G. Usoskin, et al. "Solar Activity over the Last 1150 Years: Does It Correlate with Climate?" *Proceedings of the 13th Cool Stars Workshop*, Hamburg, July 5–9, 2004, 19–22, http://www.mps.mpg.de/dokumente/publikationen/solanki/c153.pdf (accessed January 3, 2011).

[†] Usoskin, "Solar Activity," 22.

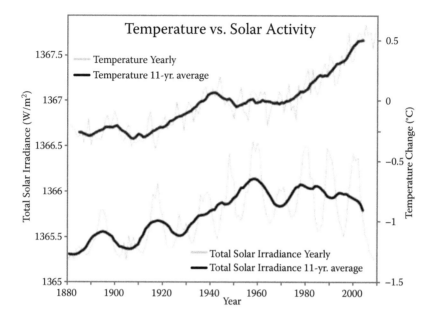

FIGURE 11.5

Global temperature change versus solar activity. (From NISS Data, John Wood, Skeptical Science, http://www.skepticalscience.com/graphics/Solar_vs_temp_500.jpg, with permission.)

In English, *irradiance* means sending forth radiant light, and if the sun is not causing the warming, something else must be causing the Earth's temperature to rise. These data are illustrated in Figure 11.5.

Of importance to the climate is the total solar irradiance, which is the amount of solar radiative energy that hits the Earth's upper atmosphere. The figure is about 1366 W/m² (watts per square meter). The amount varies with sunspots, but the change in the amount is very small, ranging from +0.06% to −0.3% or an amplitude of 0.1%. The Earth absorbs about 240 W/m² of energy from the sun, so the irradiance variation of about 0.1% causes a direct climate forcing of just over 0.2 W/m². This is a very small variation in the irradiance considering the total of 1366 W/m².

While this is enough to have some small impact, and the data from before 1960–1975 indicate there is some correlation, it is eight times less than the current 1.66 W/m² radiative forcing from human released CO_2. This is illustrated in Figure 11.6.

There is no relationship between global temperature changes and global cosmic ray counts. In fact, during periods of high sunspot and solar flare activity, there is a reduction in cosmic ray activity due to the effect of the magnetic field of the sun.

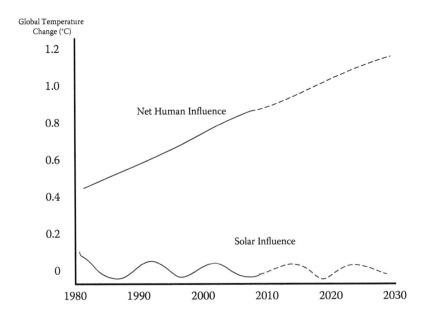

FIGURE 11.6
Relative solar influence on temperature change.

OCEANS

As goes the ocean, so goes life.[*]

—Alanna Mitchell

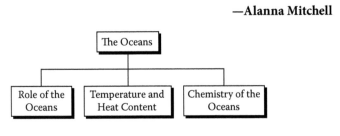

Oceans section outline.

Overlay: The oceans are important for more than boating, fishing, and transportation. They are critical to the overall well-being of all land creatures as well as those that live in the waters. Three things are

---

[*] Alanna Mitchell, *Seasick: The Global Ocean in Crisis* (Toronto, Ontario: McClelland & Stewart, Ltd., 2009), 22.

happening in the oceans and all are related to CO_2 increasing in the atmosphere: (1) they are getting warmer, (2) the waters are rising due to melting of ice and due to thermal expansion, and (3) the chemistry is changing due to absorption of CO_2 and the ocean acidification.

For a program manager, these are important conditions that should be considered in planning and implementation and risk analyses. In some areas of climate change there are options to just do nothing and adapt, but a dead ocean means a dead planet.

Role of the Oceans

Overlay: The oceans play a major role in climate and climate change. Alanna Mitchell,[*] in the prologue to her book *Sea Sick: the Global Ocean in Crisis*, summarizes the situation with the oceans. The oceans make up 99% of the living space on the planet and the atmosphere and land represent the remaining 1%. All over the world, ocean scientists are finding in every one of their specialty areas that human-caused climate change and other human actions are having a measurable effect on the ocean. "The vital signs of this critical medium of life are showing clear signs of distress."[†] This distress is due to the fact that approximately one third of the carbon dioxide that humans put into the atmosphere has eventually entered the ocean and about 80% of the extra heat generated by CO_2 through the greenhouse effect has been absorbed by the ocean. Program managers should plan for continuation of a broad pattern of disruptions and changes that are occurring that can have an adverse impact on programs dependent upon ocean resources and behavior.

---

[*] 2010 Grantham Prize winner for Excellence in Reporting on the Environment.
[†] Mitchell, *Seasick*, 8.

The chemistry and the physics of the oceans are changing, and have already changed more in the past 50 years than has occurred in the past 55 million years. The impact of these changes is the subject of hundreds of ongoing studies by oceanographers and ocean scientists. Near where I live there are at least five major scientific institutions located on or near the Chesapeake Bay that are performing ongoing bay and oceanography research. The chemistry and physics of the environment determine the nature of the biology in a system, and *future* chemistry and future physics determine *future* biology. The oceans are changing and so is the biology.

Changing also are the ocean winds and waves. A paper published in *Science Express*[*] reports that ocean wind and waves increased substantially over the last two and a half decades. Satellite altimeter measurements were used to test for trends in wave height from 1985 to 2008 and wind speed from 1991 to 2008. There was a positive trend in average wind speed and wave height, especially at higher latitudes. If the trends shown and correlation to global warming continue to prove out with further analysis, then these changes will have many obvious impacts (e.g., need for higher sea walls, stronger waves breaking up more sea ice, more wind and wave power, increased sea sickness, changes to migration patterns, etc.) and likely hundreds of others not thought of yet.

Temperature and Heat Content

Figure 11.7 illustrates where the global warming is occurring and also explains why there is a lag in atmospheric temperature increases.[†] Most of the extra heat from the heat and energy imbalance is going into the oceans that are warming, the air that is warming, and the ice that is melting. To establish a thermal equilibrium (outgoing heat equals incoming heat), the entire planetary system must reach a new higher temperature. Equilibrium cannot be reached as long as human emissions are continuing. Since most of the net heat imbalance caused by increasing CO_2 is going into the oceans, the imbalance will continue even after emissions cease and there is restoration of overall heat balance with the atmosphere. For this reason, there is a significant amount of warming still in the pipeline even if we stop adding CO_2 today.

The oceans have warmed significantly since 1950, accounting over this period for more than 80% of the changes in the energy content of the Earth's climate system. The heat capacity of the oceans is approximately 1000 times larger than that of the atmosphere, and therefore the ocean's heat uptake is many times larger than the atmosphere.[‡] Figure 11.8 presents the measured heat buildup since 1950 and compares it to the land heat buildup.

---

[*] R. Young, S. Zieger, and A. V. Babinin, Global Trends in Wind Speed and Wave Height, *Science Express*, March 24, 2011 published online, http://www.sciencemag.org/content/early/2011/03/23/science.1197219.abstract. (accessed April 26, 2011). Also see an analysis of the paper by John Bruno, April 13, 2011 at http://www.skepticalscience.com/more_wind_and_waves.html.

[†] Infographic from SkepticalScience.com, http://www.skepticalscience.com/graphics/GW_Components_1024.jpg (accessed February 5, 2011). Reproduced with permission.

[‡] IPCC4, Technical Summary, Working Group 1, 47.

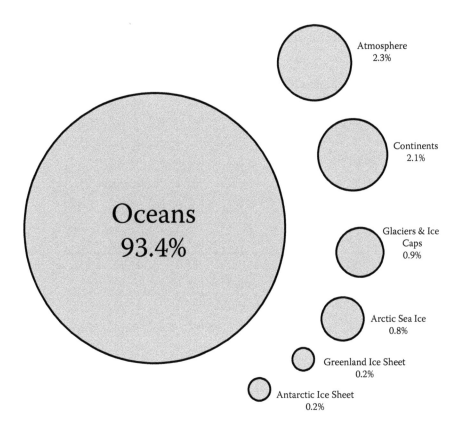

FIGURE 11.7
Global warming destinations. (From Skeptical Science, http://www.skepticalscience.com/graphics.php. With permission.)

Figure 11.7 tells us how important the ocean has been in mitigating the effects of increasing CO_2 levels and thereby protecting the human biosphere. This also indicates the probability of increasing intensity of storms as the ocean warms and the ocean itself undergoes transformations due to the changing temperatures. In addition, warmer air is able to hold more moisture, providing the source of heavier rainfalls. Storms are caused by temperature differentials and a warming ocean changes the temperature relationships with the atmosphere. Kevin Trenberth, a senior scientist in the climate analysis section at the National Center for Atmospheric Research in Colorado said: "[W]hen warmth and moisture at the surface build up, one response by the atmosphere is to transport it upward. ... That's what causes intense thunderstorms, tropical storms and hurricanes. The main driver of super-cell thunderstorms—those with deep rotating updrafts—is warm, moist air near the surface. In terms of

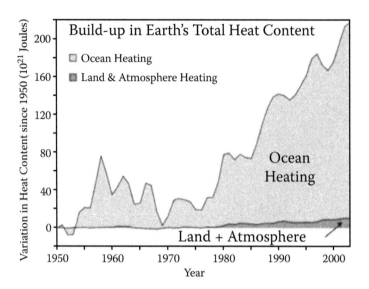

FIGURE 11.8

Build-up in total heat content of the Earth. (From John Wood, Skeptical Science, http://www.skepticalscience.com/, with permission.)

climate change, the main sources of warm moist air in the regions that were hit (in May 2011) are out of the Gulf of Mexico or out of the tropical Atlantic. This sets the stage for the atmosphere becoming very unstable."[*]

Many creatures in the oceans survive only in certain temperature strata; as the ocean warms the location of these strata changes and the dependent creatures also move. This causes a problem for other species that depend upon the creatures for food and potentially disrupts the food chain. This is one of the reasons the Adelie penguin population has decreased significantly in the last few years as the Antarctic Ocean has warmed; the ice shelves on which they live collapse and the krill upon which they depend have moved. In addition, the warmer, moister air over the Antarctic has increased the snowfall and caused problems in their nesting areas. Some other penguin species have benefitted from the changes.

Changes in timing of biological cycles are happening in the Chesapeake Bay. The warming bay is causing upsets in spawning and migration of native species and some species are forecast to disappear entirely from the bay within one or two decades.[†]

---

[*] Quoted by Renee Schoof in the *Richmond Times-Dispatch*, May 26, 2011, A8 in an article titled "A Warning of Warming?"

[†] National Wildlife Federation, *The Chesapeake Bay and Global Warming*, Reston, VA: 2007. Table 2. IS & Glick, P., Staudt, A., Inkly, D.

As an aside, the warming of the Arctic and Antarctic Oceans means that various fish and animal species that were effectively blocked from these regions by the very cold water are now moving in because the water is warming. This is not necessarily bad, but the reader should be aware that it is occurring. The waters around Greenland have been seasonally warming and the cod run has been extended to the benefit of the fishermen.

Chemistry of the Oceans

Overlay: Changing chemistry will gradually change the oceans as crustaceans lose their ability to form shells and as dissolved oxygen decreases. Planners need to expect that certain species will crash with cascading and unpredictable effects on the ocean ecosystem.

There are two significant changes occurring in the oceans resulting from the excess of CO_2 that is being absorbed: (1) decrease in pH and (2) decrease in dissolved oxygen. The first is important because the level of pH determines the ability of certain crustaceans to form shells; the second is important because minimum levels of dissolved oxygen are necessary for sea life to survive. Increasing atmospheric CO_2 concentrations lead directly to increasing acidification of the surface ocean.

It was estimated in 1994 that the CO_2 content of the oceans increased by 118±19 gigatons since the start of the Industrial Revolution in about 1750. It continues to increase by about 2 gigatons per year. (A gigaton is a billion tons.)

Projections give reductions in pH of between 0.14 and 0.35 units in this century, adding to the present decrease of 0.1 units since 1750. This translates into an increase in acidity of more than 30%. Figure 11.9 is derived from a Virginia Institute of Marine Sciences (VIMS) presentation that was used as input to the current State of Virginia Climate Change Action Plan.[*]

This very simple chart has a simple message: we are on the road to eliminating shellfish.

Historical data show that for shellfish over the past 50,000 years, during periods of higher CO_2, the animals had smaller shells evident. At present,

---

[*] Governor's Commission on Climate Change, Final Report: A Climate Change Action Plan, Secretary of Natural Resources, December 15, 2008 (Figure 23 from James E. Bauer Presentation April 2008).

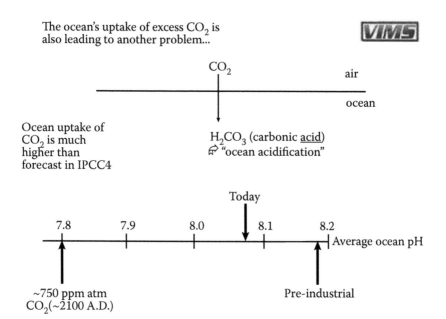

FIGURE 11.9

Ocean pH process. (From James E. Bauer, VIMS presentation, April 2008.)

the polar regions of the Arctic and southern oceans are expected to start dissolving certain shells once the atmospheric levels reach 450 ppm (~2030 under business-as-usual conditions).[*]

To continue the bad news, by 2050 the pH will be lower than it has been for 20 million years.[†] This means the basic plankton called *coccoliths* will be severely threatened. These plants make armor for themselves out of the calcium, carbon, and oxygen that they absorb from the ocean. The white cliffs of Dover are made up of coccoliths. The coccoliths are the builders that absorb the surplus carbon from the sea. They need calcium for this building process and the more acidic the sea becomes the less calcium is available for this purpose. If the coccoliths crash, the effects will cascade through the entire ocean system with unpredictable results since they are critical at the bottom of the food chain.

The other big impact of CO_2 absorption in the oceans is a continuing decrease in dissolved oxygen concentrations. Existing large equatorial

---

[*] I. Allison, N. L. Bindoff, R. A. Bindschadler, et al. *The Copenhagen Diagnosis, 2009: Updating the World on the Latest Climate Science* (Sidney, Australia: The University of New South Wales Climate Change Research Centre, 2009), 38.

[†] Mitchell, Alanna, *Sea Sick, The Global Ocean in Crises*. (Toronto: McClelland & Stewart 2009), 86.

oxygen minimum zones and dead zones in the Chesapeake Bay are expanding as the ocean water warms. Declining oxygen causes physical distress and respiratory problems for large predators and significantly compromises the ability of marine organisms to cope with acidification. Studies indicate a high risk of widespread expansion of regions lacking in oxygen in the upper ocean if increases in atmospheric CO_2 continue.[*]

TEMPERATURE

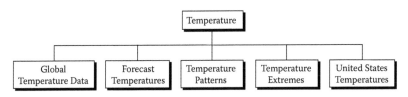

Temperature section outline.

Overlay: Global temperatures have been increasing significantly since 1980. Every decade has been warmer than the previous decade, with temperature records set every year. This is expected to continue until well after mankind ceases emitting additional greenhouse gases. It is virtually certain that over most land areas, there will be warmer and fewer cold days and nights, and warmer and more frequent hot days and nights. Warm spells and heat waves will increase in frequency over most land areas. Therefore, planners must directly take into account these increasing temperatures, which impact almost every aspect of human life and the biosphere.

Global Temperature Data

Overlay: Planners need to be aware that worldwide weather events will be more frequent and more intense due to increasing temperatures and related increases in moisture in the atmosphere.

---

[*] Allison et al., *The Copenhagen Diagnosis*, 38.

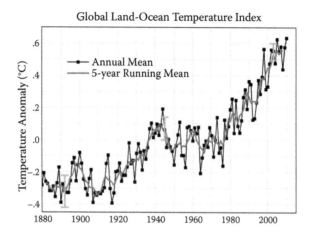

FIGURE 11.10
Global temperature.

Most of the scientific presentations of data have a vertical or y axis labeled "Anomaly." This means only that it relates to changes from some reference point that is considered "normal." In this case they use a base period of 1951 to 1980. They take an average of the temperatures for the years 1951–1980 and then plot the changes from that average. Any year or period could be chosen and the shape of the curve would be the same, only the numbers in the "y" scale would be shifted so that the zero would be the reference line.

There has been a lot of misinformation spread about regarding the current and projected changes in global temperature. In a discussion of the issue of temperature in climate change, the best place to start is with valid, reliable data. The graph in Figure 11.10 is a line plot of the global mean land-ocean temperature index, 1880 to present, with the base period of 1951–1980. The dotted black line is the annual mean and the solid line is the 5-year mean. The four lightly shaded vertical bars show the range of uncertainty in the estimates. This is the current NASA Goddard Institute for Space Studies (GISS) data from their web site.[*]

The year 2010 had the warmest January–August on record, and 2010 was tied with 2005 as the warmest year on record. This was predicted in January 2009 by the NASA GISS organization.

---

[*] See http://data.giss.nasa.gov/gistemp/graphs/ (accessed February 5, 2011).

This comes at the end of the warmest decade of global average temperature on record. Beginning in the 1980s, every decade has been warmer than the decade before, with the average for the last three decades each being higher than the record year global average temperature during the previous decade.

Because it is getting warmer, and especially during a record warm year, one would expect more record high than record low temperatures. That's exactly what we saw in 2010, with 19 nations setting their all-time record high temperatures, and Pakistan's record high was also Asia's all-time record high of 128°F.

The nations with record high temperatures range over much of the globe and include nations in South America, Africa, and Asia.

In the United States the National Climatic Data Center keeps the most dependable temperature records back to 1880 (thermometers were developed more than a century and a half before this, and through the 1800s and often before it was common practice to hang thermometers in the shade).

In the contiguous 48 states there were slightly more cold records than heat records in the 1960s and 1970s, but from January 1, 2000 to date there have been over twice as many heat records as cold records. According to analyses by Gerald Meehl at the National Center for Atmospheric Research, it is estimated that if human burning of fossil fuels is not curtailed, there could be 20 heat records for every cold record by 2050, and by 2100 the ratio could be 50 to 1.[*]

There are many other well-documented and consistent effects of temperature increase impacts, including the significant melting of 90% of the world's glaciers, increased melting of summer and early fall ice throughout the Arctic Ocean, increased severity of droughts, and more dramatic precipitation events of all kinds (including snow where it is cold enough to snow). Warming causes increased evaporation that has led to a 4% increase in the amount of water vapor since 1970, with about another 4% added for every degree of increase (Fahrenheit).

According to the 2007 IPCC4 Report, the global average temperature could increase by 3 to 10 degrees Fahrenheit by 2100. An atmosphere with 40% more water vapor than now would be unrecognizable to any human, with frequent storms of all kinds on scales we can't imagine.

---

[*] University Corporation for Atmospheric Research, Boulder, CO, "Record High Temperatures Far Outpace Record Lows across U.S.," http://www2.ucar.edu/news/1036/record-high-temperatures-far-outpace-record-lows-across-us (accessed February 6, 2011).

Climate looks at the averages of weather, and climate scientists don't claim to know what will happen in any given time and place in the months and years ahead, just as actuaries don't know what will happen to any individual, but they've typically studied the average life expectancies among various large groups, as discussed in Chapter 3. Climate scientists don't know where and when temperature and precipitation records will be broken, but they are confident that the next decade, and especially century, will have more records of all kinds broken than the last decade and century, and all on the up side.

Each year brings more records and variances from normal as the global temperature slowly rises in response to increasing CO_2. Because of normal weather variability it is difficult to state unequivocally that a particular weather event is caused by CO_2-induced temperature increases or if it is a local weather pattern aberration. However, a pattern of unusual events is occurring that points to climate change impacting weather much more severely and sooner than the scientists expected. This has caused alarm in the insurance industry as it tracks the numbers of extreme events and has seen the annual numbers increase steadily with claims. See the next section on planning for a warming future for a discussion of the insurance industry response.

Forecast Temperatures

The increase in global temperature from 2011 to 2030 is estimated to be between +1.15°F and +1.24°F. By mid-century (2046–2065) the overall estimate is between +2.3°F and +3.2°F as compared to the 1980 to 1999 base and by late century (2090–2099) a mean of +5.0°F and a range of 3.1°F to 7.9°F. Some predictions are higher and others are lower. When we consider that the "dangerous" increase is 3.6°F (2°C) it will be reached probably well before 2075. When the CO_2 in the atmosphere reaches approximately 450 ppm, in 25–30 years, the Earth is irreversibly committed to the 3.6°F dangerous level of increase. Remember from the section on the Keeling Curve that we are currently at 390 ppm and increasing 2+ ppm per year.

According to the IPCC4, the equilibrium global mean surface air temperature warming for a doubling of atmospheric carbon dioxide (CO_2), or *equilibrium climate sensitivity*, is likely to lie in the range 3.6°F to 8.1°F, with a most likely value of about 5.4°F. This is close to the same range as Arrhenius predicted in 1896. This is why this book is dedicated to my grandchildren and yours as well; this event will occur within their lifetimes.

Temperature Patterns

Geographical patterns of projected surface air temperature warming show greatest temperature increases over land (roughly twice the global average temperature increase) and at high northern latitudes, and less warming over the southern oceans and North Atlantic, consistent with observations during the latter part of the twentieth century.

Temperature Extremes

It is *very likely* (above 90% probability) that heat waves will be more intense, more frequent, and longer lasting in the coming warmer climate. Almost everywhere, daily minimum temperatures are projected to increase faster than daily maximum temperatures, leading to a decrease in the diurnal (day to night) temperature range. Decreases in the number of frost days (below freezing) are projected to occur almost everywhere in the middle and high latitudes, with a comparable increase in growing season length. Remember, this is climate change and not a prediction of a specific season's weather.

The IPCC4 report states specifically: "Cold episodes are projected to decrease significantly in a future warmer climate." However, the impact of warming in the Arctic Ocean and subsequent release of heat that disturbed the Arctic Oscillation were not predicted at the time the report was written. This phenomenon resulted in excessive cold flowing south into the United States and at the same time resulted in record high temperatures in Alaska. The IPCC4 statement is valid as an overall global set of episodes, but specific regions may have different experiences as many existing meteorological phenomena such as El Niño and La Niña, the Arctic Oscillation, the Pacific Decadal Oscillation, the North Atlantic Oscillation, and others are perturbed by the temperature changes.

United States Temperatures

Overlay: The United States is a large country. Its weather is a result of many different actions around the world. New England weather is driven by maritime events and air coming down from Arctic Canada. Louisiana depends on the Gulf and Arizona is impacted by the flows over the Rocky Mountains and straight down from Canada. We have deserts, mountains, plains, major lakes, and big cities. All are impacted by increasing temperatures but the weather responses are all different as are the living things that live in the various regions. Any programs that depend upon natural resources or predictable climate must look further into regional and other impacts.

Extensive temperature data are collected throughout the United States. Table 11.2 presents the 2010 report of NOAA,[*] which describes succinctly a currently typical meteorological year.

CRYOSPHERE: THE ARCTIC AND THE ANTARCTIC

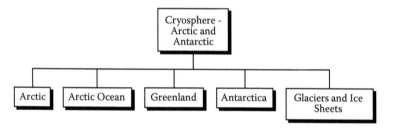

Cryosphere section outline.

Overlay: Warming of the climate has its most dramatic impacts on the cryosphere—the world of snow and ice. Three major events need to be integrated into program planning: (1) melting of ice sheets in Greenland and West Antarctica are having serious impacts on sea level rise, (2) melting of sea ice in the Arctic Ocean is opening up the area for commerce, and (3) melting of the permafrost is having significant impacts on the infrastructure and local environments.

The IPCC4 Report for snow and ice indicates just what one would expect: as the climate warms, snow cover and sea ice extent decreases, and

---

[*] NOAA, "NOAA: 2010 Tied For Warmest Year on Record," http://www.noaanews.noaa.gov/stories2011/20110112_globalstats.html (accessed February 5, 2011).

TABLE 11.2

NOAA 2010 Weather Report

- Combined global land and ocean annual surface temperatures for 2010 tied 2005 as the warmest such period on record at 1.12°F (0.62°C) above the 20th century average.
- The global land surface temperatures for 2010 were tied for the second warmest on record at 1.73°F (0.96°C) above the 20th century average.
- Global ocean surface temperatures for 2010 tied with 2005 as the third warmest on record, at 0.88°F (0.49°C) above the 20th century average.
- In 2010 there was a dramatic shift in the El Niño-Southern Oscillation (ENSO), which influences global temperature and precipitation patterns —when a moderate-to-strong El Niño transitioned to La Niña conditions by July. At the end of November, La Niña was moderate-to-strong.
- According to the Global Historical Climatology Network, 2010 was the wettest year on record, in terms of global average precipitation. As with any year, precipitation patterns were highly variable from region to region.
- The 2010 Pacific hurricane season had seven named storms and three hurricanes, the fewest on record since the mid-1960s when scientists started using satellite observations. By contrast, the Atlantic season was extremely active, with 19 named storms and 12 hurricanes. The year tied for third- and second-most storms and hurricanes on record, respectively.
- The Arctic sea ice extent had a record long growing season, with the annual maximum occurring at the latest date, March 31, since records began in 1979. Despite the shorter-than-normal melting season, the Arctic still reached its third smallest annual sea ice minimum on record behind 2007 and 2008. The Antarctic sea ice extent reached its eighth smallest annual maximum extent in March, while in September, the Antarctic sea ice rapidly expanded to its third largest extent on record.
- A negative Arctic Oscillation (AO) in January and February helped usher in very cold Arctic air to much of the Northern Hemisphere. Record cold and major snowstorms with heavy accumulations occurred across much of eastern North America, Europe and Asia. The February AO index reached −4.266, the largest negative anomaly since records began in 1950.
- From mid-June to mid-August, an unusually strong jet stream shifted northward of western Russia while plunging southward into Pakistan. The jet stream remained locked in place for weeks, bringing an unprecedented two-month heat wave to Russia and contributing to devastating floods in Pakistan at the end of July.

glaciers and ice caps lose mass owing to dominance of summer melting over winter precipitation increases. This contributes to sea level rise. There is a projected reduction of sea ice in the twenty-first century in both the Arctic and Antarctic, with the projected reduction being accelerated in the Arctic, where summer sea ice cover is expected to disappear entirely in the latter part of the twenty-first century. Widespread increases in thaw depth over much of the permafrost regions are projected to occur in response to warming over the next century.

Overlay: It is important for program managers to watch the Arctic and Antarctic for signals of major climate impacts to come. Weather temperatures in the Arctic will continue to be much warmer than average, bringing both benefits and problems. The melting ice from Antarctica is providing a significant input to overall sea level rises and will continue to do so at an increasing rate. Measurements from the GRACE satellites confirm that Antarctica is losing mass at an accelerating rate. "The important message is that it is not a linear trend. A linear trend means you have the same mass loss every year. The fact that it's above linear, this is the important idea that ice loss is increasing with time."* Antarctica mass loss is one of the biggest unknowns regarding sea level rise. Increasing losses will result in much higher seas with significant impact on low-level land infrastructure.

---

* Isabella Velicogna, "Increasing Rates of Ice Mass Loss from the Greenland and Antarctic Ice Sheets Revealed by GRACE," *Geophysical Research Letters* 36, (2009): L19503, doi:10.1029/2009GL040222, 2009; Department of Earth System Science, University of California, Irvine California, USA. Also Jet Propulsion Laboratory, California Institute of Technology, Pasadena, California, USA.

Understanding the issues of climate change at each end of the Earth is important since this is where the most dramatic changes are occurring.

Arctic

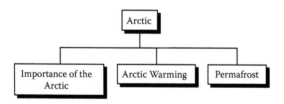

Arctic section outline.

Overlay: Climate changes and impacts are occurring more dramatically in the Arctic than almost anywhere else on Earth. Understanding and planning for these changes critical for Arctic programs as resource exploration and transportation options change.

Importance of the Arctic

An important source of data on the Arctic is the NOAA document *The Arctic Report Card,* which tracks environmental changes throughout the Arctic and is updated annually.* The 2010 version is typical and reflects the work of an international team of 69 researchers and is based upon 174 scientific references. It is supported by the International Arctic Council and the Circumpolar Biodiversity Monitoring Program (CBMP).

There are two principal reasons why the Arctic is of interest. One is the commercial interest in having the Arctic Ocean free of ice so that shipping can use this shortcut between the Atlantic and Pacific oceans. In addition, the risks of undersea exploration and exploitation of resources are reduced.

The second reason takes advantage of the warming temperatures, running 7°F to 9°F above normal. The most recent 4 years are reported to be the worst 4 on record—"worst" being subjective because the permafrost is affected, which has many negative impacts; also, the less ice coverage there is in summer, the more solar heat the Arctic Ocean can absorb, making it harder to form new ice and more difficult to maintain the thickness of old sea ice. This naturally affects wildlife. It also impacts the Arctic Oscillation, the normal cyclical weather pattern in the atmosphere over the pole that influences the southern range of the very cold Arctic air. Release of heat from the Arctic Ocean as it freezes later in the fall and winter results in shifts in the location and intensity of the normal Arctic Oscillation and brings Arctic air deep into the United States and other northern latitude countries.

Arctic Warming

Overlay: The Arctic is a bellwether of the changes that are occurring due to climate change and global warming. Significant changes are occurring that impact all aspects of life in the Arctic.

Figure 11.11 presents the Arctic air temperature changes over the past 2,010 years. Like the other temperature data for the globe, the long-term cooling trend of the Sun was slowly driving cooling. There was a significant change in the middle of the twentieth century when the warming

---

* NOAA: http://www.arctic.noaa.gov/reportcard/ArcticReportCard_full_report.pdf (accessed February 28, 2012).

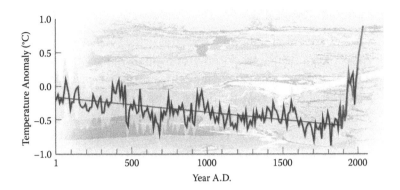

FIGURE 11.11

Arctic air temperature change. (Data from I. Allison, N. L. Bindoff, R. A. Bindschadler, et al. *The Copenhagen Diagnosis, 2009: Updating the World on the Latest Climate Science* (Sidney, Australia: The University of New South Wales Climate Change Research Centre, 2009, Figure 20, 46, with permission; and University Corporation for Atmospheric Research, Darrell S. Kaufman, David P. Schneider, Nicholas P. McKay, et al., "Arctic Warming Overtakes 2,000 Years of Natural Cooling," NCAR Press Release, September 03, 2009, http://www2.ucar.edu/news/846/arctic-warming-overtakes-2000-years-natural-cooling (accessed October 20, 2011.)

from carbon emissions changed the direction of the curve. And the line is expected to keep going upward.* Many different reconstructions of this chart by other credible organizations result in virtually the same chart, independent of the methodology used.

The Arctic is currently experiencing the impacts of a prolonged and amplified warming trend, highlighted with many record-setting events. The impact of this warming is most evident in the dramatic losses that have been observed in the ice covers that define the region.

As the air temperature increases, ice (which presents a bright, white, highly reflective surface) melts, revealing darker ocean and land surfaces that absorb more solar energy during a summer season when the sun never sets. This causes more heating, which causes more melting, continuing a positive feedback cycle and amplifies Arctic warming. The record warm temperatures cause a continued increase in the rate of ice mass loss from all glaciers and ice caps in the Arctic.

The warming air temperatures also play a major role in the observed increases in permafrost temperatures around the Arctic rim, the increase in river discharge to the Arctic Ocean, and the increase in the greenness of Arctic vegetation.

---

* Allison et al., *The Copenhagen Diagnosis*, 46.

Warming in subarctic regions such as Canada and Russia have extended the growing seasons, allowed new crops to be planted, and opened up large areas for cultivation.

Permafrost[*]

> **Overlay:** Any programs that involve any aspect of permafrost, from road construction in the Arctic to building homes, must assume that significant changes will be occurring and that the land is no longer stable. Melting of permafrost also results in the release of methane, which exacerbates global warming. Planners must be aware that warmer is not always better in the Arctic—not when people depend upon cold temperatures to provide a rigid surface for infrastructure elements.

Permafrost is defined on the basis of temperature because the layer of soil or rock that remains below 32°F throughout the year. It forms when the ground cools sufficiently in winter to produce a frozen layer that persists throughout the following summer. The layer above the permafrost is called the *active layer* and usually supports plant life of all types, including spruce, fir, and pine forests.

Each year, the layer of the ground at the surface rises above 32°F for part of the year. This active layer freezes and thaws with the changing seasons. Both the thickness of permafrost and the active layer depend on local climatic conditions, vegetation cover, and soil properties. The temperature beneath the Earth's surface increases with increasing depth at a rate of about 75° to 90°F per mile. The thickness of permafrost can be altered by changes in the climate or disturbance of the surface.

Permafrost thins and the active layer thickens when ground temperatures increase. Permafrost gets colder and thicker northward, as might be expected. Within the northern foothills of the Brooks Range, permafrost is 28° to 10°F and about 600 feet thick. On the Alaskan Arctic Plain, permafrost is as cold as 12° to 9°F and up to 2,000 feet thick.

The long-term records of the near-surface permafrost temperature, obtained from different parts of the permafrost zone in northern regions,

---

[*] This general discussion of permafrost is based on an essay prepared by Vladimir E. Romanovsky, Associate Professor Geophysical Institute UAF, Fairbanks, AK, for NOAA, http://www.arctic. noaa.gov/essay_romanovsky.html (accessed February 7, 2011).

show a significant warming trend during the last 30 years. Ground temperature trends generally follow the trends in the air temperatures, with a more pronounced warming in the lower latitudes (between 55° and 65° north). This recent climate warming brought soil temperatures to a surprisingly high level, about 2° to 5°F warmer than long-term averages. Within some areas, the permafrost temperatures are very close to 32°F and at many sites long-term permafrost degradation has already started.

A major concern of warming in the Arctic is the current thawing of permafrost.[*] There are two major problems: first, many structures and roads and airports have been built on permafrost and need to be rebuilt with different foundations; second, permafrost contains a vast amount of carbon and methane, which is currently sequestered.

> One of the more interesting of the author's projects was to be the U.S. government pipeline safety engineer assigned to oversee the Northwest Alaska Company program to bring a gas pipeline from the north slope down to Prudhoe Bay, Alaska. The pipeline was to be placed underground through a thousand miles of permafrost, so many meetings and discussions and on-site visits occurred to discuss and solve the engineering problems of digging trenches in permafrost areas.

As global temperatures continue to rise, the vast expanse of permafrost beneath much of the grasslands on the Tibetan Plateau's northern tier is also now at risk of thawing.[†] This will have effects on the watershed that feeds the Yellow and other rivers. It will also accelerate desertification and degrade the pasturelands on which traditional nomads have long depended.

But the most profound global impact of this thawing, which has already begun, will be the enormous amounts of methane gas—roughly twenty times more potent in heat-trapping capacity than CO_2—that will be released by the decomposition of once-frozen carbon-rich organic matter in the area's soil. This continued thawing threatens to turn what has been a major carbon-sink—sequestering about 2.5% of the world's soil carbon—into a huge new source of emissions.

---

[*] Victoria Barber, "Borehole Network Confirms, Permafrost Is Thawing Worldwide," *The Arctic Sounder*, August 13, 2010, http://thearcticsounder.com/article/1032borehole_network_confirms-permafrost_is_thawing_worldwide/htm (accessed August 14, 2010).

[†] Orville Schelle, "The Message from the Glaciers," *New York Review of Books*, May 27, 2010, http://www.nybooks.com/issues/2010/may/27/ (accessed May 29, 2010).

Arctic Ocean

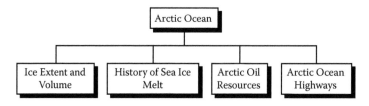

Arctic Ocean section outline.

> **Overlay:** The Arctic Ocean in the summer will be an increasingly busy place as warming continues and as oil prices rise. There will be increased shipping in the summer and more exploration for oil and gas. The environment, from every perspective, will be undergoing change. Not all will be positive.

An overview of the Arctic polar ice caps and the Arctic Ocean and the problems and opportunities resulting from the rapid melting in response to global warming are provided by Alun Anderson in the *World Policy Journal.* The problems and opportunities arise as the Arctic ice melts and as the resources of the Arctic become available.

Ice Extent and Volume

> **Overlay:** Dramatic reductions in sea ice in the summer are occurring. This potentially opens up the Arctic Ocean for shipping and resource extraction while at the same time adversely impacting wildlife that depends upon sea ice.

Ice extent refers to the coverage of the ocean by ice. It is important for three reasons: the first is that the ice reflects the rays of the sun, which results in a cooler surface and a cooler Earth; the second is the opening of the ocean for shipping; and the third is the impact on wildlife.

The September 2010 amount of Arctic sea ice extent was the third smallest of the past 30 years. This continues an ongoing trend, with the four smallest

---

* Alun Anderson, "The Great Melt: The Coming Transformation of the Arctic," *World Policy Journal*, October 15, 2010, http://www.worldpolicy.org/blog/2010/10/15/great-melt-coming-trans-formation-arctic (accessed May 3, 2011).

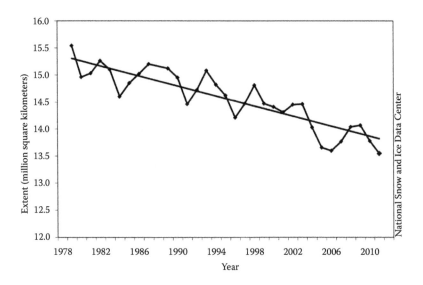

FIGURE 11.12
Average monthly Arctic Sea ice extent.

September ice extents having occurred in the past four years. Eight of the ten lowest summer minimums have occurred in the last decade. The amount of older, thicker multiyear ice was the third smallest ever, and there was a notable loss of multiyear ice in the Beaufort Sea, north of Alaska. Although happening at a slower rate, wintertime sea ice extent is also declining.

Figure 11.12 presents data regarding the extent of the loss of sea ice and the trend line. This figure was provided by the National Snow and Ice Data Center in Boulder, Colorado. January as well as February 2011 had the lowest ice extent for their months since the beginning of satellite records. The linear rate of decline for each month is −3.3% per decade.[*]

Figure 11.13, from the Polar Ice Center, presents recent variations of total Arctic sea ice volume in the context of longer-term variability. Arctic sea ice volume is an important indicator of climate change because it accounts for variations in sea ice thickness as well as sea ice extent. These data are based on observations from satellites, Navy submarines, moorings, and field measurements.

A new study finds that Arctic plankton blooms are occurring up to 50 days earlier now than they were in the late 1990s. This is due to the

---

[*] National Snow and Ice Data Center, Boulder, CO (NASA), http://nsidc.org/arcticseaicenews/, Figure 3 (accessed February 7, 2011).

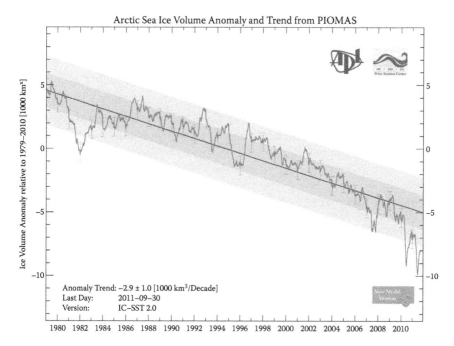

Arctic Sea Ice Volume Anomaly and Trend from PIOMAS

FIGURE 11.13
Change in Arctic ice volume.

retreat of the ice. Phytoplankton lie at the base of the marine food chain and the change in timing may have a ripple effect for other species.[*]

History of Sea Ice Melt

By using proxy measurements, such as the size and type of organic and inorganic particles buried in sea-floor sediments, scientists have looked back more than 100,000 years to find a time when the summer melt has been as dramatic as it is today. The study found the following:

> The current reduction in Arctic ice cover started in the late 19th century, consistent with the rapidly warming climate, and became very pronounced over the last three decades. This ice loss appears to be unmatched over at least the last few thousand years and unexplainable by any of the known natural variabilities.[†]

[*] Mati Kahru et al., Scripps Institution of Oceanography, "Scripps Oceanography Researchers Discover Arctic Blooms Occurring Earlier," Press Release, March 2, 2011, http://scrippsnews.ucsd.edu/Releases/?releaseID=1144 (accessed March 11, 2011).

[†] Leonid Polyak et al., "History of Sea Ice in the Arctic," *Quaternary Science Reviews* 29 (2010): 1757–1778, http://www.sciencedaily.com/releases/2010/06/100602193423.htm.

The evidence indicates there was probably no ice during the Arctic summers 7,000 years ago, and also ice-free summers during the last interglacial period 125,000 years ago. Those were due to natural factors, most notably the changes in Earth's orientation to the sun, which brought more sunlight to the Arctic in summer, as discussed earlier regarding Milankovitch Cycles. This time, there is no known natural explanation, so the conclusion is that it is due to the increase in CO_2 emissions into the atmosphere by humans.

Arctic Oil Resources

Oil companies are convinced that they will eventually be able to exploit the area. In February 2008, they bid $3.4 billion in a competition for drilling rights in the Chukchi Sea, off the city of Barrow on the northwest coast of Alaska. Shell led the pack with $2.1 billion in winning bids, followed by ConocoPhillips. At present these plans are on hold for various reasons. But as the price of oil increases, the political constraints will probably disappear, the environmental constraints will be resolved, and normal economics will take over. It is very expensive to extract oil and gas in the Arctic and get it to market. Further out into deep water there is no certainty that their claims will ever be worth anything. Although there may be oil and gas further out to sea, it may be so far from land that it will be uneconomic to exploit for many years into the future.

The exception to the U.S. situation is Russia. It has significant close-in reserves of oil and gas that it is actively exploiting, since it is the key to its wealth and power. It is rapidly adding infrastructure and building massive oil platforms and new special ships to operate in sea ice.

Arctic Ocean Highways

The expectation is that that new trans-Arctic shipping routes will open as the ice vanishes, providing short cuts across the top of the world for container traffic that currently takes manufactured goods from China, Korea, and Japan to Europe and the east coast of the United States via the Suez Canal or the southern tip of Africa.

Traffic in general is certainly going to grow, but the old dream of an easily navigable short cut between Atlantic and Pacific is likely to remain a mirage far into the future. The Northwest Passage sought by explorers runs from Baffin Bay in eastern Canada to the north coast of Alaska. There are many possible paths among Canada's northern islands, but none provides easy passage. Prevailing winds and currents mean that these channels will always be littered with chunks of winter ice, swept in from the deeper Arctic, making them a dangerous choice for all but the toughest ships. Other routes such as the northern route that runs across the other side of the Arctic and the route that stays away from the coasts of either Canada or Russia all have problems. The big disadvantage for all routes is that they will always freeze solid in winter, and the Arctic summers (while increasingly ice-free) remain short. Even by mid-century, ice-free transit will not be possible for more than a few months each year.

Greenland

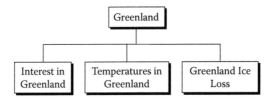

Greenland section outline.

> **Overlay:** Greenland is one of the two keys to sea level rise, the other being East Antarctica. This island needs to be carefully observed as a bellwether of the impact of global warming on low-lying lands around the world.

Interest in Greenland

Greenland is a unique place and different from the other Arctic regions. As opposed to the Arctic Ocean, Greenland is an island and therefore the ice it holds will add to sea level rise as it melts. Because of this, from a long-term perspective, what is occurring in Greenland is more significant to the world as a whole than any other Arctic phenomenon except the comparable situation in West Antarctica. Greenland is critical to monitoring the impact of global warming due to the immense amount of ice located within its ice sheets and ice cap. Melting of the Greenland ice cap can result in not inches of sea level rise, but many feet. Of course this would take a long time, centuries in fact.

Satellite and on-site measurement networks have documented increasing melting and accelerated ice flow around the periphery of the Greenland ice sheet (GIS) over the past 25 years.[*]

Temperatures in Greenland

Record warm air temperatures were observed over Greenland in 2010. This included the warmest year on record for Greenland's capital, Nuuk, in at least 138 years. The duration of the melt period on Greenland's inland ice sheet was exceptional, being 1 month longer than the average over the past 30 years, and led to an extended period of amplified summer melt. All of the additional melt water very likely contributes to a faster rate of crevasse widening, which allows surface melt water to flow down to the rock base and lubricate the movement of the glaciers and ice sheets seaward.

Greenland Ice Loss

Glacier loss along the Greenland margins has also been exceptional, with the largest single annual glacier area loss (110 square miles, at Petermann Glacier) equivalent to an area four times that of Manhattan Island. There is now no doubt that Greenland ice loss has not just increased above past decades, but has accelerated. The implication is that global sea level rise projections will again need to be revised upward, as discussed in the subsection on sea levels in Chapter 12.

The latest data from the GRACE satellites, which measure the change in gravity around the Greenland ice sheet, is shown in Figure 11.14 in terms of differences from a 2007 baseline.[†]

The Greenland ice mass anomaly is a measure of the deviation from the average ice mass over the 2002–2010 period. Note: this does not mean that the ice sheet was gaining ice before 2006, but only that the ice mass was above the 2002–2010 average.

---

[*] IPCC4, Working Group I, 776.

[†] Mr. Tenney Naumer from the Climate Change: The Next Generation blog and Dr. John Wahr at the University of Colorado analyzed the GRACE data and granted permission to reproduce it on SkepticalScience.com.

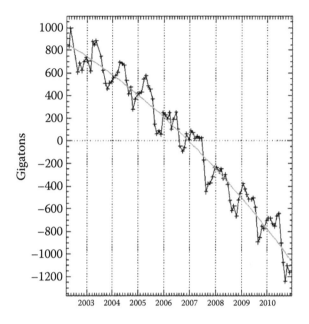

FIGURE 11.14
GRACE satellite data; Greenland ice loss. (From SkepticalScience,com, with permission.)

Antarctica

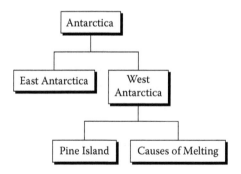

Antarctica section outline.

Overlay: The Antarctic is of interest primarily because of the impact the melting has on global sea level rise. The Antarctic holds 90% of the world's ice.

FIGURE 11.15
Antarctic continent. http://en.wikipedia.org/wiki/File:Antarctica.org (From Wikimedia Commons and NASA.)

Antarctica is a continent lying chiefly within the Antarctic Circle and asymmetrically centered on the South Pole. It is the largest of the Earth's ice zones, or *cryosphere*, is 1.5 times the size of the United States (including Alaska), and some 95% is covered in ice, in places to a depth of 3 miles. Figure 11.15 is a map of Antarctica prepared by NASA.

East Antarctica

Two-thirds of Antarctica is a high, cold desert, and known as East Antarctica. It is very cold; the Soviet Antarctic base, Vostok, on July 21, 1983 measured the temperature as −128.6°F, which is the lowest temperature ever recorded on Earth. The polar plateau, where explorer Robert Scott perished, routinely records temperatures of −70°F or −80°F in winter. This section of Antarctica has an average altitude of about 1.2 miles, higher than the American Colorado Plateau and Denver, and from approximately sea level on up it is all ice. It will be quite some time before the heart of Antarctica's vast ice dome begins to melt. However, if all of this ice melted, it would raise global sea levels by about 200 feet. However, it appears that little if any surface warming is occurring over East Antarctica. Radar and laser-based satellite data show a little mass loss at the edges of East Antarctica, and even this is being partly offset by accumulation of snow in the interior. Although some early studies have shown that most of Antarctica is cooling slightly, the most comprehensive recent survey shows that Antarctica overall warmed by 1°F between 1957 and 2007.[*]

---

[*] Eric J. Steig et al., "Warming of the Antarctic Ice-Sheet Surface since the 1957 International Geophysical Year," *Nature* 457 (January 22, 2009): 459–462, http://www.nature.com/nature/journal/v457/n7228/full/nature07669.html (accessed February 8, 2011).

Also, changing atmospheric circulation patterns around Antarctica due to the increasing ozone hole have, in places, brought more frigid air off the polar plateau and cooled some parts of the continent. One portion of the Ross Sea, for example, is colder and has actually seen sea ice grow in recent years.

However, recent satellite data suggest that since 2006 there has been more ice loss from East Antarctica than previously thought.* Possible melting of the periphery is a serious matter and any steady warming there has the potential to raise global sea levels many feet and to affect global ocean circulation. Overall, however, the available data do not indicate much is going on in East Antarctica, but it bears watching.

The Antarctic accumulated its volume of ice because it is a continent surrounded by ocean—the Southern Ocean—which acts like a great, insulating moat around the South Pole. The Arctic, by contrast, is an ocean surrounded by continents whose landmasses moderate the polar climate.

The Antarctic is also the location of the ozone hole that has reduced the greenhouse effect and kept the continent colder. Ironically, ongoing efforts to reduce the ozone hole will increase the temperatures and the melting in the Antarctic Peninsula.

West Antarctica

West Antarctica is very different from East Antarctica. It is an important consideration in any risk analysis involving sea level rise. Instead of a single land mass, it is a series of islands covered by ice. Much of the West Antarctic ice sheet is actually sitting on the floor of the Southern Ocean, not on dry land. Parts of it are more than 1 mile below sea level.

Since 1950, winter temperatures have increased by 11°F and annual average temperatures by 5°F at a research base originally built by the British and now run by the Ukrainians on the peninsula. Ninety percent of 244 glaciers along the western Antarctic Peninsula have retreated since 1953.† Sea ice now blankets the Southern Ocean off the western Antarctic Peninsula three fewer months a year than in 1979, according to satellite data.

Pine Island

Pine Island is the largest of the islands, and the largest ice stream in West Antarctica is called Pine Island Glacier. The West Antarctic ice sheet,

---

* J. L. Chen et al., "Accelerated Antarctic Ice Loss from Satellite Gravity Measurements," *National Geoscience* 2 (2009): 859–862 (2009).
† Op. cit. SCAR, p. xviii.

if it melted completely, would raise sea level by between 16 and 23 feet. Approximately 10% of that would be from the Pine Island Glacier.

The Pine Island ice shelf is thinning at a rate of 160 feet a year, and the melting has loosened the grip of the Pine Island Glacier on the sea floor, causing the enormous river of ice behind it to accelerate in its movement into the sea. The Pine Island Glacier is now sliding into the Amundsen Sea at a rate of about 2 miles a year.

Recently, a British group revisited the Pine Island Glacier and found that its rate of retreat had quadrupled between 1995 and 2006.[*] Its melting in 2009 was 50% faster than measured in 1994. The Pike Island Glacier and smaller glaciers that flow into it contain enough ice to boost sea levels by 9 inches.[†]

Causes of Melting

One of the fundamental laws of thermodynamics is that heat always goes from warm to cold. Not only are air temperatures rising, changing atmospheric and oceanic circulation patterns around Antarctica have caused the deep Antarctic Circumpolar Current to be funneled up onto the continental shelf in western Antarctica. In winter, that water can be as warm as 37°F, which sounds cold, but in fact is considerably warmer than the surface water, which hovers around 32°F, and vastly warmer than air temperatures, especially in winter. This huge volume of relatively warm water on the continental shelf is having an enormous impact, since water holds 1,000 times more heat than air.

This Antarctic Circumpolar Current water is playing a key role in the warming of the Antarctic Peninsula and the melting of ice shelves, glaciers, and sea ice. Melting of the Pine Island Glacier has been from the bottom up, as the warmer water from the deep ocean enters the cavity beneath the ice shelf where the ice is thickest. The current level of warming in Antarctica is far more severe than global warming in Antarctica of the past century. One major reason is that the warming of land masses and oceans to the north has set up a sharper contrast with Antarctica's intense cold. That has led to a strengthening of northerly winds, pulling far warmer air down

---

[*] D. J. Wingham et al., "Spatial and Temporal Evolution of Pine Island Glacier Thinning, 1995–2006," *Geophys. Res. Lett.* 36 (2009): L17501.

[†] Alex Morales, "West Antarctica's Biggest Glacier Is Melting 50% Faster than 17 Years Ago," Bloomberg, http://www.bloomberg.com/news/2011-06-26/antarctica-s-pine-glacier-melting-50-faster-study-indicates.html (accessed June 27, 2011).

from the south Pacific and south Atlantic onto the Antarctic Peninsula. Satellite data show that Antarctica has been losing more than 24 cubic miles of ice each year since 2002 and at an accelerating rate.[*]

Glaciers and Ice Sheets

> **Overlay:** In one word: *melting.* This will have two impacts that planners need to accommodate: rising sea levels and a shortage of fresh water where the population depends on glacier melt.

Mountain glaciers around the world, nearly everywhere, are retreating. Glacier National Park in Montana contained more than 100 glaciers when it was established in 1910. Today, just 26 remain, and at the current rate of decrease it is estimated that by 2030 there will be no glaciers in Glacier National Park.[†] Lonnie Thompson from The Ohio State University, one of the world's leading glacier climatologists, states:

> Glaciers serve as early indicators of climate change. Over the last 35 years, our research team has recovered ice-core records of climatic and environmental variations from the Polar Regions and from low-latitude high-elevation ice fields from 16 countries. The ongoing widespread melting of high-elevation glaciers and ice caps, particularly in low to middle latitudes, provides some of the strongest evidence to date that a large-scale, pervasive, and, in some cases, rapid change in Earth's climate system is underway.

He has documented glacier shrinkage in the Andes, the Himalayas. and Mt. Kilimanjaro. His efforts have been described in detail in Mark Bowen's *Thin Ice* listed in the bibliography. The primary problem of loss of glaciers is the loss of fresh water supplies and resulting impact on the ecosystem. People on dry land need the fresh water that is running into the sea and the hydroelectric power that comes from mountain streams that are fed by mountain glaciers and ice fields.

---

[*] Basic material for description of the Antarctic provided by Erik Conway, NASA/Jet Propulsion Laboratory, NASA Web Page: http://www.nasa.gov/topics/earth/features/20100108_Is_Antarctica_Melting.html (accessed February 7, 2011).

[†] Lonnie Thompson, "Climate Change: The Evidence and Our Options," *The Behavior Analyst* 33, no. 2 (2010): 153–170.

Polar ice sheets are also melting and the Greenland ice sheet has experienced dramatic ice melt in recent years. The sea ice in Antarctica is melting and especially the West Antarctic ice sheet. The concern about the ice sheet melting is the impact on sea level rise. As mentioned earlier, a large proportion of the rise in sea levels is due to ice sheet melting, and this proportion is expected to increase. In addition to the danger of flooding, rising sea levels bring saltwater into rivers, spoil drinking wells, and turn fertile farmlands into useless fields of salty soil.

12

Climate Change Overlays

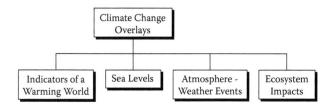

Chapter 12 outline.

INDICATORS OF A WARMING WORLD

Climate change overlay applicability occurs at two levels: existing and ongoing events and phenomena that occur at an organization and country level, and global mitigation and adaptation activities that occur at the macro or U.N. level. In this section we address the lower-level items first, and then address the macro. Figure 12.1 lists some of the indicators of a warming world. They are grouped by increasing and decreasing indicators.

The following discussion contains some of the specific projections of the probable impacts of the climate changes documented in the previous chapters. The source is the Intergovernmental Panel on Climate Change (IPCC), *Climate Change 2007: The Physical Science Basis* (IPCC4) Working Group 1 report, Section 10, "Global Climate Projections," pages 747–845. More recent data, especially that documented in *The Copenhagen Diagnosis Report* (Allison et al.; prepared to update the IPCC4 report in preparation for the international conference at Copenhagen in 2009), indicates that almost every indicator presented in the IPCC4 report shows the projections and the IPCC4 data to be too conservative. This includes almost

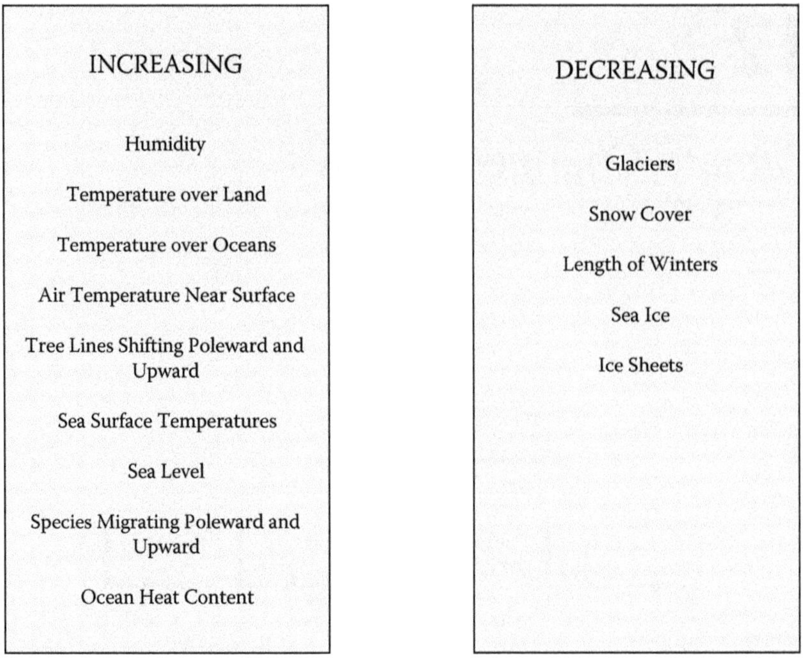

INCREASING	DECREASING
Humidity	Glaciers
Temperature over Land	Snow Cover
Temperature over Oceans	Length of Winters
Air Temperature Near Surface	Sea Ice
Tree Lines Shifting Poleward and Upward	Ice Sheets
Sea Surface Temperatures	
Sea Level	
Species Migrating Poleward and Upward	
Ocean Heat Content	

FIGURE 12.1

Indicators of a warming world. (From John Wood, Skeptical Science, with permission. www.skepticascience.com/graphics.php)

all the data in this discussion, summarized from the IPCC4 report. *Conservative* means cautious in projecting severe impacts or deviations from normal trends. As actual data are gathered, in virtually all cases the changes are more severe than forecast.

The IPCC4 contains some regional climate predictions; however, the models used for these projections have wider margins of error than the general predictions included in this discussion. One of the foci of the upcoming IPCC5 report is to include more information on likely regional impacts based on more recent data and more sophisticated modeling and forecasting capabilities. It is recommended that program managers watch for the release of this report or release of regional reports in advance of IPCC5 for updates on the projections. A recommended and typical report is the current *Global Climate Change Impacts in the United States,* published in 2009 and prepared by the U.S. Global Change Research Program, a U.S. government entity that provides updated data for the United States.[*]

---

[*] Thomas R. Karl et al., eds., *Global Climate Change Impacts in the United States* (Cambridge: Cambridge University Press, 2009), available online at http://www.globalchange.gov/usimpacts.

Another example is the report *Climate Change and the Chesapeake Bay*, from the intergovernmental Chesapeake Bay Program, Science and Technical Advisory Committee.* More recently the National Academy of Sciences published a report on America's climate choices.†

The following sections address only the more important of the extensive list of impacts on the world's environment.

SEA LEVELS

Overlay: Cities, communities, and property owners with tidal waterfront property must prepare for a conservatively estimated global sea level rise of between 4 and 7 feet by the end of the century. For long-range planning, some are predicting double these numbers. Communities should restrict construction within the Federal Emergency Management Agency (FEMA) 100-year flood plain or modify and adapt protective infrastructure for higher water levels. The *100-year flood* is no longer a 1% statistical probability, but represents an area at much higher risk from frequent storms. Problems of sea level rise such as erosion and flooding are exacerbated by storm surges and increasing tidal ranges. Rain storms with high precipitation will increasingly result in inland rivers exceeding historic flood stages.

The global sea level rose by about 400 feet during the several millennia that followed the end of the last ice age (approximately 21,000 years ago), and stabilized between 3,000 and 2,000 years ago.‡ It appears from various sea level indicators that global sea level did not change significantly from then until the late nineteenth century. Satellite observations available since the early 1990s provide relatively accurate sea level data with nearly global coverage. Since 1993, sea level has been rising at an average rate of around

---

* STAC Publication #08-004, September 2008, Edgewater, MD, Chesapeake Research Consortium, Inc., available from http://www.chesapeake.org/stac.
† National Research Council, Committee on America's Climate Choices, *America's Climate Choices*, (Washington, DC: National Academies Press, 2011), available from http://www.nap.edu/catalog/12781.html in a PDF format).
‡ Intergovernmental Panel on Climate Change (IPCC), *Climate Change 2007: The Physical Science Basis* (New York: Cambridge University Press, 2007), Working Group 1, 409.

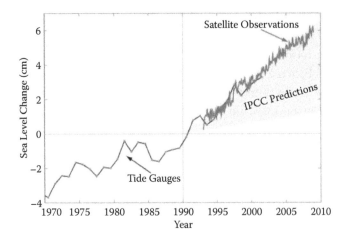

FIGURE 12.2

Sea level changes. (From I. Allison, N. L. Bindoff, R. A. Bindschadler, et al. *The Copenhagen Diagnosis, 2009: Updating the World on the Latest Climate Science* (Sidney, Australia: The University of New South Wales Climate Change Research Centre, 2009), Figure 16, 39.

1/8 inch (3 mm) per year globally, and this rate is significantly higher than the average during the previous half century. It is important to qualify this figure—this is a global average and it may be much higher in some regions and much lower in others. There have been recent studies analyzing the regional impacts and it is suggested that these be researched if you are interested in any particular narrow geographic area. At the Chesapeake Bay, there is a subsidence phenomenon that adds another 0.12 inches (2.7 mm) per year to the sea level rise and the opposite is occurring in southeastern Alaska, where sea level is dropping about 10 mm per year due to the land rising after the retreat of the weight of the glaciers.[*]

Climate change has been causing changes in sea levels from the expansion of the oceans as they warm up and the melting of glaciers all over the world combined with the melting of the Greenland, Arctic, and Antarctic ice sheets. Figure 12.2 illustrates what has been occurring to date and Table 12.1 shows how this breaks down by sources of the rise.

Except for a period from 1985 to 1990, as shown in the figure, the sea level has been increasing constantly. In 1990 the IPCC predictions for the next decade were for lower levels than actually occurred. There has been an increase of 10 centimeters since 1970; this is about 4 inches worldwide or an inch a decade.

---

[*] NOAA Tides and Currents, "Frequently Asked Questions: What Is Sea Level?", http://tidesand-currents.noaa.gov/sltrends/faq.shtml#q1 (accessed March 10, 2011).

TABLE 12.1

Sea Level Rise in Millimeters per Year (1993–2003)

Sea Level Rise	
Source	**Amount**
Thermal Expansion	1.6 ± 0.5
Glaciers and Ice Caps	0.77 ±0.22
Greenland Ice Sheet	0.21±0.07
Antarctic Ice Sheet	0.21±0.35
Other[a]	0.3±1.0
Total Observed	3.1±0.7

[a] Recent studies have shown that this is deep ocean thermal expansion.
Source: Intergovernmental Panel on Climate Change (IPCC), *Climate Change 2007: The Physical Science Basis* (New York: Cambridge University Press, 2007), Working Group 1, Table 5.3, 419.

Table 12.1 presents the breakdown of the causes of the sea level rise per year over the decade 1993 to 2003. As shown in the table, thermal expansion accounted for approximately two thirds of the rises in 2003 when you include the deep ocean data. The IPCC4 report forecast that by 2100 the total average sea level rise would be approximately 2 feet. However, an update to the IPCC4 report prepared for the conference in Copenhagen in 2009 revised and updated the estimate to between 14 inches and as much as 4 feet (36–120 cm), about double the earlier IPCC4 estimate.[*] So instead of a 12- to 21-inch rise by 2100, it is now predicted to be approximately 14–42 inches by 2100. Again, this is an *average* range and in local regions this may be much higher or other regions can be lower, as described earlier. According to one study, sea levels in the Chesapeake Bay, for example, are projected to rise between 0.7 and 1.6 meters (27–63 inches) by the end of this century. [†] The midpoint is almost a 4-foot rise in sea level. Higher sea levels also cause a bigger risk from the problem of storm surge—Hurricane Isabel in 2005 had a maximum storm surge of 9 feet in the Bay, and it had only 65-mph winds when it arrived. Hurricane Irene in 2011, on the other hand, had almost no storm surge.

A 2011 study by NASA's Jet Propulsion Laboratory indicates that even this estimate of sea level rise is too low because of recent data showing higher rates of melting of the ice sheets in Greenland and the West Antarctic. (This is why we spent so many pages in Chapter 11 on the cryosphere.) Just the ice sheet melting is now estimated to add 6 inches to

---

[*] Allison et al., *The Copenhagen Diagnosis*, 40.
[†] Chesapeake Bay Program, Science & Technology Advisory Committee, Pub #08-004, September 2008.

worldwide sea level rise by 2050. Considering thermal expansion and the other factors listed in Table 12.1, it appears that global average sea level rise will be as much as 12.6 inches from current levels by the year 2050.[*]

Much of the melting that has occurred and that gets much press is the melting in the Arctic Ocean. This is important for many reasons, among which is the economic impact of a Northwest Passage; however, this is melting of ice that is floating and it has no impact on sea levels.

> The National Oceanic and Atmospheric Administration (NOAA) tells us that "sea levels provide an important key to understanding the impact of climate change, not just along our coasts, but around the world. By combining local rates of relative sea level change for a specific area based on observations with projections of global sea level rise (from IPCC4, 2007), coastal managers and engineers should begin to analyze and plan for the impacts of sea level rise for long-range planning."[*]

[*] Rignot et al., "Acceleration," concluding sentence in FAQ section.

For risk management it is important to monitor melting rate changes in the ice caps and ice sheets and local conditions if your programs are near coastal waters. This is where the big changes in the future will occur and where there is some uncertainty regarding predicting the rate of melting. These data are generally available from NOAA sites or from research institutions. For example, the Virginia Institute for Marine Science (VIMS) recently published a study of the land subsidence and sea level change in the Chesapeake Bay that indicated the absolute increase in sea level was less than the worldwide IPCC4 data but the subsidence more than made up for it, and therefore sea levels were rising faster than the IPCC4 data.[†] The thermal expansion numbers can be calculated relatively accurately now that data are available from the deep ocean. Expansion can be predicted

---

[*] E. Rignot et al., "Acceleration of the Contribution of the Greenland and Antarctic Ice Sheets to Sea Level Rise," American Geophysical Union, *Geophysical Research Letters* 38 (2011): L05503, doi:10.1029/2011GL046583. Also described in Joanna Zelman, "Melting Ice Sheets Now Largest Contributor to Rising Sea Levels: Study," *The Huffington Post*, http://www.huffingtonpost.com/2011/03/10/melting-ice-sheets-sea-level_n_833517.html (accessed March 10, 2011).

[†] John D. Boon et al., *Chesapeake Bay Land Subsidence and Sea Level Change: An Evaluation of Past and Present Trends and Future Outlook* (Gloucester Point, VA: VIMS November 2010, Special Report No. 425 to the U.S. Army Corps of Engineers, Norfolk, VA), http://web.vims.edu/GreyLit/VIMS/sramsoe425.pdf?svr=www (accessed March 11, 2011).

As reported in an update to the IPCC4 Working Group 1 report, "the largest unknown in the projections of sea level rise over the next century is the potential for rapid dynamic collapse of ice sheets." The most significant factor in accelerated ice discharge in both Greenland and West Antarctica over the last decade has been the ungrounding of glacier fronts from their bed, mostly due to submarine ice melting. Changes to base lubrication by melt water, including surface melt draining through moulins (vertical conduits) to the bottom of the ice sheet, also affect the ice sheet dynamics in ways that are not fully understood. The major dynamic ice sheet uncertainties are largely in one direction: they can lead to a faster rate of sea level rise, but are unlikely to significantly slow the rate of rise. Although it is unlikely that total sea level rise by 2100 will be as high as 2 meters (7 feet), the probable upper limit of a contribution from the ice sheets remains uncertain.[*]

Rob Young and Orrin Pilkey write in *Yale e360* that the message for the world's leaders and decision makers is that sea level rise is real and is only going to get worse. Governments and coastal managers should assume the inevitability of a 7-foot rise in sea level.[†] This number is not a prediction, but they believe that 7 feet is the most prudent, conservative long-term planning guideline for coastal cities and communities, especially for the siting of major infrastructure. A number of academic studies examining recent ice sheet dynamics have suggested that an increase of sea level of 7 feet or more is not only possible, but likely, if not by 2100 then shortly thereafter. Certainly, no one should be expecting less than a 3-foot rise in sea level this century.

---

[*] Allison et al., *The Copenhagen Diagnosis*, 28.
[†] Rob Young and Orrin Pilkey, "Opinion: How High Will Seas Rise? Get Ready for Seven Feet," Yale e360, January 14, 2010.

reasonably well for different levels of CO_2 emissions and for increases in average global temperatures. Expansion due directly to warming will soon account for less than a third of the rise as more ice sheets and caps melt faster and faster.

The data are very straightforward and the conclusions are obvious. The water levels in the ocean are rising. Fortunately, the governments of many shoreline communities are aware of what is coming and are acting responsibly in their planning. If you act on the assumption that the rise will occur as expected and even put in a margin of safety, the worst that happens is that the threat does not materialize on the time scale expected, but your organization or the community has updated their plans and adaptive measures are in place. If no action is taken and the threat does materialize, then it will be far more costly to adapt—or move.

ATMOSPHERE: WEATHER EVENTS

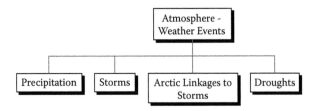

Atmosphere section outline.

Precipitation

> **Overlay:** Increasing temperatures in the atmosphere result in more moisture being retained. Storms will contain more moisture and precipitation will increase in those areas where precipitation is normal; this includes snowfall. The world is in the process of setting new "normals." Flood prevention infrastructure and other structures in flood plains need to be evaluated for higher flood levels and more frequent floods. Flood plains should also be redefined and rezoned accordingly.

For the future warmer climate, the current predictions are that precipitation generally increases in the areas of tropical monsoons and over the tropical Pacific in particular, with general decreases in the subtropics.* There will be increases in precipitation at high latitudes (Paris, New York, San Francisco, Tokyo, etc.) as a consequence of a general intensification of the global hydrological cycle. This means that as a global average, the atmosphere will be holding more moisture, which will come from evaporation. Rainfall will increase simply because there is more water in the

---

* IPCC4 Working Group 1 Report, Section 10, "Global Climate Projections," 747–845.

atmosphere to fall as precipitation. Individual regions will be impacted differently and as a generality, areas that get heavy rainfall will get even more and areas that are drought prone will get even less.

Even in areas where mean precipitation is expected to decrease (most subtropical and mid-latitude regions), and precipitation intensity is projected to increase, there would be longer periods between rainfall events. There is a tendency for drying of the mid-continental areas during summer, indicating a greater risk of droughts in those regions. Precipitation extremes are forecast to increase more than does the mean in most tropical and mid- and high-latitude areas. These precipitation extremes are likely to cause local flooding.

Storms

> **Overlay:** Storms. That is the one word that will best characterize the twenty-first century climate.[*] It is difficult to prove that any given weather event is related to global warming or climate change. A decade or more of data usually needed to definitively show a trend that would validate a hypothesis of a permanent climate change. However, there is enough data that a prudent planner would assume that there will continue to be stronger weather events as time goes on and as CO_2 levels continue to increase. Therefore, the weather overlay should include expectations of more heat waves, more flooding, more tornadoes, stronger hurricanes, and heavier snowfalls. The specific event relating to the part of the country or world where the program is located.
>
> _____
> [*] James Hansen, Makiko Sato, and Pushker Kharecha, *Earth's Energy Imbalance and Implications* (New York: NASA Goddard Institute for Space Studies, August 26, 2011), 250, 253.

John Cook of SkepticalScience.com wrote in the U.K. *Guardian* that Queensland experienced two 1-in-a-100-year weather events within a few weeks in early 2011, which might lead one to conclude that they are unlikely to reoccur for the next two centuries.[*] Unfortunately, that is not

_____
[*] John Cook, excerpted from "Australia's Recent Extreme Weather Isn't So Extreme Anymore," SkepticalScience.com, http://www.guardian.co.uk/environment/blog/2011/feb/09/australia-extreme-weather-flooding-drought/print (accessed February 11, 2011).

how probabilities work, and that is not the case when the probabilities are in the process of changing.

As the climate gets warmer, more water evaporates and the air holds more moisture, as mentioned previously. Over the past 40 years, the amount of water vapor in the atmosphere has risen by 4%. All that extra water vapor increases the chance of an extreme rainfall event.

Our physical understanding of climate tells us global warming will cause the water cycle to grow more intense. This means both more heavy downpours and more intense drought. As temperatures rise, the ground dries out faster, causing droughts to get worse. So we find ourselves swinging from one extreme to another, like an ever-deepening rollercoaster ride. But increased drought and heavy downpours aren't just predictions from a climate model. They're happening in the real world. Dr. Lynton Land, a geoscientist, explains the stronger storms very simply: there is a latitudinal imbalance between the heat received from the sun and the heat back-radiated, as discussed in the section on the greenhouse effect. Therefore the atmosphere, and ocean, must transport more heat pole-ward as the Earth warms, hence stronger storms; simple thermodynamics.

Global warming is expanding arid areas of the Earth. Warming at the equator drives a climate system called the Hadley Cell. Warm, moist air rises from the equator, loses its moisture through rainfall, moves north and south, and then the air falls to the Earth at 30° north and south latitude, creating deserts and arid regions. There is evidence that over the last 20 years the Hadley Cell has expanded north and south by about 2 degrees of latitude, which broadens the desert zones.* Therefore, droughts are expected to become more persistent in the American southwest, the Mediterranean, Australia, South America, and Africa.

Arctic Linkages to Storms

Overlay: Very cold winter weather in lower latitudes and climate change are closely related. Abnormal Arctic temperatures and record snowfalls are caused by disturbances to the upper atmosphere caused by increased temperatures and moisture.

---

* Lonnie Thompson, "Climate Change: The Evidence and Our Options," *The Behavior Analyst* 33, no. 2 (2010): 153–170.

A common lament is, "If there is global warming, how come it is so cold this winter or why is there so much snow?" There is an answer, but it is complex.

A study by Ian Simmonds and Kevin Keay, at the University of Melbourne in Australia, finds connections between the decline in September sea ice extent and the characteristics of Arctic storms. As ice extent has decreased, Arctic storms have shown a tendency to become more intense, especially in the last few years. The study suggests that low September ice extent, with extensive areas of open water, provide more energy to autumn storms, allowing them to become stronger. The stronger storms also help to break up the ice.

The linkage between changes in the Arctic and the very cold temperatures in the winter in North America and Europe is also addressed in the NOAA *Arctic Report Card*.[*]

Dr. James Overland of the NOAA Pacific Marine Environmental Laboratory (PMEL) recently noted a link between low sea ice and a weak polar vortex in 2005, 2008, 2009, and 2010, all years with very low September sea ice extent.[†] Earlier work by Jennifer Francis of Rutgers University and colleagues also identified a relationship between autumn sea ice levels and mid-latitude winter conditions.[‡]

The warm conditions in the Arctic and cold conditions in northern Europe and the United States are linked to the strong negative mode of the Arctic Oscillation.[§] Cold air is denser than warmer air, so it sits closer to the surface. Around the North Pole, this dense cold air normally causes a circular wind pattern called the *polar vortex*, which helps keep cold air trapped near the poles. When sea ice has not formed during autumn and winter, heat from the ocean escapes and warms the atmosphere. This appears to weaken the polar vortex and allow air to spill out of the Arctic and into mid-latitude regions, bringing cold winter weather to lower latitudes.

[*] J. Richter-Menge and J. E. Overland, eds., "Arctic Report Card 2010: Update for 1022," http://www.arctic.noaa.gov/reportcard (accessed February 7, 2011).

[†] Overland, J.E., and M. Wang, Large-scale atmospheric circulation changes are associated with the recent loss of Arctic sea ice, Tellus, 62A, doi: 10.1111/j.1600-0870.2009.00421.x, 1–9 (2010) http://www.pmel.noaa.gov/publications/search_abstract.php?fmContributionNum=3302 (Accessed February 28, 2012)

[‡] Jennifer A. Francis, Elias Hunter, Drivers of declining sea ice in the Arctic winter: A tale of two seas. American Geophysical Union, GEOPHYSICAL RESEARCH LETTERS, VOL. 34, L17503, 5 PP., 2007 doi:10.1029/2007GL030995

[§] See National Snow and Ice Data Center, http://nsidc.org/arcticseaicenews/ (accessed February 7, 2011).

Droughts[*]

> **Overlay:** Areas of the world currently experiencing drought conditions, such as the U.S. western deserts, parts of Australia and China, the Sahel in Africa, and others, are expected to not only have the droughts continue, but to get more intense and cover wider areas. Planners should expect that this will have many impacts on programs that involve these geographic areas.

The areas covered by droughts have increased in various parts of the world. The regions where they have occurred seem to be determined largely by changes in sea surface temperatures, especially in the tropics, and through changes in the atmospheric circulation and precipitation. Increased evaporation from land into the atmosphere and drying associated with warming are additional factors in drought increases, but decreased precipitation is the dominant factor. In the western United States, diminishing snowpack or early snowpack melt and subsequent summer soil moisture reductions have also been a factor. In Australia and Europe, direct links to warming have been inferred through the extreme nature of high temperatures and heat waves accompanying drought.

The IPCC4 Working Group 2 identified the major impacts of areas affected by drought increases to be as follows:[†]

- **Agriculture, forestry, and ecosystems:** Land degradation, lower yields/crop damage and failure, increased livestock deaths, increased risk of wildfire
- **Water resources:** More widespread water stress
- **Human health:** Increased risk of food and water shortage, increased risk of malnutrition, increased risk of water- and food-borne diseases
- **Industry, settlement, and society:** Water shortages for settlements, industry, and societies, reduced hydropower generation potentials, potential for population migration

Closely related to drought are the overall fresh water resource problems. These are discussed in detail by Fred Pearce in his book *When the Rivers Run Dry.*

---

[*] IPCC4, Working Group 1, 317.
[†] IPPC4 Working Group 2, "Impacts, Adaptation and Vulnerability," 18.

Ecosystem Impacts

Three clear, observable connections between climate and terrestrial ecosystems are (1) the seasonal timing of life cycle events or phenology, (2) responses of plant growth or primary production, and (3) biogeographic distribution.[*] Examples of specific ecosystem impacts follow.

Global daily satellite data, available since 1981, indicate earlier onset of spring "greenness" by 10–14 days over 19 years, particularly across temperate latitudes of the Northern Hemisphere. Field studies confirm these satellite observations. Many plant species are expanding leaves or flowering earlier. Consider these changes:

- Earlier flowering in lilac: 1.8 days/decade, 1959 to 1993, 800 sites across North America
- Honeysuckle: 3.8 days/decade, western United States
- Leaf expansion in apple and grape: 2 days/decade, 72 sites in northeastern United States
- Trembling aspen: 2.6 days/decade since 1900, Edmonton
- The area burned in wildfires has increased dramatically over the last three decades.
- Warmer springs have led to earlier nesting for 28 migrating bird species on the east coast of the United States and to earlier egg laying for Mexican jays and tree swallows.
- In northern Canada, red squirrels are breeding 18 days earlier than 10 years ago.
- In lowland California, 70% of 23 butterfly species advanced the date of first spring flights by an average 24 days over 31 years.
- Red foxes have expanded northward in northern Canada, leading to retreat of competitively subordinate Arctic foxes.
- Worldwide, the tree lines are shifting and species are migrating pole-ward and upward.

Hundreds of additional ecosystem impacts have been documented. It is incredible to believe any literate person reading these reports can deny the existence of climate change.

---

[*] IPCC4, Working Group 2, 622.

13

Planning for a Different Future:
An Overlay of Adaptation and Mitigation

It is difficult to get a man to understand something when his job depends upon not understanding it.

—Upton Sinclair

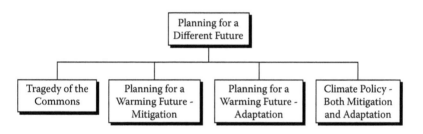

Chapter 13 outline.

Overlay: It is important to be aware that the future will be different from the past. Not simply an extrapolation as we have been able to do for the past several decades. There are four planning approaches that take climate change into account: mitigation or adaptation and their combination, or simply do nothing.

This section is based on the conclusions expressed by the many organizations listed in Appendix A, "The Scientific Community Positions on Climate Change and Global Warming."

At this point in our scientific understanding, there is no question the future will continue to be one of warming.*

---

* See Appendix A.

TRAGEDY OF THE COMMONS

Overlay: Our atmosphere and oceans are public "commons" and there are no costs attributed to their usage. They are free. The fish and animal resources are harvested without any payment for the privilege or consideration of long-term impacts, and they are used as dumping grounds for all types of waste—they are grossly misused.

In England, villages typically had open, public areas referred to as *commons* like, for example, the Boston Commons.

In 1968 Garrett Hardin wrote an essay titled the "Tragedy of the Commons," which was published in *Science*.[*] It quickly became a classic. He described a situation where farmers were using a commons as a place to graze their cattle. Over time, more and more farmers took advantage of this free resource with larger and larger herds. Each farmer rationalized, "If I don't let my cattle graze there, someone else will do so anyway, so it doesn't make sense for me to back off. And why should I pay for grazing land elsewhere when it is free in the commons?"

This individual rationalization leads to an outcome where everyone is worse off. If overgrazed, the resource will crash or become depleted and all lose. There are examples of the use of commons all around—fishermen harvesting fish or crabs in a certain part of the ocean or bay, oystermen harvesting oysters, or the extraction of fresh water from an aquifer. There are also many examples of where the commons have been preserved and examples where they have been lost.

Our atmosphere is a commons, just like our oceans and major segments of our land areas such as the state and national parks or the Great Lakes. People use them as sources of enjoyment or for sources of food or waste disposal.

The classic "Tragedy of the Commons" problem is resolved by one or more of the following three classic solutions:[†]

1. An outside force enforces quotas
2. Privatize the resource—divide into individually owned parcels

---

[*] Garret Hardin, "The Tragedy of the Commons," *Science*, New Series 162, no. 3859 (December 13, 1968): 1243–1248.

[†] See Jared Diamond, *Collapse: How Societies Choose to Fail or Succeed* (New York: Penguin Books, 2005), 428–430 for a discussion of the alternatives and rational bad behavior.

3. Users recognize common interests to preserve the commons and negotiate a solution

There is always the "Do Nothing" option, which in this case means eventual loss or collapse of the commons; this is often the default option when the potential collapse is beyond the planning horizon of the "herders."

The Chesapeake Bay is a commons that is threatened on many fronts and some action is slowly being taken by the federal and state governments (Solution 1: enforcing quotas regarding fishing, waste disposal, fertilizer usage, and other regulatory instruments is the current choice to preserve the Bay. There is also a lot of voluntary action by concerned citizens.)

At present there is no cost (or very little cost) perceived to be associated with the emissions of CO_2 or other greenhouse gases into the atmosphere. The people and industries involved are able to "graze" for free and will do so until there is recognition that the atmosphere is a commons; it is being destroyed and must be protected. There is a measure of where we are on the pathway to collapse due to carbon emissions from around the globe: it is the Keeling Curve. All countries have signed on to a 450 ppm = 3.6°F (2°C) increase in global temperature is the point at which the climate change becomes dangerous. There are three current solutions that are available for whenever the world decides to take action. These are organized by the classic solutions to the general commons problem.

1. An outside force enforces quotas
   i. Regulatory Instruments: mandated targets, emission controls, Corporate Average Fuel Economy (CAFÉ) standards, etc.
   ii. Economic Instruments: subsidies, fees, taxes, tax exemptions, cap and trade, U.N. programs with commitments and method of enforcement, etc.
2. Privatize the resource: divide into individually owned parcels; not applicable since the atmosphere won't recognize borders.
3. Users recognize common interests to preserve commons and negotiate solution:
   i. Policy Processes: voluntary agreements, dissemination of information, etc.
   ii. Research and Development: expand the commons; change demand for use of the commons.

4. Do nothing: Business as usual: adaptation to the effects of climate change to the extent possible. Let the commons collapse, in other words.

An open question is why countries have been so reluctant to address CO_2 emissions when the data are so convincing. One logical explanation is provided by Dr. Angel Cabrera of the Thunderbird School of Global Management. He attributes the foot dragging to "carbon lock-in," which refers to the "self-perpetuating inertia created by interlocking institutional forces and cultural norms that inhibit efforts to develop alternate energy systems."[*] In English, this means that we have a major difficulty in moving away from fossil fuels because any alternative would create a loss for an important constituency. This would include private and public institutions, automobile manufacturers, coal companies, oil companies and refiners, miners, farmers, consumers, and others. From a global perspective we are talking about nations agreeing to a common plan or set of emissions reductions and methods of enforcement. Constituencies include leaders within China, India, Brazil, and the European Union and of course the U.S. Populations with much lower standards of living than the United States naturally want to increase their standards of living and this requires energy, which in today's world means carbon dioxide emissions.

The simplest approach to resolving the global atmosphere misuse of the commons is to make the use of the commons more expensive: to reduce demand and make the cost of using the commons part of the price of the unit of energy involved. Either by a regulatory instrument or economic instrument, no matter how it is done it will translate into a tax or fee on carbon.

The impact of any tax, fee, or regulation of carbon, no matter what the form, would be immediate and personal while the benefits would be long term and may not accrue to those paying the cost. The beneficiaries would be our grandchildren. That is why Dr. Hansen's book is titled *Storms of My Grandchildren*. As discussed in the section on oil in Chapter 5, the current and previous generations have been living a relatively idyllic life-style due to cheap oil and any attempt to moderate that would be strongly resisted, as Dr. Calvera stated. One perspective is that because our standard of living is higher in the United States, we might have to bear most of the costs and therefore there is more resistance to

---

[*] Steven Pearlstein and Raju Narisetti. "On Leadership; Carbon and Climate Change: Why Are We Behind?" *Washington Post*, August 8, 2010, G2.

change. On the other hand, the costs of doing nothing are so high and in the long run the United States really has so much to lose that the relatively small costs are inexpensive insurance against future major climatic disturbances. More extensive and deeper discussions of this issue are included in Professor Mike Hulme's book *Why We Disagree About Climate Change*.

Change will occur only when there is strong support from the bottom up or strong leadership from the top down, and neither is apparent on the horizon. The entities that would be adversely impacted have been very successful in propagating the myth that there is no problem in the commons.

In his 50th contribution over 5 years, one of the frequent contributors to the Skeptical Science blog points out that it is necessary to "always come back to the risk assessment and management perspective. Climate change poses one of the greatest potential risks the human race has ever faced. From a risk management standpoint, even if you're personally unconvinced by the scientific evidence, it just makes no sense to risk the future of human society and a great many of the species on Earth on the slim probability that the scientific experts are wrong and you're right. The risks and consequences are just too great. We're on track for a potential mass extinction event ..."[*]

And further, he concludes: "Ultimately it's not about proving which side is right, because we can't know that until future events play out. It's all about mitigating risk." As Lonnie Thompson put it, "we're committed to a certain amount of climate change, and the only question is how much we will mitigate, adapt, and suffer.[†] Personally, I'd like to reduce the risk of suffering as much as possible. I don't want to bet public health and welfare on the off chance that the "skeptics" are right. And I think those who are actively trying to prevent us from taking the steps to reduce that risk of suffering are doing our country, human society, and the world a great disservice."

The following two sections briefly address what has boiled down into two simultaneous action trajectories: mitigation of carbon emissions to save the commons combined with various adaptation schemes. It is known that the scientific data to date are correct; they have been verified many times, so if the projections are valid, then at some point it will become apparent the business-as-usual and do-nothing scenarios are untenable.

---

[*] Skeptical Science, http://www.skepticalscience.com/danas-50th-why-blog.html, March 28, 2011 (accessed March 28, 2011).

[†] Lonnie Thompson, "Climate Change."

PLANNING FOR A WARMING FUTURE: MITIGATION OF CO$_2$ EMISSIONS

Section outline.

Overlay: Actions will eventually be taken by the United States and other countries to try to mitigate climate change. Planners need to be aware of this probability. The situation is such that the longer the time before some serious action is taken, the more drastic the action must be.

Although science can cause problems, it is not by ignorance that we will solve them.

—Isaac Asimov

This section is divided into two parts: the first is what actions have been taken internationally to mitigate emissions and the second is what typical actions are needed to provide the level of mitigation that the scientific and international communities recommend. Please understand that these two sections are boiled down to the minimum that a program manager should be aware of and that volumes have been written on these subjects. As in the rest of this book, the intent is to provide facts so that the reader can understand the forces structuring the future so as to more effectively plan for the future.

International Actions

A large amount of energy has been expended by the international community on the subject of global warming and climate change. These activities are outlined in upcoming text.

Overlay: The world should not expect some organized international action to seriously address climate change until the United States, partnering with China, takes the lead. It is apparent by their actions that the leaders of the world do not believe any real actions to mitigate carbon emissions are necessary at this point. They are capable of acting when they need to, as evidenced by the Montreal Agreement, where they did act and act effectively when threatened with an enlarging ozone hole. However, that agreement did not involve any real sacrifice or culture change.

In 1972, at the U.N. Conference on the Environment in Stockholm, Principle 6 from the agreements reached stated the following: "The discharge of toxic substances or of other substances and the release of heat, in such quantities or concentrations as to exceed the capacity of the environment to render them harmless, must be halted in order to ensure that serious or irreversible damage is not inflicted upon ecosystems."[*]

Twenty years later, at the Earth Summit in Rio de Janeiro in June 1992, the United Nations Framework Convention on Climate Change, (UNFCCC) had the following objective: "to achieve stabilization of greenhouse gas concentrations in the atmosphere at a low enough level to prevent dangerous anthropogenic interference with the earth's climate system …"[†]

The resulting treaty included provisions for updates (called *protocols*) that would set mandatory emission limits. The principal update was the Kyoto Protocol. Actions were aimed primarily at industrialized countries, with the intention of "stabilizing their emissions of greenhouse gases at 1990 levels by the year 2000; and other responsibilities would be incumbent upon all UNFCCC parties."[‡]

The Kyoto Protocol, which has received an inordinate amount of media coverage, was adopted in 1997 and went into force in 2005. It included the following goals: Between January 2008 and 2012, Annex I Countries were to reduce collective emissions by 5% below 1990 levels. The First World

---

[*] United Nations Environment Programme, Stockholm m 5-16 June 1972, Declaration of the United Nations Conference on the Human Environment. http://www.unep.org/documents.Multilingual/Default.asp?DocumentID=97&ArticleID=1503&l=en (accessed February 28, 2012).

[†] United Nations, United Nations Framework Convention on Climate Change, 1992, FCCC/Informal/84 GE.05-62220 (E) 200705 Article2, page 4.

[‡] National Academy of Sciences, Climate Change Science" An Analysis of some Key Questions, 2001. http://www.nap.edu/catalog/101039.html, Summary Page 1. Accessed February 27, 2012.

countries were in Annex I. China, India, and others were developing countries and excluded. There were several problems and the United States did not sign on. One was the base year of 1990, which would have been relatively easy for the European Union to achieve and difficult for the United States. Since part of the Kyoto Protocol was a "cap and trade" system with a compliance mechanism, it became apparent that while in principle that approach was acceptable, the specific implementation ground rules were very disadvantageous to the United States and the overall benefits were questionable. (In 1997, the U.S. Senate rejected it 95 to 0.)

In December 2007, at the next big U.N. conference in Bali, where the purpose was to provide the ground rules for the Kyoto Protocol beyond 2010, they decided to wait to see what a new U.S. administration policy might be because of the leadership role of the United States and also its role as the leading CO_2 emissions country at that time. In their final report they stated that the countries recognize that "deep cuts in global emissions" will be required and they called for a "long term global goal for emissions reduction."[*]

Next was a G8 meeting in July 2008 where the participants, including the United States, signed on to the following statement:[†]

> Seeking to share with all parties of the UNFCCC the vision of moving to a low-carbon society, and together with them to consider and adopt the goal of achieving at least a 50 percent reduction of global emissions by 2050, recognizing the need for contributions by all major economies;
> Recognizing that an effective post-2012 climate change regime will require all major economies, developed and developing, to commit to meaningful mitigation actions bound in a new international agreement.

There were two problems with this enigmatic statement: the first was that the scientific community was saying specifically that an 80% reduction from 2008 levels by 2050 is needed to stay at or below the danger level of 3.6°F above the 1980–1999 base.[‡] The second was that it was all voluntary; there were no binding commitments.

The next big meeting was scheduled for Copenhagen in December 2009. The results of that highly publicized meeting, called the Copenhagen Accord, are summarized as follows:

---

[*] http://uncff.int/resource/docs/convkp/conveng.pedf (Accessed February 28, 2012).
[†] Kyoto Protocol to the united Nations Framework Convention on Climate Change, Article 3, 11 December 1997. http://unfcc/int/resource/docs.convkp/kpend.html (Accessed
[‡] IPCC4,, Working Group 2, 16.

- Keep the increase in global temperature less than 3.6°F.
- Commit to implement individually or jointly the targets for 2020 submitted 31 January 2010. Provide status reports every 2 years.
- Commit to $30 billion in 2010–2012 to assist countries adversely impacted by warming and to protect rain forests; have a goal of $100 billion a year by 2020.
- Perform an assessment of the Accord by 2015 regarding a 2.7°F (1.5°C) increase in global temperatures.

Table 13.1 presents selected Annex I Country commitments that they agreed to submit by 31 January 2010. The United States commitment was generally consistent with the goals recommended by the scientific community.
Of particular interest were China and India's commitments:

China will endeavor to lower its carbon dioxide emissions per unit of GDP [gross domestic product] by 40–45% by 2020 compared to the 2005 level, increase the share of non-fossil fuels in primary energy consumption to around 15% by 2020 and increase forest coverage by 40 million hectares and forest stock volume by 1.3 billion cubic meters by 2020 from the 2005 levels.

India will endeavor to reduce the emissions intensity of its GDP by 20–25% by 2020 in comparison to the 2005 level.

TABLE 13.1

Copenhagen Accord Commitments, 2009

Selected Annex I Countries Copenhagen Commitments

- United States: 17% reduction by 2020, 30% by 2025, 42% by 2030 toward 83% by 2050 from 2005 base
- EU: 30% by 2020 from 1990 levels
- Japan: 25% by 2020 from 1990 levels
- Russia: 15–25% by 2020 from 1990 levels
- Australia: 25% by 2020 from 2000 levels

In both cases it is good to reduce the emissions intensity, which is CO_2 per unit of GDP. However, in a high-growth society, this is achieved easily by a rising GDP but meanwhile the absolute value of emissions is rising unabated. The easiest way to explain this is to put it in the form of a simple formula:

$$Emission\ Intensity = \frac{CO_2\,(Gigatons)}{GrossDomesticProduct\,(\$Trillions)}$$

As long as GDP increases faster than CO_2 emissions, the emission intensity will decrease. But the CO_2 emissions are still increasing and that is the important measure.

An analysis of the commitments of all the governments of the world calculates out to an increase of 7°F (3.9°C) by 2100 versus a business-as-usual increase of 8.6° F.[*] This is a long way from the goal of keeping the temperature increase below 3.6° F (2°C).

The Union of Concerned Scientists is recommending that the United States as the leader of the world cut its emissions and aim for at least an 80% drop from the 2005 levels by 2050, which is close to the U.S. commitment.[†]

Actions Required to Meet Mitigation Objectives

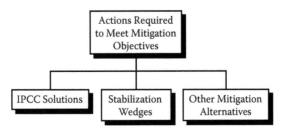

Section outline.

Overlay: The actions required in the current world and national situation to meet the scientists' estimates of what is needed to keep emissions below the 450 ppm CO_2 level are technically feasible, practically difficult, and politically impossible. It is important to monitor progress and adapt the program planning accordingly.

In this section we will illustrate the size of the problem in reducing emissions to avoid further climate change and related impact and provide an indication of the magnitude and difficulty of the mitigation alternatives. This section only touches briefly on the many, many actions required or possible to reduce emissions to the levels deemed safe by scientists or to mitigate the many negative effects of a changing climate.

---

[*] ClimateInteractive.org; C-ROADS Simulator (accessed December 20, 2009).

[†] Rachel Cleetus et al., "Executive Summary," *Climate 2030: A National Blueprint for a Clean Energy Economy* (Cambridge, MA: Union of Concerned Scientists, 2, http://www.ucsusa.org/assets/documents/global_warming/Climate-2030-Blueprint_executive-summary.pdf).

"Mitigation" comes in two forms: the reduction of emissions as well as reducing or adapting to the effects of climate change.

IPCC Mitigation Solutions

> **Overlay:** As described by the International Panel on Climate Change (IPCC), the problem of reducing emissions to acceptable levels is very large and virtually all of the alternatives are required in varying degrees and in different countries and regions of the world. The planners need to take an "all of the above" pathway. Their Working Group III Report, *Mitigation of Climate Change*, has 851 pages of contributions to the solution.

The IPCC4 Working Group III *Mitigation of Climate Change* presents a broad suite of actions relative to climate change that include both mitigation of emissions and the reduction of the effects of climate change.* It aims to answer essentially five questions relevant to policymakers worldwide:

1. What can we do to reduce or avoid climate change?
2. What are the costs of these actions and how do they relate to inaction?
3. How much time is available to realize the drastic reductions needed to stabilize greenhouse gas concentrations in the atmosphere?
4. What are the policy actions that can overcome the barriers to implementation?
5. How can climate mitigation policy be aligned with sustainable development policies?

The report does not recommend any specific strategy or technologies to be pursued, but rather lays out the options.

Stabilization Wedges

> **Overlay:** The concept of *stabilization wedges* is brilliant in its ability to present the problem of emissions reduction in a format and terms

---

* Intergovernmental Panel on Climate Change (IPCC), Fourth Assessment Report (IPCC4), *Climate Change 2007: The Physical Science Basis* (New York: Cambridge University Press, 2007), Working Group 3, ix of Preface. This is an 851-page document.

that normal people can relate to. They clearly illustrate the magnitude of the problem and provide solutions and opportunities. The concept uses technologies and actions that can be initiated today. These are all opportunities for long-term programs and provide an overview of what types of programs will most likely get support.

One of the easiest ways to get across the magnitude of the problem is to use Pacala and Socolow's "wedge" concept as a basis for discussion.[*] Figure 13.1 presents a graphic of the amount of carbon emitted globally each year.

Carbon emissions are projected to double in the next 50 years from the current annual approximate 900 billion tons of CO_2 ($BtCO_2$), keeping the world on a course to more than triple the atmosphere's CO_2 concentration from its preindustrial level of 287 ppm (660 $BtCO_2$) and to exceed an annual rate of 16 Bt/year CO_2. The preferred path for emissions is the one showing a decrease in emissions starting almost immediately in order to keep the CO_2 below 450 ppm. (A 3.6°F temperature increase). In order to follow the flat path, emission reductions need to match the prospective growth in emissions with technologies that emit little or no carbon. In other words, all growth in energy supply needs to be from carbon-free sources or current sources need to be converting to carbon-free sources.

Note that the figure does not present total CO_2, but is an annual figure that is growing at a high rate. This growth is a continuation of what has been occurring since World War II as population has been growing and energy use has been growing and the standard of living worldwide has been increasing, but more so in the Western world. It is China and India and other developing nations' turn at growth and they are doing so.

Figure 13.2 illustrates the wedge concept and why it is called a *wedge*. The so-called stabilization triangle is the area under the top curve of Figure 13.1, which needs to be addressed to shift the curve down to the flat path or preferably the decreasing CO_2 path.

Socolow and Pacala have developed an educational game based on their concept of stabilization wedges. Each wedge or strategy would reduce

---

[*] See *National Geographic*, http://ngm.nationalgeographic.com/2007/10/carbon-crisis/img/stabilization_wedges.pdf and Princeton University, http://cmi.princeton.edu/wedges/intro.php (accessed February 14, 2011).

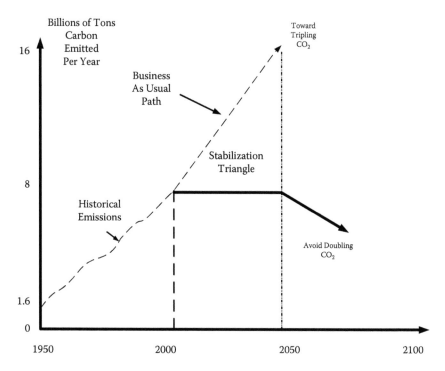

FIGURE 13.1
Annual carbon emissions. (Figure as a result of work done by the Carbon Mitigation Initiative, Princeton University.)

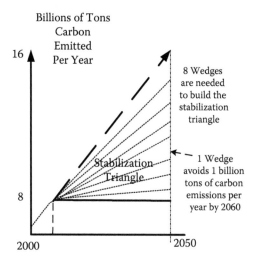

FIGURE 13.2
Stabilization wedges. (Figure as a result of work done by the Carbon Mitigation Initiative, Princeton University)

annual carbon emissions by a billion metric tons per year by 2060 and they provide a list of 15 stabilization wedges and their costs that are available for the player (or the national policymaker) to select. As can be seen from the figures, if the total annual emissions are to remain constant at approximately 8 Bt/year, then 8 wedges worth of reductions are needed to keep the total from rising above that to a level of 16 Bt/year. Some typical wedges are described as follows:

1. Improve fuel economy of the 2 billion cars expected on the road by 2057 to 60 mpg from 30 mpg.
2. Reduce the miles traveled annually per car from 10,000 miles to 5,000 miles.
3. Introduce systems to capture CO_2 and store it underground at 800 large coal-fired plants or 1,600 natural gas plants.
4. Replace 1,400 large coal-fired power plants with natural gas plants.
5. Triple the world's nuclear capacity by 2050.
6. Increase wind-generated power to 25 times current capacity.
7. Increase solar power to 700 times current capacity.

Socolow and Pacala believe that all the technologies described are available today, although scaling up in many cases, such as carbon sequestration, is still questionable. But the point here is not to question the availability of the technology, but to impress on the reader that just staying even in annual emissions is a major task and reducing the annual level is even more Herculean. Look at the list and what needs to be achieved. In the Chapter 5 of this book we address the technologies and opportunities and necessity of achieving major portions of these wedges. While the technologies may not be available or developable on Socolow and Pacala's timetable, there certainly will be pressures, eventually very strong market and political pressures, to develop technologies to meet two mitigation goals: (1) reduce the annual demand for carbon-intensive fuels, (2) produce alternative sources of energy, and (3) work on the wedges.

Figures 13.1 and 13.2 also have another message: Each year of delay it gets more and more difficult and expensive to reach the target of keeping the warming below the danger level of 3.6°F. More wedges are needed and the time periods over which they need to be implemented are shortening.

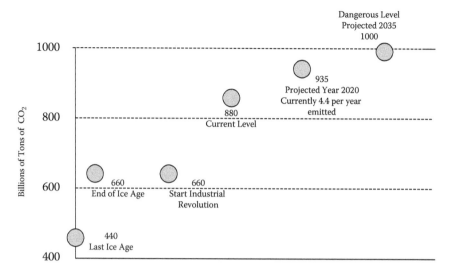

FIGURE 13.3
Atmospheric CO_2.

Another way to look at the problem is based on data presented by Fred Pearce[*] in Figure 13.3. Note the previous charts were in units per year. The data in Figure 13.3 are totals.

Pearce prefers to track the amount of CO_2 emitted in tons rather than parts per million and provide targets in terms of these data. He believes these units are more understandable.

The 2006 level of CO_2 was at 880 billion tons of CO_2 ($BtCO_2$). The U.N. IPCC4 danger level of 3.6°F (2°C) is 935 $BtCO_2$ which is projected to be reached in 2020 at the current rate of emissions. To hold the 935 $BtCO_2$ level the world would need to peak by 2015 and reduce by 50% in the next 50 years and continue reducing. In 2007 Pearce believed the world was too late to achieve this. He believes the really critical amount of CO_2 is the 1 trillion tons expected to be reached under the current business-as-usual scenario by 2035.

Most of the things worth doing in the world have been declared impossible before they were done.

—**Louis D. Brandeis**

---

[*] Fred Pearce, *With Speed and Violence*, 242, 243.

Other Emissions Mitigation Alternatives

> **Overlay:** In addition to the technology and conservation alternatives, there are several alternatives that are designed to reduce demand and shift the user to less carbon-intensive forms of energy. Long-range planners need to monitor government activities since these may have significant impact on carbon-intensive industries and at the same time generate many significant opportunities for programs that reduce emissions.

There are several alternatives that governments can take to reduce emissions besides technology. Many are designed to reduce demand and to shift the user to alternate forms of energy.* Four of the most common are as follows:

- Carbon Tax: Tax all fossil fuels and emissions to reduce demand.
- Gasoline Tax: Add a tax at the pump to encourage alternate forms of energy and reduce demand.†
- Renewable Energy Standard (RES): Require a specified percentage use of an alternative to fossil fuels. This eliminates cost as a barrier to implementation of new technologies.
- Cap and Trade: Establish a firm upper limit of carbon emissions, a cap, and require carbon emitters that exceed the specified limits to buy credits from those that under-run. This is a semi-free-market system that penalizes the use of carbon-intensive technologies.

In general, economists favor the carbon tax as being the most direct and transparent and effective. How the taxes are used is an important issue;‡ there are several alternatives that have been presented. The level of a carbon tax may have to be modified on a trial-and-error basis after the more or less exact impact on total emissions is determined.

---

* See Thomas L. Friedman, *Hot, Flat, and Crowded: Why We Need a Green Revolution and How It Can Renew America* (New York: Farrar, Straus and Giraux, 2008), 251–266.
† At the time of this writing, the cost of gasoline in Europe was 2½ that of the United States for this reason.
‡ Hansen recommends a rebate to all taxpayers of the funds received. This would offset higher gasoline prices and favor conservation focused companies and persons.

Environmentalists favor cap and trade since it is possible to set a hard ceiling on emissions based on science. The problem is its complexity and the legislation is open to considerable mischief in the provision of exemptions, time periods, credit exchanges, offsets, and the like. The gasoline tax and the mandate are only partial solutions since they do not really address the total emissions. They are a start that does directly impact consumer demand.

Dr. Jim Hansen of the National Aeronautics and Space Administration Goddard Institute for Space Studies (NASA GISS) did an analysis of the impact of phasing out coal. His study assumed that all coal emissions are phased-out linearly over the 20-year period of 2010–2030. In that study, CO_2 would peak about 2025 at around 400 ppm. Coal would be replaced by gas or oil and alternate energy sources as fast as the technology would permit. The result would be CO_2 levels stabilizing below 450 ppm.[*] His complete plan includes a rising fee on the price of carbon applied at the source with the fee redistributed uniformly to consumers via the Internal Revenue Service (IRS) database. Petroleum fuel would be reserved for transportation needs.

An interesting study by the Carnegie Institution of Washington in California concluded that even if no new CO_2-emitting sources were built, the world's existing energy infrastructure would emit 500 gigatons of CO_2 until these current sources go out of service over the next 50 years. That amount would stabilize atmospheric CO_2 levels below 430 ppm and level off the average global temperature at 1.3°C above the preindustrial mean. The researchers had expected those figures to be above the threshold values of 450 ppm and 2°C, which climate scientists believe will trigger major climate disruption.[†]

This means that all new energy sources must be greenhouse gas emissions free.

Unfortunately, much of future energy demand must be met by traditional CO_2-emitting sources. The energy sources whose emissions will cause the worst impacts have yet to be built and it will take decades to distance ourselves from CO_2-emitting technologies. This study reinforces just how difficult it will be to move away from fossil fuels and meet emission targets.

---

[*] Hansen, *Storms of My Grandchildren*, 174–185.

[†] Steven J. Davis, Ken Caldeira, and H. Damon Matthews, "Future CO_2 Emissions and Climate Change from Existing Energy Infrastructure," *Science* 329, no. 5997 (September 10, 2010): 1330–1333, doi: 10.1126/science.1188566.

PLANNING FOR A WARMING FUTURE: ADAPTATION

Observe constantly that all things take place by change and accustom thyself to consider that the nature of the Universe loves nothing so much as to change the things which are, and to make new things like them.

—**Marcus Aurelius**

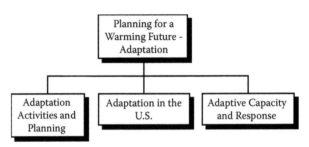

Section outline.

Three categories of adaptation activities that mitigate the effects of a changing climate are addressed in this section.

Adaptation Activities and Planning

Overlay: The conservative approach to planning considering the risks is to assume there will be the necessity for adapting to the impacts of climate change, no matter where in the world your programs are. This is especially the case if the programs involve infrastructure and ecosystems. It is likely that any serious mitigation efforts will come in the decades after this one.

Societies have a long record of adapting to the impacts of weather and climate through a range of practices that include crop diversification, irrigation, water management, disaster risk management, and insurance. But current climate change poses novel risks that are often outside the range of experience, such as impacts related to long-term drought, severe heat waves, accelerated glacier retreat, and hurricane intensity, which heretofore were treated as "acts of God" or a "hundred year storm." These were assumed to be part of some long-range cycle, like drought, which was expected to change and get better if we waited long enough. With increasing emissions and CO_2 in the atmosphere, the set of impacts will only get worse.

Some adaptation measures to current climate change are currently being implemented, on a limited basis, in both developed and developing countries. These measures are undertaken by a range of public and private organizations through policies, investments in infrastructure and technologies, and behavioral change. Examples of adaptations to observed changes in climate include:

- Changes in livelihood strategies in response to permafrost melt by the Inuit in Nunavut (Canada)
- Increased use of artificial snow-making by the Alpine ski industry (Europe, Australia, and North America)
- Coastal defenses upgraded in the Maldives and the Netherlands
- Water management in Australia
- Government responses to heat waves in some European countries
- Flood and storm gates at Venice

There is also a limited but growing set of adaptation measures that explicitly consider scenarios of future climate change. Examples include consideration of sea level rise in the design of infrastructure, such as the Confederation Bridge in Canada and a coastal highway in Micronesia, as well as in shoreline management policies and flood risk measures, for example, in Maine and the Thames Barrier (UK). As a program manager you should look forward to many more projects designed specifically to accommodate climate change events such as expected sea level rise and storm surges.

Many actions that facilitate adaptation to climate change are undertaken to deal with current extreme events such as heat waves and hurricanes. Often, planned adaptation initiatives are also not undertaken as stand-alone measures, but embedded within broader sectoral initiatives such as water resource planning, coastal defense, and other risk reduction strategies.

Examples include consideration of climate change in the National Water Plan of Bangladesh and the design of flood protection and cyclone-resistant infrastructure in Tonga.

Adaptation in the United States

Overlay: The U.S. Global Change Research Program recently published a report that discusses the impacts of climate change on the United States in general and in detail for the regions within the United States. The specific adaptive strategies are included. These are the overlays to use for your region and your programs.

The U.S. Global Change Research Program published a recent report that "summarizes the science of climate change and the impacts of climate change on the United States, now and in the future."[*] The lead organization was NOAA and it was supported by the National Science and Technology Council, all the major departments of the federal government, and supported by a large team of knowledgeable scientists from many of the major universities in the country. In their assessment, they identify in detail the areas of the country at risk that need adaptation strategies. For example, it is stated with the appropriate graphic: "Within 50 to 100 years, 2,400 miles of major roadway are projected to be inundated by sea-level rise in the Gulf Coast region."[†] In the agriculture section, the report discusses the impacts on crop yields and the reduction in effectiveness of herbicides as CO_2 levels rise.[‡] This 188-page report is full of sector (water resources, energy supply, transportation, agriculture, ecosystems, human health, and society) and regional (Northeast, Southeast, Midwest, Great Plains, Southwest, Northwest, Alaska, Islands, and Coasts) impacts of climate change, and for many of these impacts, a near- and long-range adaptation or mitigation strategy is identified and is required.

Adaptation is necessary for past emissions, which are estimated to involve some unavoidable warming (about a further 1.1°F by the end of the century relative to 1980–1999) even if atmospheric greenhouse gas concentrations remained at year 2000 levels, and we are many years past that date. There are some impacts for which adaptation is the only available and appropriate response since emissions mitigation actions occur too late.

There are individuals and groups within all societies that have insufficient capacity to adapt to climate change. For example, women in subsistence

---

[*] Karl et al., *Global Climate Change*, 7.
[†] Karl et al., *Global Climate Change*, 62.
[‡] Karl et al., *Global Climate Change*, 75.

farming communities are disproportionately burdened with the costs of recovery and coping with drought in southern Africa.

The capacity to adapt is dynamic and influenced by economic and natural resources, social networks, entitlements, institutions and governance, human resources, and technology. It of course also depends on the severity and scope of the adverse impact.

Adaptive Capacity and Response

Overlay: Adaptation is not simple. Barriers exist in many forms. New planning processes are attempting to overcome barriers at local, regional, and national levels in both developing and developed countries. For example, Least Developed Countries are developing National Adaptation Plans of Action (NAPA) under the auspices of the U.N. and some developed countries have established national adaptation policy frameworks. This overlay includes solutions to barriers to adaptation. With a new governor in Virginia, the previous governor's plan for adapting to climate change was rejected as being unnecessary; regardless, the military are taking actions to protect the fleet in Norfolk. In the United States, the National Academies of Science published a report titled *America's Climate Choices* in 2011. The data are there, the plans and recommendations of many smart people are available, but there is no political will at present.

High adaptive capacity does not necessarily translate into actions that reduce vulnerability. For example, despite a high capacity to adapt to heat stress through relatively inexpensive adaptations, residents in urban areas in some parts of the world, including in European cities, continue to experience high levels of mortality. The use of the wealth of the United States for adaptation projects is dependent upon the willingness of the electorate and the political processes, and, of course, recognition that some adaptation is necessary in the first place.

The array of potential adaptive responses available to human societies is very large, ranging from purely technological (e.g., sea defenses), through behavioral (e.g., altered food and recreational choices), to managerial (e.g., altered farm practices), and to policy (e.g., planning regulations).

Although many early impacts of climate change can be effectively addressed through adaptation, the options for successful adaptation diminish and the associated costs increase with increasing delay and increasing climate change.

There are significant barriers to implementing adaptation. These include both the inability of natural systems to adapt to the rate and magnitude of climate change, as well as formidable human environmental, economic, informational, social, attitudinal, and behavioral constraints. There are also significant knowledge gaps for adaptation as well as impediments to flows of knowledge and information relevant for adaptation decisions.

For developing countries, availability of resources and building adaptive capacity are particularly important. Some examples and reasons are given below:

a. The large number and expansion of potentially hazardous glacial lakes due to rising temperatures in the Himalayas. These far exceed the capacity of countries in the region to manage the flooding risks resulting from the collapse of the berms that contain the lakes.

b. If climate change is faster than is anticipated, many developing countries simply cannot cope with more frequent/intense occurrence of extreme weather events, as this will drain resources budgeted for other critical purposes. This also applies to communities in the United States where increased frequency of floods and snow and weather events are occurring and expected to continue.

c. Climate change will occur within the life cycle of many major infrastructure projects (coastal dykes, bridges, sea ports, etc.). Strengthening of the infrastructure based on new design criteria may take decades to implement. In many cases, retrofitting would not be possible.

d. Due to physical constraints, adaptation measures cannot be implemented in many estuaries and delta areas. An example is the marine loss of major wetlands in the Blackwater Refuge in the Chesapeake Bay due to sea level rise. Tangier Island and Smith Island and their inhabitants are threatened.

New planning processes are attempting to overcome these barriers at local, regional, and national levels in both developing and developed countries. For example, Least Developed Countries are developing National Adaptation Plans of Action (NAPA) under the auspices of the U.N. and some developed countries have established national adaptation policy frameworks.

CLIMATE POLICY: BOTH MITIGATION AND ADAPTATION

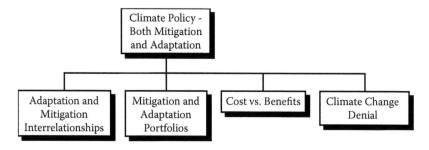

Section outline.

> **Overlay:** Unmitigated climate change would, in the long term, be likely to exceed the capacity of natural, managed, and human systems to adapt.[*] The interrelationships between adaptation and mitigation strategies need to be incorporated into planning, including strategies for portfolio choices that include both adaption and mitigation.
>
> ---
> [*] IPCC4, Working Group 2, 71.

There is nothing impossible to him who will try.

—Alexander the Great

Adaptation and Mitigation Interrelationships

Both adaptation and emissions mitigation strategies need to be implemented together to reduce the risks of climate change to nature and society. It appears to be too late to realistically use emissions mitigation alone; its effects vary over time and place. CO_2 mitigation will have global benefits but, owing to the lag times in the climate and biophysical systems, even with the most aggressive mitigation policies of the previous section, the efforts will hardly be noticeable until around the middle of the twenty-first century. As mentioned before, this is one of the major problems in abating emissions—costs are now and benefits are in the future. Regardless, there has to be a start; most economists agree that mitigation steps to reduce greenhouse gas emissions are necessary—the debate is not whether we need to put a price on carbon emissions, but how high the price should be and how we do it.

The benefits of adaptation are on a different time scale. They are largely local to regional in scale, but they can be immediate, especially if they also address vulnerabilities to current climate conditions. Increasing the height of seawalls and levees is an adaptation strategy. Changing coastal residential subdivision requirements considering sea level rise is an adaptation strategy. Setting aside land using reservoir overlays within the zoning regulations is an adaptation strategy.

Given these differences between adaptation and mitigation, climate policy is not about making a choice between *adapting* to climate change or *mitigating* climate change. Any risk management analysis would conclude: if key vulnerabilities to climate change are to be addressed, some adaptation is necessary because even the most stringent mitigation efforts cannot avoid further climate change in the next few decades.

Mitigation is also necessary because reliance on adaptation alone could eventually lead to a magnitude of climate change to which effective adaptation is possible only at very high social, environmental, and economic costs. If sea levels are allowed to continue to rise, new sea walls alone will not suffice.

In September 2010, the National Climate Adaptation Summit Committee submitted to the Executive Office of the President, Office of Science and Technology Policy, a report that included "seven high priority near-term actions to help better prepare our nation for a changing climate."* It was prepared by University Corporation for Atmospheric Research (UCAR).†

The 180 persons who participated in this activity started with the following two premises that are the same as documented previously.

Atmospheric concentrations of greenhouse gases continue to grow rapidly, and there is mounting evidence that the United States and other nations

---

* National Climate Adaptation Summit Committee, National Climate Adaptation Summit, September 29, 2010, http://www.joss.ucar.edu/events/2010/ncas/summit_report.html (accessed February 16, 2011).

† UCAR is a nonprofit consortium of 75 universities dedicated to understanding the atmosphere and the complex processes that make up the Earth system, from the ocean floor to the sun's core. UCAR manages the National Center for Atmospheric Research (NCAR) on behalf of the National Science Foundation and the university community. It also provides real-time weather data; digital library services; training for forecasters, hydrologists, and other professionals; field research support; and other services through the UCAR Community Programs (http://www2.ucar.edu/).

are already experiencing significant impacts from a changing climate, as documented in many reports, assessments, and analysis from the National Academy of Sciences, the US Global Change Research Program (USGCRP), the Intergovernmental Panel on Climate Change (IPCC), and other organizations.

Options for responding fall into two broad categories that are not mutually exclusive. Our nation can adapt to observed and expected changes by making adjustments in behavior and management to limit harm and exploit beneficial opportunities, and we can mitigate the amount of change we experience by reducing greenhouse gas emissions and concentrations. The ever-increasing disruption of our planet's climate argues for a well thought out and comprehensive portfolio of adaptation and mitigation measures. The National Climate Adaptation Summit, which resulted in this report, was organized to help inform the definition of such measures.

Mitigation and Adaptation Portfolios

As discussed previously, even the most stringent mitigation efforts cannot avoid further impacts of climate change in the next few decades, which makes adaptation essential, particularly in addressing near-term impacts.

This means the portfolio needs to include a mix of strategies that include mitigation, adaptation, technological development (to enhance both adaptation and mitigation), and research (on climate science, impacts, adaptation, and mitigation).

Such portfolios should combine consideration of policies with incentive-based approaches and actions at all levels, from the individual citizen through to national governments and international organizations. These actions should include technological, institutional, and behavioral options, the introduction of economic and policy instruments to encourage the use of these options, and research and development to reduce uncertainty and to enhance the options' effectiveness and efficiency. Many different stakeholders are involved in the implementation of these actions, operating on different spatial and institutional scales. Mitigation activities primarily involve economic areas where the emissions need to be reduced, including the energy, transportation, industrial, residential, forestry, and agriculture sectors, whereas the stakeholders involved in adaptation represent a large variety of other interests, including agriculture, tourism and recreation, human health, water supply, coastal management, urban planning, nature conservation, and others where the impacts of climate change will fall on the stakeholders.

Increasing adaptive capacity can be achieved by introducing the consideration of climate change impacts in development planning, for example, by doing the following:

- Including adaptation measures in land-use planning and infrastructure design
- Including measures to reduce vulnerability in existing disaster risk reduction strategies

These measures are in process in some places in the United States. For example, the *Miami Herald* reported on joint efforts of the U.S. Corps of Engineers, the South Florida Water Management District, and the SW Florida Regional Planning Council and Charlotte Harbor National Estuary Program to plan for a serious rise in sea levels.* South Florida includes Collier, Lee, and Miami/Dade counties. They are investigating effects on water supplies, regional flood control, fisheries, and the like and how to offset them.

This means that any remaining debate, complacency, or indecision government agencies once had about the threat of climate change has given way to urgency.

The Water Management District report states: "The question for Floridians is not whether they will be affected by global warming, but how much—that is, to what degree it will continue, how rapidly, what other climate changes will accompany the warming, and what the long-term effects of these changes will be."

However, not all Floridians feel the same. Because of a change in governors, the new governor, Rick Scott, does not believe climate change is real and therefore there is no problem for Florida.† However, there are big issues to be settled, said Peter Harlem, a research ecologist with Florida International University who has been studying rising sea levels since the 1980s—for instance, what to do about saving Florida Power & Light's nuclear plant at Turkey Point from being swamped. Dealing with those issues would be easier if the governor and legislature were involved again, he said. "While they're playing politics," Harlem said, "the water's still coming up."

---

* *Miami Herald*, January 31, 2010.
† Craig Pittman, *Tampa Bay Times*, May 16, 2011, http://www.tampabay.com/news/environment/once-a-major-issue-in-florida-climate-change-concerns-few-in-tallahassee/1169860.

Costs versus Benefits*

Overlay 1: Eventually, the world will have to face up to the fact of climate warming (and the direct effects of sea level rising, more intense storms, droughts, and floods), and the mitigation and adaptation measures that are required. The costs of mitigation are climbing as no actions are taken and massive amounts of carbon continue to be released into the atmosphere. This will require increasing investment in adaptation that will have severe impacts on the abilities of countries to grow and support their increasing populations.

The prudent path is to attempt to significantly reduce global greenhouse gas emissions to support mitigation plans. Analyses of global carbon emission reduction scenarios all show that the benefits outweigh the costs by trillions of dollars.

Overlay 2: The first step in evaluating new programs is often to do a cost–benefit analysis. It is important to incorporate the impact of the CO_2 emissions occurring as a result of the program when selecting between programs or preparing program plans. The methodology frequently used is to analyze the benefits that would accrue from a reduction of CO_2 such as better health, improved grain yields, fewer storm losses, and so on. This is equivalent to the cost of CO_2.

Most of the media and political attention has focused on the costs of mitigation and adaptation. This is no surprise since the costs are immediate and the benefits are in the future. It is relatively easy to identify the costs; it always is in cost–benefit analyses.

Cost–benefit analyses are easily misused. They are commonly used to assist in a decision process where you are choosing between investment alternatives. The quantitative analyses are not normally used in a stand-alone mode because of the difficulty and inability to quantify some of the qualitative costs and many of the qualitative benefits. When making a choice between alternatives, these items are often common to all the

---

* Adapted from the SkepticalScience.com blog written by Dana Nuccitelli, "Moncton Myth #11: Carbon Pricing Costs vs Benefits," February 14, 2011, http://www.skepticalscience.com/monckton-myth-11-carbon-pricing-costs-vs-benefits.html.

choices, and therefore need not be quantified. The do-nothing alternative is always one of the options and there are costs and benefits associated with it.

The cost of doing nothing in the face of increasing carbon emissions and a changing climate can be viewed as the equivalent of the benefit of reducing greenhouse gas emissions since these are real costs that are avoided. *The Stern Review on the Economics of Climate Change* is perhaps the most well-known evaluation of this cost.[*] It is a comprehensive 700-page report released for the British government on October 30, 2006 by economist Nicholas Stern. He is the chair of the Grantham Research Institute on Climate Change and the Environment at the London School of Economics (LSE) and also chair of the Centre for Climate Change Economics and Policy (CCCEP) at Leeds University and LSE. The report discusses the effect of global warming on the world economy. Although not the first economic report on costs of climate change, it is significant as the largest and most widely known and discussed report of its kind.

The *Stern Review*'s main conclusion is that the benefits of strong, early action on climate change considerably outweigh the costs.

The *Stern Review* estimated that taking no action to reduce greenhouse gas emissions would cost 5% to 20% of the global gross domestic product (GDP) by 2100.[†] The *Stern Report* also estimated that reducing greenhouse gas emissions to avoid the worst impacts of climate change can be limited to around 1% of global GDP each year.[‡] The specific wording from the Executive Summary is as follows:[§]

> Resource cost estimates suggest that an upper bound for the expected annual cost of emissions reductions consistent with a trajectory leading to stabilization at 550 ppm CO_{2e} is likely to be around 1% of GDP by 2050.

In June 2008, Dr. Stern increased the estimate for the annual cost of achieving stabilization to 2% of GDP to account for faster than expected current climate change and therefore more difficulty in

---

[*] Report available at http://webarchive.nationalarchives.gov.uk/+/http:/www.hm-treasury.gov.uk/sternreview_index.htm.

[†] *Stern Report*, "Executive Summary," ix, http://webarchive.nationalarchives.gov.uk/+/http://www.hm-treasury.gov.uk/sternreview_index.htm.

[‡] *Stern Report*, http://webarchive.nationalarchives.gov.uk/+/http://www.hm-treasury.gov.uk/sternreview_index.htm.

[§] *Stern Report*, "Executive Summary," xii, http://webarchive.nationalarchives.gov.uk/+/http://www.hm-treasury.gov.uk/sternreview_index.htm.

reducing emissions to safe levels. This is the same reason Pacala and Socolow have increased the number of wedges it takes to stabilize emissions, as discussed earlier. Since emissions are continuing to increase under a business-as-usual regime, it is logical to assume that the longer no action is taken, the higher the cost to achieve some designated level of stabilization.

The *Stern Review* also has the following conclusion regarding opportunities:[*]

> There are also significant new opportunities across a wide range of industries and services. Markets for low-carbon energy products are likely to be worth at least $500 bn per year by 2050, and perhaps much more. Individual companies and countries should position themselves to take advantage of these opportunities.

Not everyone agrees with the conclusions of the *Stern Review*. Other than those who think climate change is a myth, there are many criticisms of methodology, discount rates, and other factors, but it still stands as the gold standard of analyses. The conclusions are generally accepted.

Other assessments of proposed climate legislation in the United States have also concluded that they would significantly reduce the country's greenhouse gas emissions at a cost on the order of 1% of national GDP.[†] Most economists who study the economics of climate change agree that action to reduce greenhouse gas emissions is necessary. According to Robert Mendelsohn (professor of forest policy and economics at Yale University), "The [economic] debate is how much and when to start." Some economists believe that we should immediately put a high price on carbon emissions, while others, like Yale's William Nordhaus, believe we should start with a low-carbon price and gradually ramp it up.

Nordhaus, whose models project a smaller economic impact than most, said that regardless of whether the models showing larger or smaller economic impacts from climate change are correct, "We've got to get together as a community of nations and impose restraints on greenhouse gas emissions and raise carbon prices. If not, we will be in one of those gloomy scenarios."[‡]

[*] *Stern Report*, "Executive Summary," xvi, http://webarchive.nationalarchives.gov.uk/+/http:/www.hm-treasury.gov.uk/sternreview_index.htm.

[†] See summary at Skeptical Science, http://www.skepticalscience.com/economic-impacts-of-carbon-pricing.html (accessed February 19, 2011).

[‡] January 6, 2011, posted as a feature article in Yale University's Environment360 web page, http://e360.yale.edu/feature/calculating_the_true_cost_of_global_climate_change__/2357/.

One shortcoming in these studies that mixes economics and social costs and benefits is that it's very difficult to put a price on things like biodiversity, cultural diversity, human life, and so on. Many of the side effects, such as rising sea levels that eliminate small island nations like Tuvalu or for a drought-related famine in Africa, the loss of life and culture in these cases won't have much impact on the global economy, but there is a significant noneconomic loss associated with these types of events. We all see the pictures of the polar bears used to raise funds for environmental organizations; if they are truly lost, only a few Arctic residents will be impacted. There will be little impact on the economies of Alaska or Canada. Likewise, even if a large number of species fails to adapt to the rapidly changing climate and becomes extinct, the real non-dollar loss associated with this reduction in biodiversity goes beyond whatever small economic impact is included in the economic studies. After all, who needs marmots?

Cost–benefit analyses of proposals to reduce greenhouse gas emissions have consistently concluded that the benefits far outweigh the costs. In the United States the direct benefits of the legislation that was passed by the House of Representatives in 2009 (but later not acted on by the Senate) would have outweighed the costs by a factor of 2 to 9 (a net savings of at least $1 trillion by 2050), under conservative assumptions (ignoring indirect benefits such as reduction of co-pollutants and ocean acidification).

There is a considerable amount of effort being put into determining, in more detail, the impact of various mitigation and adaptation scenarios and also the real cost of doing nothing. In the latter case, do nothing, the costs are based on the forecast adverse impacts of some level and rate of temperature rise. Typical of the ongoing work is a National Academy of Sciences study that looks at the methodologies used in modeling with the goal of improving the data provided to policymakers.[*]

Climate Change Denial

> Everyone is entitled to his own opinion, but not his own facts.
>
> **—Daniel Patrick Moynihan**

---

[*] K. John Holmes, Rapporteur; National Research Council, *Modeling the Economics of Greenhouse Gas Mitigation: Summary of a Workshop* (Washington, DC: National Academies Press, 2010), http://www.nap.edu/catalog/13023.html.

Retired General Anthony C. Zinni of the Marine Corps, former com-
mander-in-chief of Central Command, and member of a Military
Advisory Board,* placed the challenge into perspective when he said:
*"The point is if you just write off the science, if you don't accept what
seems to me to be the majority view, then you are saying you're going
to roll the dice and take the chance. I think if you look at the potential
outcomes of that, we would see that for our children and our grandchildren that that would be a disaster, and they'll look back at us and
will say **you should have seen this, you should have taken a prudent
course and prepared for this. You should have taken the action to
lessen the impact.**"*

---

* In 2006 the Center for Naval Analyses convened a Military Advisory Board of 11 retired
three-star and four-star admirals and generals to assess the impact of global climate
change on key matters of national security and to lay the groundwork for mounting
responses to the threats found.

Finally, and importantly, we must stop listening to disinformation.
Arguments contrary to the reality of dangerous climate change have been
repeatedly shown to be false and misleading. Claims that climate change is
a hoax, or a conspiracy, or that climate scientists have deceived the public,
are an inversion of the truth. Climate change denial is the propaganda.
Ninety-eight percent of scientists agree that climate change is happening;
the remaining 2% are not active in peer-reviewed science. The peer-reviewed
evidence is overwhelming; see Appendix A. The time for skepticism about
climate change has passed. There are many well-documented incidents of
the same persons who defended the tobacco industry now leading the climate denier charge, and they are funded by special interests.*

Skepticism is a good thing; all scientists are skeptics. People should
critically examine evidence and motivations. A good place to begin is the
following. What is more plausible? Tens of thousands of scientists have
been fabricating evidence and theory for over a hundred years (since before
Arrhenius in 1896 or Tyndall in 1849) in a conspiracy to achieve some
mysterious goal? Or certain industries and their partners are sponsoring a

---

* See James Hoggan, *Climate Cover Up: The Crusade to Deny Global Warming* (Vancouver BC,
Canada: Greystone Books, 2009), and/ Naome Oreskes and Erik M. Conway, *Merchants of Doubt:
How a Handful of Scientists Obscured the Truth on Issues from Tobacco Smoke to Global Warming*
(New York: Bloomsbury Press, 2010).

disinformation campaign because they stand to lose billions of dollars in profits if people should use less, or alternative forms of, energy? These are the ones who are despoiling the commons.

Who stands to lose the most if the scientists' warnings are acted on? The cost of prevention now is far less than the cost of trying to fix the damage later.

There is a problem in the Congress of the United States:

I don't know of any other government in the world in a major country where a party that's in control of one of the houses of the legislature basically has as the party line position to reject the findings of a major branch of modern science. (Richard Somerville, Climate Scientist and Professor Emeritus, Scripps Institution of Oceanography March 17, 2011.*)

* Bruce Lieberman, *Teaching … and Re-Teaching… Climate Science 101*. Yale Forum on Climate Change and the Media, http://www.yaleclimatemediaforum.org/2011/03/teaching-and-re-teaching-climate-science-101/ (accessed March 22, 2011).

Section III

Energy Overlay

14

Energy Constraint Overlay

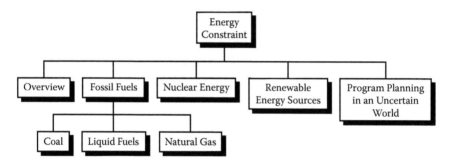

Section 3 outline.

The diagram presents the outline of Section 3, which deals with the energy constraint overlay. The overview is included in this chapter and the other six chapters include the three fossil fuels plus the nuclear energy and renewable energy sources, followed by a chapter that integrates the information and data.

Overlay: Population expansions in the past have been directly related to availability of cheap energy and abundant harvests and this continues to be the situation in the world today. Energy usage worldwide is expected to keep pace with or exceed population growth. The current energy infrastructure is built around a major dependence upon fossil fuels for energy—oil, coal, and natural gas—to drive the world's engines and power plants and to provide fertilizer and pharmaceuticals. Coal is expected to be a major source of energy until the end of the century unless replaced by fuels with less carbon emissions, primarily driven by demand for energy in Asia. There is no world shortage of coal. Natural gas is increasing in importance with its increasing availability and there is a lot of pressure to increase the usage of renewable energy sources. Nuclear energy is expected to increase (but slowly) to meet increasing demands for CO_2 free energy sources.

These are the current energy considerations in planning—basically business as usual for the short term, but significant changes in the medium to long term.

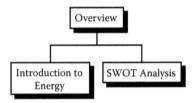

Section outline.

INTRODUCTION TO ENERGY

The third major constraint the world will be addressing the remainder of this century is energy.* The worldwide drive for an increasing standard of living requires a comparable increasing amount of energy—energy usage is a surrogate measure of standard of living. There are three current determinants of the demand for energy:

1. The existing population and its current needs to maintain its current standard of living
2. The desire of the world's population in second and third world countries in addition to the West to increase its standard of living and then increase its ability to pay for it
3. An increasing population that needs energy to live.

---

* Actually, there is an additional major constraint and that is fresh water. Unfortunately, that is beyond the scope of this book at this time and is briefly addressed in the population section. Similarly, there is an evolving shortage of many important minerals, including gold, silver, diamonds, indium, arsenic, thallium, lead, zinc, cadmium, strontium, tin, and mercury, according to Holland in his book *Living Dangerously*.

Energy is the ability to do work and comes in many forms:

- Heat (thermal)
- Light (radiant)
- Motion (kinetic)
- Electrical
- Chemical
- Nuclear
- Gravitational

We use some form of energy for everything we do and we can store energy when not needed. The law of "conservation of energy" says that energy is neither created nor destroyed. When we use it, we convert it from one form to another.

We have many sources of energy and it is important to differentiate renewable from nonrenewable energy sources. Most of our energy currently comes from nonrenewable sources, that is, once they are used up they are gone. These include coal, petroleum, natural gas, propane, and uranium. All except uranium were formed millions of years ago from the remains of ancient plants or animals. The renewable sources of energy include biomass, geothermal energy,* hydropower, solar energy, and wind energy.

This third overlay of the triple constraints concerns the availability and form of energy in the coming decades that will support the growing population and the increasing world per-capita usage of energy. As the nonrenewable resources become depleted, other energy sources must be available as replacements. In a perfect world, as a particular nonrenewable resource started to have supply problems, the price would increase and an alternate would be developed by the market. The concern is that the rate of supply deterioration may exceed the ability of the market to produce an adequate replacement.

The analysis of energy also must include reference to the emissions that occur when the energy is generated because of the concerns raised in Chapter 4. Many policy decisions are currently being made worldwide by various governments and businesses based on assumptions that relate to carbon emissions. Emissions are a serious consideration and impact decision making. Therefore, it is difficult to discuss energy usage separate from carbon emissions.

---

* Technically it is not renewable, only that there is a virtually unlimited source of heat under the ground.

The readers of this book and their parents and perhaps grandparents have been living in the golden age of cheap energy. The first phase of this age began with the invention of the Newcomen engine in 1712 that enabled water to be pumped out of the coal mines of England and Wales. This provided access to large quantities of coal to be mined for the furnaces of England and enabled the rapid expansion of energy usage in what is now called the Industrial Revolution. The golden age really began in earnest in 1901 when Al Hammil and his brother Curt successfully brought in the Spindletop oil gusher in Beaumont, Texas. Since that time, energy has been cheaper and more plentiful than at any other time since the beginning of man.

The development of gasoline and diesel fuel enabled the wondrous development of engines for transportation—the automobile, diesel engines for railroads, and several different types of aircraft engines. But there is a problem, actually many problems, that result from the energy bonanzas of coal and oil.

First, there are the unequal distributions of oil, natural gas, and coal around the world.

Second, there are finite limits to the most useful of the sources of energy—oil. There are limits to all fossil fuels, although coal and natural gas will likely be available for at least three generations.

Third, there are byproducts of their use that can cause problems.

Some energy sources are sustainable, such as hydroelectric power (as long as we protect the sources of water) and the use of biomass, and some are renewable, such as wind and solar power. Nuclear power is almost in a class by itself as uranium ore is available in large quantities at various locations, including ocean water (although at a high cost).

Naturally, all persons on Earth wish to increase their standard of living and take advantage of any low-cost energy, and total demand also increases simply as the population increases. People need shelter, food, electricity, transportation, water, and so forth. The ability to take advantage of available sources of energy depends on the economics of the individual situation.

There are limits on the energy sources and these limits in some cases are reflected in increasing prices and in other cases simply by technology or nature. Some energy sources have limited application; for example, the use of the energy of coal to propel aircraft requires a relatively expensive conversion to a form that can be utilized by aircraft engines.

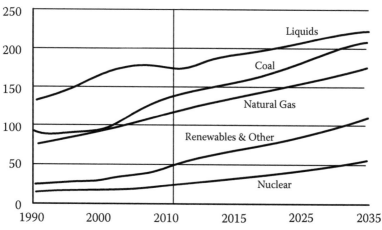

FIGURE 14.1
World marketed energy use by fuel type.

Figure 14.1 illustrates the types of energy fuel in today's world and their forecasted change over the next 25 years. The forecasts were made by the U.S. Energy Information Administration (EIA) and assume basically a business-as-usual future with recognition of the impacts of some carbon regulation and relative price changes of oil and natural gas.

There are three significant messages from Figure 14.3:

1. There is a major dependence upon fossil fuels for energy—oil, coal, and natural gas—to drive the world's engines and power plants.
2. Coal is expected to be a major source of energy over the next several generations, primarily driven by demand for energy in Asia.
3. Energy usage worldwide is expected to grow from the total of 495 quadrillion Btu's in 2010 to 740 in 2035, an approximate 50% increase, and to keep growing as the population grows toward 9+ billion in 2050.

The relative costs of the various sources of energy in the form of electricity are of paramount importance as steps are taken to find replacements for coal in the generation of electricity. Oil is not an issue, as virtually all oil-fired electricity generation plants have been retired or replaced by coal or gas.

Table 14.1 presents the estimated levelized cost of new generation resources as expected in 2016. Levelized cost is a convenient summary

TABLE 14.1

Estimated Levelized Cost of New Generation Resources, 2016

Plant Type	Capacity Factor (%)	Levelized Capital Cost	Fixed O&M[a]	Variable O&M (including fuel)	Transmission Investment	Total System Levelized Cost
				U.S. Average Levelized Costs (2009 \$/megawatthour) for Plants Entering Service in 2016		
Conventional Coal	85	65.3	3.9	24.3	1.2	94.8
Advanced Coal	85	74.6	7.9	25.7	1.2	109.4
Advanced Coal with CCS	85	92.7	9.2	33.1	1.2	136.2
Natural Gas-fired						
Conventional Combined Cycle	87	17.5	1.9	45.6	1.2	66.1
Advanced Combined Cycle	87	17.9	1.9	42.1	1.2	63.1
Advanced CC with CCS	87	34.6	3.9	49.6	1.2	89.3
Conventional Combustion Turbine	30	45.8	3.7	71.5	3.5	124.5
Advanced Combustion Turbine	30	31.6	5.5	62.9	3.5	103.5
Advanced Nuclear	90	90.1	11.1	11.7	1.0	113.9
Wind	34	83.9	9.6	0.0	3.5	97
Wind, Offshore	34	209.3	28.1	0.0	5.9	243.2
Solar PV	25	194.6	12.1	0.0	4.0	210.7
Solar Thermal	18	259.4	46.6	0.0	5.8	311.8
Geothermal	92	79.3	11.9	9.5	1.0	101.7
Biomass	83	55.3	13.7	42.3	1.3	112.5
Hydro	52	74.5	3.8	6.3	1.9	86.4

[a] O&M = operations and maintenance. [b] CCS = carbon capture and storage. [c] PV = photovoltaic.

Source: Energy Information Administration, *Annual Energy Outlook 2011*, December 2010, DOE/EIA-0383(2010).

measure of the overall competiveness of different electricity-generating technologies. It represents the present value of the total cost of building and operating a generating plant over an assumed financial life and duty cycle, converted to equal annual payments and expressed in terms of constant dollars to remove the impact of inflation. It is a form of life cycle cost and is useful for the comparative analysis of Table 14.1.

The costs shown in Table 14.1 are national averages. However, there is significant local variation in costs based on local labor markets and the cost and availability of fuel or energy resources such as windy sites. For example, regional wind costs range from $82/MWh in the region with the best available resources in 2016 to $115/MWh in regions where the best sites have been claimed by 2016. Costs shown for wind include additional costs associated with transmission upgrades needed to access remote resources, as well as other factors that markets may or may not include in the market price for wind power.[*]

To convert from dollars per megawatt-hour to cents per kWh, move the decimal point in the table one spot to the left (for example, conventional coal is 9.48 cents per kWh on average).

The current energy constraint is quite simply a matter of the finite nature of oil, natural gas, and coal in the face of increasing demand from increasing income levels and increasing populations in major sectors of the world. Oil from traditional wells is the source most at risk of early depletion.

Natural gas advanced combined cycle systems (gas turbines combined with steam recycling) will tend to replace coal at power plants because of lower prices and expected regulations constraining carbon emissions, but coal will remain the primary source of electrical power throughout the world until alternatives are developed and come on line at production levels. Market economics will continue to set a relatively high price on petroleum and it will tend to lose market share in sectors where it is currently strong due to price increases from supply constraints and the high costs of extraction. Automobile energy needs will slowly transition to alternate transportation fuels such as natural gas, fuel cells, and electricity as the related technology becomes economical and available and as the price of gasoline inevitably increases. With new sources of oil coming on

---

[*] A full description of the methodology and the full report are available at http://www.eia.doe.gov/oiaf/aeo/index.html. The specific assumptions for each of these factors are given in the *Assumptions to the Annual Energy Outlook*, available at http://www.eia.doe.gov/oiaf/aeo/assumption/index.html.

ENERGY SOURCE OVERVIEW

- Coal is abundant in the United States, China, Russia, and India and various other parts of the world, but coal has emissions problems in its byproducts. There is no supply shortage forecast, but there are many pressures to reduce usage and thereby reduce emissions.
- The world started with a total of approximately 2–2.5 trillion barrels of oil in the ground when modern human civilization began some 12,000 years ago. Since then we have used approximately 1 trillion barrels, mostly since January 1901. There is an estimated roughly 1 trillion accessible barrels left in the ground worldwide. At the rate we are currently using oil, 27 billion barrels a year, and considering the probability of new finds, we will theoretically run out in less than 40 years. However, this does not reflect the newfound ability to extract oil from shale in fairly large quantities. Therefore, the amount available may be significantly larger, albeit expensive.
- The availability and usage rates of natural gas provide an optimistic picture; capabilities to extract gas from shale formations at economic rates have improved and there are large known reserves in the United States and elsewhere.

line from shale, this may take a long time. Alternate energy using renewable sources will continue to come on line to help meet the worldwide increasing demand for energy, but they are not expected to exceed 20% of the total energy usage. As can be seen from Table 14.1, the alternative energy systems (except hydropower) are all more expensive than coal. So the cost of energy will increase.

Program and portfolio managers of projects that depend upon low-priced energy, as has been the case for the past 100 years or more, will need to recalibrate their thinking and strategies.

The following parts of the energy constraint section amplify the preceding discussion of fossil fuels, nuclear, and renewable energy sources and conclude with a cross-cutting planning discussion.

For each we include a description of the energy source and the situation worldwide and in the United States, and their strengths, weaknesses, opportunities, and threats—a SWOT analysis.

Four things come not back: The spoken word, the sped arrow, the past life, and the neglected opportunity.

—Arabic Proverb

SWOT ANALYSES

SWOT analysis is a tool used in marketing and business analysis to assist in strategic planning. The acronym stands for strengths, weaknesses, opportunities, and threats. It includes specifying the objective of the entity under analysis and identifying the internal and external factors that are favorable or unfavorable in meeting the objective.

A SWOT analysis starts with a statement of the objective, then identifies the following characteristics:

- **Strengths:** The internal characteristics of the entity that give it an advantage over competitors or provide a beneficial output
- **Weaknesses:** The internal characteristics of the entity that place the entity at a disadvantage over competitors or inhibit the entity
- **Opportunities:** The external circumstances that are favorable to the continued existence and benefits provided by the entity
- **Threats:** The external elements in conditions and factors surrounding the entity that could cause trouble for the entity

The results of a SWOT analysis are frequently arrayed in a 2 × 2 matrix, as illustrated in Figure 14.2. In our analyses we will not provide the SWOT matrix as shown in the figure, but instead provide a risk matrix.

Strengths:
- (describe)
- Etc.

Weaknesses:
-
-
-

Opportunities:
-
-
-
-

Threats:
-
-
-

FIGURE 14.2
SWOT analysis matrix.

15

Coal

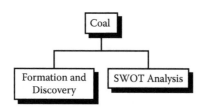

Chapter 15 outline.

FORMATION AND DISCOVERY

Overlay: The world has vast quantities of coal still in the ground. It has been used as a fuel since the Bronze Age and is widespread in the world, although the quality coal is not spread evenly.

Coal began as layers of plant matter accumulated at the bottom of a body of water protected from biodegradation and oxidization, usually by mud or acidic water. The wide shallow seas of the Carboniferous period 800 million years ago provided such conditions. This trapped carbon, including absorbed CO_2, was in immense peat bogs that were eventually deeply buried by sediments and transformed into coal by time, elevated temperatures, and the pressure of overlying strata. The chemical and physical properties of the plant remains were changed by geological action to create layers of a solid, readily combustible sedimentary rock. The harder forms, such as anthracite coal, become metamorphic rock because of later exposure to elevated temperature and pressure. Coal is composed primarily of carbon along with variable quantities of other elements, chiefly sulfur, hydrogen, oxygen, and nitrogen.

The Age of Coal, which started in the Bronze Age (3000–2000 BC) and drove the Industrial Revolution in the eighteenth century, continued until the start of the twentieth century when the event occurred in Beaumont Texas that introduced the competing Age of Oil.

SWOT ANALYSIS: COAL

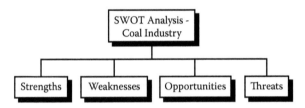

SWOT analysis section outline.

> **Overlay:** Coal is the primary source of energy in the world today. However, the CO_2 and other gases emitted into the atmosphere by burning coal need to be eliminated. This could be accomplished by a combination of carbon capture and storage (CCS) and the replacement of coal-burning facilities by other energy sources. This will occur over time, with the specific timetable based on the ability to replace the coal energy with alternatives that meet the needs of a growing population, and on the mechanisms used to increase the cost of burning coal. Therefore, there must be strong emphasis on developing alternatives to meet supply requirements and on increasing the cost of coal to dampen demand. This industry will be under strong pressures.

The objective of this strengths, weaknesses, opportunities, and threats (SWOT) analysis is to assess the long-term viability of the coal industry.

Strengths

Coal provides approximately 25% of the world's energy and provides almost 50% of the electricity for the United States.

Overlay: *Coal Reserves.* Worldwide, compared to all other fossil fuels, coal is the most abundant and more widely distributed energy source across the continents. Currently, total world recoverable coal reserves are estimated at approximately 900 billion short tons. (A short ton is a unit of weight equal to 2,000 pounds.) Based on current world coal production rates, the resulting ratio of coal reserves to production is approximately 130 years. Coal will eventually run out, almost certainly by the end of the next century.

Overlay: *World Outlook.* There is strong demand for coal in the world, especially in India and China and the less-developed nations. There is no alternative fuel available that can substitute for coal at a competitive cost. The amount of coal used each year is projected to increase significantly through 2035 and beyond. Unfortunately, the higher-quality coal in places like China has been mined, so lower-quality, even dirtier coal is coming out of the ground.

Even if there were a strong international desire to reduce emissions from coal, there is a large amount of inertia in the system. Unless some dramatic actions, such as a global agreement to discontinue the use of coal to generate energy by a certain date, are implemented, it is unlikely there will be much change in the projections in Figure 14.1.[*]

It is not easy to provide alternative fuels that can replace coal or even to accommodate the expected increase in world demand for electricity. Energy Information Administration (EIA) projections, although basically conservative, show a stable consumption through 2035 in the first world due to steady erosion of the market by natural gas and renewable sources. This assumption of little growth includes recognition that the United States will add another 100 million or so persons to the economy. Continuing growth of the use of coal in China and India where large quantities of cheap coal exist are necessary to generate power for an increasingly upward mobile population seeking a higher standard of living. The strength of coal is in its ubiquity in the United States, China, and Russia and its ease of extraction and distribution and resulting low cost.

---

[*] See Hansen, *Storms of My Grandchildren*, for such a situation.

In China, coal is the inexpensive energy source needed to support a rapidly growing economy and it is wishful thinking to expect this to change any time soon.

An example of the optimism of the industry for continuing coal production is the case of Australia. Already the world's leading exporter of coal, Australia is expected to dominate future international coal trade as it continues to improve its inland transportation and port infrastructure to expedite coal shipments to international markets.[*] New and expanded port facilities are expected to significantly increase its annual export capacity. Australia remains the primary exporter of metallurgical coal to Asian markets, estimated to supply three quarters of Asia's import demand for coking coal in 2035, an increase from today's levels. Similarly, the U.S. coal industry is planning on increasing the capacity of West Coast ports in the Seattle area to facilitate increased exports from the United States. As U.S. emissions regulations dampen the U.S. market, China will increasingly become an important destination. The quality of U.S. coal is generally superior to that found in China and the higher quality is needed for the coke to manufacture iron and steel.

Solar and wind power are going to be important, but it is really difficult to move them beyond 10% of total power supply. It has been a significant engineering achievement to raise the efficiency of solar photovoltaic (PV) cells from about 25% to about 30%, but to be competitive with coal, the cost of PV power has to be reduced from the current approximately 18 cents per kilowatt-hour to 6 cents. You are not going to run a steel or aluminum plant with solar panels.

It is very difficult to believe there can be significant reduction in carbon emissions without some plan or technology to enable people to continue to use coal. It is by far the most prevalent and efficient way to produce electricity. Fallows from *Atlantic Monthly* quotes Julio Friedmann of Lawrence Livermore Laboratories who said, regarding coal, "People are going to use it. There is no story of climate progress without a story for coal. In particular, U.S.–China progress on coal."[†]

Weaknesses

The biggest weakness is the large quantity of carbon emissions that occur when coal is burned. A leading climate scientist has written: "Coal

---

[*] EIA/International Energy Outlook 2009, p. 56.
[†] Op. cit. James Fallows, *Atlantic Monthly*, p. 10.

Overlay: *Emissions.*—The enormous amount of emissions of CO_2 from coal suggests the technical challenges ahead. As one climate scientist was reported to state: "To stabilize the CO_2 concentration in the atmosphere, the whole world on average would need to get down to the Kenya level"—a 96% reduction for the United States.[*]

There is a major ongoing effort from environmental organizations and others to reduce the usage of coal and therefore the emissions. Program planners should be looking at alternate sources of energy and at opportunities to reduce coal emissions.

---

[*] Fallows, *Atlantic Monthly.*

emissions must be phased out as rapidly as possible or global climate disasters will be a dead certainty."[*] His focus is on coal emissions, not coal use, and he would phase out coal emissions linearly between 2010 and 2030. This means 50% would be phased out by 2020. This would be accomplished through carbon capture and storage (CCS), technology, or replacing all existing coal plants with less carbon-intensive alternatives.[†]

There is increasing demand for some sort of carbon tax or comparable mechanism to reflect the cost to the environment of carbon emissions. Coal is seen as the primary culprit and the coal industry is expected to bear the brunt of the resulting increases in costs due to regulation worldwide. This will make coal more expensive and less competitive with alternate sources of energy and encourage more rapid development of alternatives.

Another weakness is the current low probability of a successful CCS technology evolving in the near future. Major problems in sequestration sites exist both from not in my back yard (NIMBY) and geological difficulties.

The biggest issue facing the coal industry is that of carbon dioxide emissions. The leading technology candidate to address this issue is the development of CCS technology. The MIT study titled *The Future of Coal* stated:

> We conclude that CO_2 capture and sequestration (CCS) is the critical enabling technology that would reduce CO_2 emissions significantly while also allowing coal to meet the world's pressing energy needs.[‡]

---

[*] James Hansen, *Storms of My Grandchildren* (New York: Bloomsbury, 2009), 172.
[†] CCS is the process of capturing CO_2 from coal-burning plants and sequestering or storing it underground for indefinite periods of time.
[‡] James Katzer et al. "Executive Summary," in *The Future of Coal: Options for a Carbon Constrained World* (Cambridge, MA: MIT, 2007), x.

With regard to the status in 2007, the report states:

> At present government and private sector programs to implement on a timely basis the required large-scale integrated demonstrations to confirm the suitability of carbon sequestration are completely inadequate.[*]

In 2010, the Department of Energy (DOE) released its third *Carbon Sequestration Atlas of the United States and Canada*.[†] The atlas identifies over 3,400 billion metric tons of long-term underground carbon dioxide storage potential in oil and gas reservoirs, coal seams, and saline formations.

A study in March 2008 found that the United States will need to drill over 100,000 (and perhaps up to three times that number) injection wells to inject enough carbon dioxide in order to keep total emissions at 2005 levels.[‡] The study was based on data from the petroleum industry, which has been injecting CO_2 for enhanced oil recovery for more than 30 years. As a comparison for feasibility, approximately 40,000 oil and gas wells are drilled each year in the United States. All told, the total cost of such carbon dioxide sequestration efforts could easily top $1.5 trillion per year.

> **Overlay:** *Carbon capture and storage.* CCS technology appears to be two or more decades away from viability as a true remover of CO_2 from the emissions from coal. Based on current progress and problems, it appears unlikely that CCS will be available at significant sites to make a significant impact on total emissions before the end of the century. As a result, this technology can be considered as still in the conceptual phase of the program life cycle.[*]
>
> ---
>
> [*] To emphasize this, due to financial difficulties, the EU countries have recently withdrawn funding for CCS pilot programs.

Opportunities

Major opportunities exist to find ways to use the heat content of coal, yet limit or eliminate the escape of CO_2 emissions into the atmosphere. In China

---

[*] Katzer et al., "Executive Summary," xii.

[†] U.S. Department of Energy, National Energy Technology Laboratory, *Carbon Sequestration Atlas of the United States and Canada*, 3rd ed., http://www.netl.doe.gov/technologies/carbon_seq/refshelf/atlasIII/2010atlasIII.pdf, 22.

[‡] Energy Information Administration. *International Energy Outlook 2011*. Report Number DOE/EIA-0484 (2009). May 2009. p. 55. http://www.eia.gov/forecasts/archive/ieo09/pdf/0484(2009).pdf. (Accessed February 29, 2012).

Overlay: *U.S. Outlook.* The United States is going to add another 100 million people by 2050, and they all are consumers. They all need electricity to maintain their standard of living. There will be increased generation from coal-fired power plants in order to meet overall energy demand in spite of environmental concerns. However, the share of the market may be reduced as subsidized renewables come on line.

and India in particular it is important that they find a carbon-free source of baseload electric power that is competitive in price with coal. Today, coal is the fuel of choice by the industry for electricity generation and may be the source of an extensive synthetic liquids industry (synfuels) in the future.

There are several technologies being proposed, tested, and scaled up to remove the carbon that results from combustion. All of these technologies need further explorations. China also needs to find technologies to curb emissions from coke used in the manufacture of pig iron and steel.

A strategy for the coal industry is to be involved in the negotiation of new legislation or international agreements that protect them in two ways: (1) to generate funding dollars for CCS and related technology, which would allow coal to produce power while sequestering its carbon emissions; and (2) to participate in the setting of a price on carbon when required that enables the coal companies to remain in business. The strategy is simple: if you are not at the table, you will be on the table.*

Threats

The threats to coal are all based on its carbon emissions role. The EIA projections show coal's market share in the United States set to decline significantly in the coming decade as electricity companies switch to natural gas and combined cycle gas turbine (CCGT) systems and renewables for power generation. As shown in Figure 15.1, coal has been the nation's number one source of electric power, supplying about half the nation's electricity, while natural gas and nuclear energy generated about 20% each, with renewables making up the rest.

But power companies say changes in the regulatory landscape and in the nation's fuel supply mix are about to alter that. New and tougher

---

* The basic philosophy of government lobbyers.

Quadrillion Btu

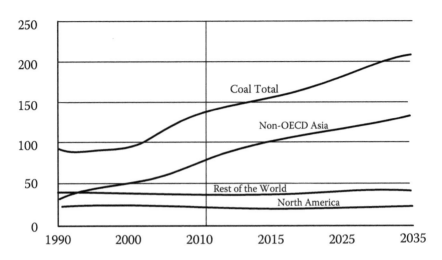

FIGURE 15.1

World coal consumption by region. (Data from Energy Information Administration [EIA], International Energy Outlook 2011 data. *International Energy Outlook 2011*. Report Number: DOE/EIA 0484 (2011). September 2011. p. 64. http://205.254.135.24/forecasts/ieo/pdf/0484(2011).pdf. (Accessed February 29, 2012.)

Environmental Protection Agency (EPA) regulations on coal pollutants such as acid rain–causing sulfur dioxide, mercury, and nitrogen oxide will have an impact. In addition, public reaction to mountain-top mining is increasing. Also in store are new Clean Water Act regulation changes, as well as a number of new mining safety regulations. Increasingly, environmental and local organizations are marching and demonstrating against new coal-fired power plants and there are some indications these are being effective. However, in the current political climate, these regulations may be delayed. The focus is on smaller government and less regulation and not on the benefits to the public.

There are indications that China and India are having second thoughts about their rapid increase of coal-fired power plants due to their current pollution problems. However, their necessity to provide power for demands for increasing standards of living ensure that coal will be in strong demand worldwide for many years.

It is obvious that any mandatory requirements for CCS or any other scheme to reduce the CO_2 emissions from coal must add to the price of coal and diminish its economic margins.

TABLE 15.1

Coal Industry Risk Matrix Based on Threats[a]

No.	Risk Event	P1	P2	Px
1	Tougher EPA CO_2 emissions regulations that would increase costs significantly	2	3	6
2	Carbon tax on fossil fuels	1	3	3
3	Switch to natural gas CCGT systems	4	3	12
4	Significant delay in CCS technology development and demonstrations	4	4	16
5	Renewables incentives reduce comparative advantage of coal	2	2	6

[a] See Appendix C.
Note: P1 = likelihood of risk event occurring; P2 = probable impact on the industry if P1 occurred; Px = product of P1 and P2 to assign ranking.

Table 15.1 presents a sample risk matrix based on the threats listed in this chapter. The range of values for P1 and P2 is 1–5.

Our off-the-cuff analysis would indicate that the biggest risks are that CCS would fail and that the market for coal would change as there is increasing switching to CCGT systems. Increased regulation of carbon and increased renewables incentives are a diminishing near-term threat.

> **Overlay:** The bottom line for coal in the energy leg of the new triple constraint is that there is no foreseeable shortage of the resource or significant reduction in the demand or usage; it will remain the lowest-cost fossil fuel to extract and deliver to market. However, its carbon emissions will result in it becoming increasingly expensive due to regulation and incentives provided to competing sources of energy. Coal will lose market share. It appears unlikely that carbon capture and storage will become a commercially feasible technology in the foreseeable future.
>
> The Age of Coal is far from over, even though its younger competitor, discussed in the next section, is proceeding apace. Until nuclear, water, wind, and solar, combined with conservation can provide enough energy to maintain our current levels of comfort and convenience, coal will play a major role in our lives.
>
> Coal must be used in less damaging, more sustainable ways than it is now, because there is no other plausible way to meet the world's unavoidable energy demands and climate imperatives.

16

Liquid Fuels

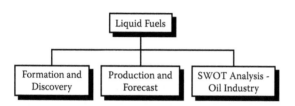

Chapter 16 outline.

> **Overlay:** The availability of oil is critical to the economies of the world. It is an essential ingredient for maintaining or increasing the standards of living of not only the new 3 billion persons coming in the next decades but the existing 6 billion as well. The concern is the supply constraint that exists and the rate of depletion of the world's supply that may cause serious price increases.

Liquid fuels are defined by the Energy Information Agency as 95% conventional liquids or oil and 5% unconventional liquids. The latter includes extra-heavy oil, bitumen, coal to liquids, gas to liquid, shale oil, and biofuels. Bitumen occurs naturally or is obtained by distillation from coal or petroleum and is used for surfacing roads and for waterproofing. The conventional liquids category includes conventional crude oil, lease condensate, natural gas plant liquids (NGPL), and refinery gain.

FORMATION AND DISCOVERY

"The end of the coal age began on the morning of January 10, 1901, just outside Beaumont, Texas, on a small hill called Spindletop."* This well and

---
* Paul Roberts, *The End of Oil* (New York: Houghton Mifflin Co., 2005), 31.

many more discovered shortly thereafter in Texas and Oklahoma ushered in the age of oil—of cheap energy—and the dramatic increase in standards of living that occurred over the next 110 years and is still occurring.

Oil, like coal and natural gas, is an ancient substance. While coal is formed largely from dead plant matter, oil was formed over 50 million years ago from millions of algae and plankton dying and accumulating along with sediment on ocean floors, especially in anoxic (dissolved oxygen-free) environments. Animals contain more fats than plants and contain more hydrogen, which under great pressure forms liquid hydrocarbons and gases. Within the pressure cooker of the hydrocarbons, the gases expand and crack the source rock and the combination slowly moves or floats upward toward the surface. Because of the different density, the gases usually separate as they rise through the microscopic pores of the rock above. Some continue to the surface and others are blocked by impervious layers of rock or other material. In the case of Spindletop, the blocking layer was a super-hard layer of limestone and the petroleum formed a reservoir under the limestone. New technology of the time in the form of a rotary drill enabled the drillers to penetrate the limestone not only there in Texas, but subsequently in Oklahoma, Mexico, and Venezuela.

When oil became available in large quantities, prices fell and many coal users switched to oil. Of course Henry Ford introduced the gasoline engine in his Model A in 1903. This was the true beginning of the golden age of oil.

Worldwide demand for oil moved from 500,000 barrels a day in the early 1900s to 1.25 million in 1915, to 4 million by 1929, and to 85 million barrels a day today. Of this the United States consumes approximately 20 million barrels per day, or about ten supertanker loads.

PRODUCTION AND FORECAST

Overlay: Demand for worldwide production of conventional oil is expected to increase by almost 20% by 2035. Meeting this demand is dependent upon potential supply constraints. Some experts are forecasting a decrease of supply of the same amount in the same time period.

TABLE 16.1

World Liquid Fuels Production

World Liquid Fuels Production (Million barrels per day)		
Liquid Type	**2008**	**2035**
Conventional Liquids	81.7	99.1
Unconventional Liquids		
Extra-heavy crude oil	0.7	1.5
Oil sands	1.5	4.8
Coal to liquids	0.1	1.7
Gas to liquids	0.1	0.3
Shale oil	0.0	0.1
Biofuels	1.5	4.7
World Total	**85.7**	**112.2**

Source: Energy Information Administration, International Energy Outlook 2011, Report Number: DOE/EIA-0484 (2011) September 2011. Table 3, page 26. http://205.254.135.24/forecasts/ieo/pdf. (Accessed February 29, 2012.)

This section is included because of the importance of oil to the United States and world standard of living and world economies.

The Energy Information Administration (EIA) forecasts world demand to increase from a total of 87 million barrels a day of all liquid fuels to approximately 110 million barrels per day in 2035. Demand for unconventional liquids is estimated to increase from approximately 5% today to 12%. The breakdown is shown in Table 16.1.

This table presents the conventional and unconventional liquid fuels and clearly indicates the relatively small impact of the various unconventional liquids on the world totals today but an increasing importance as time goes on.

Figure 16.1 presents the world oil consumption since 1965. The recent slowdown is due to the economy. Data are from BP, which is a reliable major source of worldwide data on the oil industry.

Figure 16.2 illustrates the production forecast of the EIA. It is organized into Organization of Petroleum Exporting Countries* (OPEC) and non-OPEC production. OPEC controls its production as a bloc, usually trying to maintain a constant market share. The non-OPEC countries operate independently, with their policies varying from country to

---

* Organization of the Petroleum Exporting Countries (OPEC): Algeria, Angola, Ecuador, Iran, Iraq, Kuwait, Libya, Nigeria, Qatar, Saudi Arabia, the United Arab Emirates, and Venezuela.

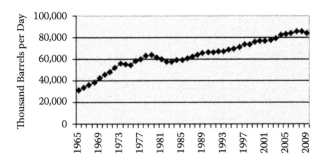

FIGURE 16.1

World oil consumption. Data from British Petroleum BP Data 2009 Report. *Statistical Review of World Energy.* June 2009. p. 12. http://www.bp.com/liveassets/bp_internet/globalbp/globalbp_UK_English/reports_and_publications/statistical_energy_review_2008/STAGING/local_assets/2009_downloads/statistical_review_of_world_energy_full_report_2009.pdf. (Accessed February 29, 2012.)

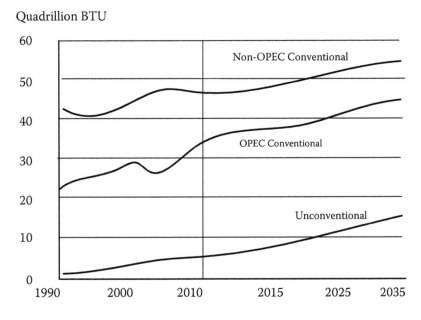

FIGURE 16.2

World liquid fuels production 1990–2035. (Reproduced from Energy Information Administration (EIA), *Annual Energy Outlook 2011*, http://www.eia.gov/forecasts/aeo/source_oil.cfm, Figure 28.)

country. Most try to extract as much oil as possible but are constrained by depleting reservoirs.

The forecast assumes the world economies recover fully from the effects of the recession after 2 years of declining demand. The EIA stated world liquids consumption is expected to increase from the recession levels and strengthen thereafter. Note that the steeper increases in production, as illustrated in Figure 16.2, are in OPEC conventional sources and from unconventional sources. The non-OPEC fields for the most part are in decline, so it is difficult to increase production.

In the forecast, the price of light sweet crude oil in the United States (in constant 2009 dollars) rises from $79 per barrel in 2010 to a projected $108 per barrel in 2020 and $125 per barrel in 2035. This translates roughly to $2.77, $3.79, and $4.38 per gallon of regular, also in constant 2009 dollars. This is an increase of $2 per barrel per year approximately. Please note this assumes no unusual activities that might cause disruptions in supply or price spikes.

Tables 16.2 and 16.3 present the detailed data from the EIA estimates on production from each region, from selected countries, and from OPEC. The tables present the situation in the 2011 report and illustrate the dependence of the world on OPEC and the Persian Gulf states for oil. Of particular interest is the expected growth in unconventional liquids—the oil shales and sands that are primarily in North America. Table 16.3 presents selected countries to provide an indication of where the major sources of oil are at present and what is expected in 2035. The increase in production in the United States is all from offshore wells; onshore well production has been declining since the 1970s. The data for 2035 are expected to change

TABLE 16.2

World Total Liquid Production (MBD)

World Total Liquids Production (MBD)				
	Conventional		Unconventional	
Region	2008	2035	2008	2035
OPEC	35.0	45.0	0.7	1.7
OECD North America	12.8	13.3	2.3	8.1
OECD Europe	5.0	2.8		
OECD Asia	0.8	0.7		
Non-OECD	28.2	37.1	0.9	3.3
World Total	**81.7**	**99.1**	**3.9**	**13.1**

TABLE 16.3

Selected Countries, Total Conventional Liquids Production (MBD)

World Total Liquids Production Selected Countries (MBD)		
	2008	2035
Saudi Arabia	10.7	15.4
Iran	4.2	3.9
Venezuela	2.0	1.2
United States	7.8	9.9
Canada	1.8	1.8
Mexico	3.2	1.6
Russia	9.8	13.3
China	4.0	4.3
Brazil	2.0	4.8
World Total	**81.7**	**99.1**

Source: Data from Energy Information Administration (EIA), *Annual Energy Outlook 2010*, http://www.eia.gov/forecasts/aeo/source_oil.cfm.

as oil sands and shale extraction quantities increase in the United States and Canada. Table 16.3 provides a preliminary estimate of the increases. The uncertainty in the market due to supply sources is reflected in the next text box. Of note is the drop in oil prices over the 6 months following the date of the article to approximately $80 per barrel.

A slowdown in consumption is expected in Organization for Economic Cooperation and Development (OECD) regions due to declining

WASHINGTON POST, MARCH 6, 2011

The laws of supply, demand and panic. Oil prices surged as Libya's bloody rebellion escalated and anxiety grew that the instability would trigger unrest in other oil-exporting nations, including Algeria, Oman, Yemen, Saudi Arabia and Nigeria.

U.S. crude oil futures settled at $104.42 a barrel, their highest mark since September 2008. And Saudi Arabia raised output in response to Libya's disruption. Oil experts said there is enough oil in storage and spare capacity worldwide to meet short-term needs.

Fed Chairman Ben S. Bernanke said the agency was prepared to respond if rising oil prices feed inflation. Gas prices set records in Europe and tipped past $4 per gallon in California. Economists warned higher prices could hurt the U.S. economic recovery.

populations and much slower overall economic growth rate compared to China and India and the other third world countries outside Africa. In addition, growth in consumption in OECD countries is constrained by government policies, by conservation efforts, and by legislation aimed at increasing efficiency of trucks and automobiles. Older populations also use less energy.

The EIA forecast of 112 million barrels per day (MBD) in 2035 as made in the 2010 report has been questioned by Dr. Kjell Aleklett, a professor of physics at Uppsala University in Sweden and author of a report titled *The Peak of the Oil Age. He* claims crude production is more likely to be 75 MBD by 2030 than the "unrealistic" amount projected for 2030 by the IEA.* Since the current usage is approximately 87 MBD, this is a cause for concern and is discussed further in the section "Weaknesses."

Sustained high prices provide an economic basis to develop the unconventional sources of shale and oil sands as well as the use of enhanced oil recovery techniques in existing wells. New exploration and extraction techniques for high-risk and expensive projects, such as very deep water in the Gulf of Mexico, the U.S. continental shelf, the Arctic, and off Iceland and West Africa, also become economically attractive.

Unconventional liquids are expected to play an increasing role between now and 2050, especially if oil production slows as expected. Unconventional liquids will be needed to fill the gap between normal oil production and the increasing demand to meet transportation requirements.

Unconventional liquids from both OPEC and non-OPEC sources become increasingly competitive in the *EIA 2011* analyses. They indicate unconventional petroleum liquids production development faces some difficulties, such as environmental concerns for Canada's oil sands projects and investment restrictions for Venezuela's extra-heavy oil projects. Production of nonpetroleum unconventional liquids, such as biofuels, coal to liquid, and gas to liquid, is spurred by sustained high prices for crude oil. However, their development also depends on country-specific programs or mandates. World production of unconventional liquids, which in 2008 totaled only 3.9 million barrels per day or about 5% of total world liquids production, is estimated to increase to 13.1 million barrels per day in 2035, when it accounts for 12% of total world liquids production.

The EIA expects that the largest increase in unconventional supply will come from non-OPEC sources in the United States, Canada, Russia, and

* Terry Macalister and Lionel Badel, *The Observer*, August 22, 2010, http://www.guardian.co.uk/business/2010/aug/11/peak-oil-department-energy-climate-change. (Accessed February 29, 2012.)

Brazil because of the OPEC pricing policies and perhaps an inability of non-OPEC sources to ramp up production much beyond current amounts.

The unconventional sources will become increasingly competitive due to effort put into research and development (R&D) and subsidies. The possible exception is the Canadian oil sands and the Venezuelan extra-heavy oil where environmental concerns and investment limitations may suppress the development.

The Canadian oil sands development is continuing rapidly and may be assisted by the completion of a pipeline to the refineries in Texas.

Overall production is very difficult to estimate for these reasons:

- Declines in production capability due to depletion of resources are often hidden by governments
- Tax policies that provide disincentives to investment
- Unfavorable investment terms by controlling governments
- Lack of technical expertise combined with restrictive laws
- Lack of financial strength to develop potential deep water sites
- Requirements that the relevant government be given a large equity interest
- Progress in developing technology to increase yields from mature fields is unpredictable
- Legislative constraints on drilling in environmentally sensitive locations
- Laws to reduce greenhouse gases make projects uneconomical by increasing the cost of carbon
- Territorial disputes, transportation blockages, and contractual changes that make the investment environment uncertain
- Lack of transportation routes (pipelines) or capacity
- International sanctions on oil supplying countries

Logic would indicate that these barriers will probably disappear if demand and prices increase sufficiently.

SWOT ANALYSIS: OIL INDUSTRY

The objective of this SWOT analysis is to assess the long-term viability of the oil industry as a major component of the energy constraint.

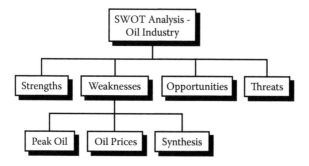

SWOT analysis section outline.

Overlay: The oil industry has led the tremendous increase in standard of living in our country. However, planners should assume that we have reached peak oil, and from now on the oil will be harder and more costly to produce, and the commodity will be supply constrained. This means prices will increase faster than demand increases. Supply will remain constant and eventually decrease. Use of oil for energy should be limited to transportation needs and alternatives used for all other energy needs. Alternative fuels must be developed rapidly to replace falling supplies.

Strengths

The oil industry is one of the largest and best organized sectors of our economy. It has been a critical component of the dramatic rise in our standard of living and in the current strength of the world economy. The investment in oil infrastructure in the United States and around the world is immense and therefore the political strength of the industry is immense. Table 16.4 presents the current and forecasted demand for oil in the United States.

A major strength is its essential role in transportation, as indicated in Table 16.4. While substitutes can be found for its use as a fuel for homes and industry and other uses, there is no ready substitute for its primary role in transportation in the near future. As shown in the table, the EIA is forecasting a small increase in the consumption of liquids over the next 25 years. The use of natural gas, batteries, or fuel cells has limited application in trucks or cars at present and there is no real alternative power source in aircraft to the jet engine. Biofuels are increasing, but only at a level to approximately offset growth in demand. The production capacity

TABLE 16.4

Current and Forecasted Consumption

United States Delivered Liquids Consumption Quadrillion Btu		
Sector	2008	2035
Residential	1.2	0.86
Commercial	0.64	0.53
Industrial	8.9	8.9
Transportation	27.2	30.8
Electric Power	0.47	0.47
Total Liquids Energy Consumption	**38.4**	**41.7**

Overlay: The U.S. production of oil is forecast to increase from approximately 7.8 to nearly 10 million barrels per day (BPD) by 2035. This assumes world oil prices will remain high since the extraction of oil from offshore and the Arctic is increasingly expensive as is the further recovery of oil from smaller deposits and once-abandoned wells.

of biofuels and synfuels at this time is a long way away from being able to substitute significantly. Transportation requirements make it important to find alternatives for nontransportation usages and to conserve oil for these future high-value requirements.

The U.S. production of oil depends upon the price structure and technology, as mentioned previously. Technology is important since it is needed to recover oil from existing wells that are otherwise depleted and to assist in the exploration and extraction of oil from remote locations, such as deep offshore underwater and the Arctic.

The increases in production in the United States come from additional deepwater wells in the Gulf and offshore because the basic conventional wells within the continental boundary have been in decline since 1970. High oil prices induce the oil companies to drill to recover the offshore oil in the deeper areas of the Gulf, from offshore, and from the Arctic. Low oil prices significantly reduce supply since many of the existing sources are in expensive locations.

Figure 16.3 shows that oil provides approximately 40% of the U.S. energy needs. Market share is expected to drop as time goes on due to diminishing supply and increasing prices combined with the availability of alternate energy sources.

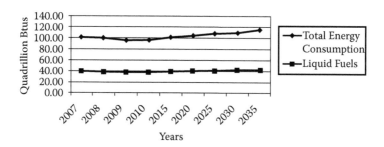

FIGURE 16.3

Total energy versus liquid fuels consumption. (Data from Energy Information Administration (EIA), *Annual Energy Outlook 2010*, Reference case.)

U.S. crude oil production, both onshore and offshore, is sensitive to future world oil prices and advances in technology. The remaining onshore resources typically require more costly secondary or tertiary recovery techniques. High-cost projects are undertaken when world oil prices are high. However, long lead times from discovery to production, on the order of 10 years, limit the increases in production, especially for offshore fields.

Oil companies hold many leases for potential offshore sites in the Gulf and elsewhere, but they are not worth drilling until prices rise enough to make them profitable.

Different assumptions about rates of technology improvement also have significant effects on projections of crude oil production in the United States. Advances in horizontal drilling, hydraulic fracturing, and enhanced oil recovery techniques as well as equipment improvements contribute to increases in domestic production. This has contributed to slowing the decline in U.S. crude oil production and increasing the amounts of recoverable oil.

A final strength is the role of increased U.S. production in reducing reliance on foreign sources. Although U.S. consumption of liquid fuels is expected to continue to grow through 2035 according to the EIA estimates, reliance on petroleum imports as a share of total liquids consumption decreases. Total U.S. consumption of liquid fuels, including both fossil fuels and biofuels, rises from about 18.8 million barrels per day in 2009 to 21.9 barrels per day in 2035. The import share, which reached 60% in 2005 and 2006 before falling to 51% in 2009, is forecast to fall to 42% in 2035.[*]

---

[*] EIA, "Oil/Liquids, Executive Summary," *Annual Energy Outlook 2011*, http://www.eia.gov/forecasts/aeo/source_oil.cfm (accessed September 27, 2011).

Weaknesses

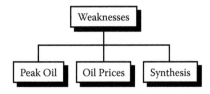

Weaknesses section outline.

The diagram presents an outline of this section. This section is expanded from the typical discussion of weaknesses to address peak oil and oil prices in more detail due to the importance of the topics and the personal interest most program managers have in the subjects.

There are four weaknesses in the reliance on oil in the coming decades. The first is the ongoing peak oil plateau and the eventual decline in supply, which will eventually result in price instability and other problems, as discussed previously. The second is the increasing costs of exploration and extraction that will provide upward pressure on oil prices. The third is that it is a fossil fuel and burning it has a negative environmental effect due to the carbon that is emitted. The fourth is the dependence upon OPEC for the much of the world supply, which puts the economic destiny of many countries in potentially unstable hands and any rational allocation of the resources as the total pool declines is highly improbable. Also, many countries are entering into bilateral long-term contracts with supplying countries. This reduces the amount of oil available for free market adjustments in prices. We will focus on two of these factors, peak oil and prices.

Peak Oil

In 1956, the geologist M. King Hubbert predicted that U.S. oil production would peak in the early 1970s. At the time, almost everyone inside and outside the oil industry rejected his analysis.* It turned out to be correct; the peak year for U.S. production was 1970 at a production rate of approximately 40 million barrels per day. Hubbert's methodology was based on a combination of discovery rates and production rates. He showed that the discovery curve led the production curve by approximately 40 years. That

---

* Kenneth S. Deffeyes, *Hubberts's Peak: The Impending World Oil Shortage* (Princeton, NJ: Princeton University Press, 2009, Reissue), 1.

Overlay: Most studies estimate that oil production will peak sometime between last year (2006) and 2040. This range of estimates is wide because the timing of the peak depends on multiple, uncertain factors that will help determine how quickly the oil remaining in the ground is used, including the amount of oil still in the ground; how much of that oil can ultimately be produced given technological, cost, and environmental challenges as well as potentially unfavorable political and investment conditions in some countries where oil is located; and future global demand for oil. Demand for oil will, in turn, be influenced by global economic growth and be affected by government policies on the environment and climate change and consumer choices about conservation.*

---

* General Accounting Office Report GAO-07-293, *Crude Oil: Uncertainty About Future Oil Supply Makes It Important to Develop a Strategy for Addressing a Peak and Decline in Oil Production* (Washington, DC: U.S. Government Printing Office, February 2007), GAO Summary, 2.

is, changes in the annual amount discovered were reflected in the amounts produced some 40 years later when these data were plotted as curves.

His methodology also involved an estimate of the total amount of discoverable oil to be found by conventional means. The discovery rate peaked in 1930, as illustrated by a graphic plot of the amount of new oil discovered each year. Extending the same methodology to the world situation is a little more complex due to the games played with the amount of declared and proven reserves in each country. It is to some countries' advantage to exaggerate the amount of proven reserves. It then becomes a political estimate. Also, there is an incentive within the OPEC bloc in particular to have high estimated reserves since it influences the OPEC formula for allocating production. Higher reserves mean higher production is permitted and therefore greater income.

In 1982, in his last published paper, Hubbert estimated the total world amount of recoverable oil to be 2.1 trillion barrels and a peak occurring in 2003–2004. His analysis also used the world discovery curve, which peaked in 1960. The 2.1 trillion barrels was later confirmed by a detailed analysis performed by Colin J. Campbell.* A collaborator of Hubbert,

---

* Colin J. Campbell. *The Coming Oil Crisis* (Brentwood, Essex UK: Multiscience Publishing Company, 1997), 201.

Dr. Kenneth Deffeyes, estimated the peak to be 2005, and in the preface to his 2008 edition of his book *Hubbert's Peak,* he indicates that the peak arrived as he estimated in an "I told you so" essay as a prologue to the latest edition. He provided some qualifications based on changing reserve estimates and improved technology, which put 2009 as the latest date for peak oil. In a 1999 paper, Duncan and Youngquist cited seven forecasts that all identified the peak as occurring by 2013 or earlier, and one as late as 2020.[*]

A General Accounting Office (GAO) study for Congress in 2007 addressed government readiness for peak oil and subsequent decline.[†] The conclusions of the GAO were that peak oil would occur between 2007 and 2040. Included in the report were the results of 21 studies of the timing of peak oil.[‡] Many of the studies used current reserve estimates as the basis for their conclusions. The Overlay statement at the beginning of this section is an excerpt from the summary of that report.

The EIA estimates assume that existing fields will be depleted but production will be maintained from other sources. It is important to understand that many fields have already been depleted and abandoned, and more are being abandoned each year, even after trying to use the existing infrastructure and to extract as much oil as possible with advanced recovery techniques. Figure 16.4 demonstrates this concept, which is the assumption in the reference case of the IEA estimates. The heavy line is the current forecast from producing wells and the very top line reflects the estimate of the world demand. Please note the area descriptors and consider the probabilities of the various sources being available in time to meet the demand. The area labeled "fields yet to be developed" is the expensive deep water and remote areas of the world. And the area labeled "fields yet to be found" is an important assumption based on history and the optimism of the oil industry. Since demand is the top line of this set of areas, and if anything is too low, it is easy to see the risk involved in the projections of supply.

Ibraham Nashawi and others from Kuwait University estimate the world oil production to peak in 2014 at a rate of 79 MBD. As a reference and reminder, the U.S. production is approximately 7 MBD. OPEC production

---

[*] Richard C. Duncan and Walter Youngquist, "Encircling the Peak of World Oil Production," Minnesotans for Sustainability, June 1999, 5. Originally published in *Natural Resources Research* 8, no. 3 (June 25, 1999).
[†] General Accounting Office Report GAO-07-293, *Crude Oil.*
[‡] General Accounting Office Report GAO-07-293, *Crude Oil,* 18.

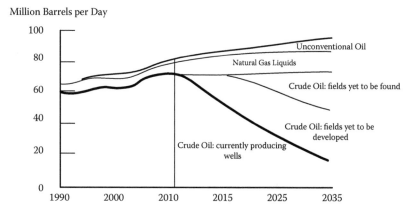

FIGURE 16.4

World oil production by type. (Based on International Energy Agency [IEA], *World Energy Outlook 2010* [Paris: IEA], Key Graphs, number 7.)

is estimated to peak in 2026 at a rate of 53 MBD. And they calculate the depletion rate of the world's oil reserves to be 2.1% per year.* At this rate, 50% would be depleted in 20 years using compound interest tables; this is a higher negative slope than that shown for the heavy line in Figure 16.4.

> **Overlay:** The general belief is that the next decade will see a series of oil price spikes and drops followed by stabilization of production due to interplay of the OPEC policies, world economic conditions, exploration and technology, the U.S. economy, and geopolitics.

Oil Prices

> **Overlay:** Oil prices are expected to increase significantly in the coming decades due to supply constraints and increasing demand. There is only one direction for oil prices to go and that is up. The concern is the amount and rate and impact on the economy and the point in time when supply from conventional sources starts to drop rapidly.

Predicting world oil prices is a complex undertaking. The EIA has developed a set of estimates out to 2035 that also includes a high oil price and

---

* Ibraham Nashawi et al., "Forecasting World Crude Oil Production Using Multicyclic Hubbert Model," *Energy & Fuels* (2010): 1000204085653081, doi: 10.1021/ef90124lp (from Abstract).

a low oil price based on alternate scenarios or sets of assumptions. Their reference case is the EIA most likely scenario.

The EIA baseline or reference case reflects an assumed decision by OPEC members to maintain the organization's aggregate production at approximately 40% of world liquids supply. To retain that share of world liquids supply, OPEC would have to increase production by 12.6 million barrels per day from 2007 to 2035, or about one-half of the projected total increase in world liquids supply. Not many analysts believe that OPEC has this capability due to perhaps having already reached their production peaks or reaching it well before 2035.[*] This doesn't mean the EIA estimate is wrong, only that the user of the data needs to be aware of the limitations. The EIA has no basis to reduce OPEC output below what OPEC states they can achieve.

Light sweet crude was listed at $76 per barrel in October 2010 and gasoline was selling at an average of $2.75 per gallon. There was a spike in March 2011 and it increased to $102 per barrel and $3.90 per gallon. If it increases to $133 per barrel in 2035 as forecast, this could translate into approximately $5 per gallon in 2008 dollars.[†]

Synthesis of Weakness

The overall oil situation does not look good. Richard Heinberg's collapse scenario[‡] is even worse and goes something like this for later in this century:

> Energy shortages will begin to become significant, perhaps as soon as 2020, which will lead to economic turmoil, frequent and longer power blackouts and serious population unrest. Over time, food production will drop due to fertilizer shortages or high prices resulting in widespread famine. Regional wars will break out frequently. Climate and ecological problems result in water shortages, rising sea levels and severe storms. The constant disasters will wear down the ability to respond and governments will collapse. Instead of population growth between 2020 and 2100, there will be an overall decline from 2020 levels.

Not everyone is this pessimistic or fearful and most approach the future with optimism, such as outlined by Jared Diamond in his book *Collapse*, mentioned in the prologue of this book.

---

[*] Roberts, *The End of Oil*, 56.
[†] See www.eia.gov/petroleum/gasdiesel/ and www.nyse.tv/crude-oil-price-history.htm. (Accessed February 29, 2012.)
[‡] Heinberg, *Power Down*, 149.

Overlay: In the United States, alternative fuels and transportation technologies face challenges that could impede their ability to slow or halt the consequences of a peak and decline in oil production, unless sufficient time and effort are brought to bear. For example, although corn ethanol production is technically feasible to replace gasoline, it is more expensive to produce than gasoline and will require costly investments in infrastructure, such as pipelines, storage tanks, and more land, before it can become widely available as a primary fuel. Key alternative technologies currently supply the equivalent of only about 1% of U.S. consumption of petroleum products, and the Department of Energy (DOE) projects that even by 2015, they could displace only the equivalent of 4% of projected U.S. annual consumption. In such circumstances, an imminent peak and sharp decline in oil production could cause a worldwide recession. If the peak is delayed, however, these technologies have a greater potential to mitigate the consequences. The DOE projects that the technologies could displace up to 34% of U.S. consumption in the 2025 through 2030 time frame, if the challenges are met. The level of effort dedicated to overcoming challenges will depend in part on sustained high oil prices to encourage sufficient investment in and demand for alternatives.* It also may depend upon the availability of government money.

---

* General Accounting Office Report GAO-07-293, *Crude Oil*, 2.

We should not necessarily expect the worse scenario, but also we must not blindly assume that any problem will either go away or correct itself based on free market principles without some government policy intervention. On the other hand, it would be shortsighted to rely on government policies to positively resolve the problem of oil shortage. The concept of peak oil has been around for several years, with many geologists and engineers and analysts identifying actions to be taken. To date there is minimal indication that any leader in any country has aggressively addressed or planned for the eventuality, or even talked about it. Program and portfolio managers need to watch oil production and prices as a key indicator of future growth or decline of the industry and react accordingly. Any risk management analysis would show that some action is needed now to either provide insurance or develop workarounds or options. The best approach is to assume little change in present government policies of doing nothing and to act accordingly. There are many sources available to investigate the situation more deeply and to provide insight into possible defensive strategies for your organization.

Kenneth D. Worth has an interesting book on this same subject, and discusses the consequences of peak oil, rising prices and the economy, and the likelihood of hyperinflation and a major economic depression.[*] Christopher Steiner presents an analysis of the probable impacts on the economy and our lives as the price of gasoline increases from $4 per gallon to $20 per gallon.[†] He describes likely impacts in $2 increment price increases. Since we reached $4 in 2008 and again in 2011, this is his starting reference point.

So, while demand will remain strong, the ability of the industry to meet it over the coming decades is questionable and it will revert to an industry in decline. There will be increasing efforts to find substitutes.

The arithmetic is pretty clear; even using the most optimistic estimates of the amount of recoverable oil, it is not likely to fill the gap shown in the chart. New production takes at least 10 years and there are not sufficient projects actually in the works today to make up the declines expected in the next 10 years from existing sources. Closing new offshore areas for exploration only exacerbates the situation—even assuming there are significant reservoirs awaiting development, which is questionable, and whether the oil companies are really ready to start drilling.

Back to the chart of production, Figure 16.4: as demand increases, at some point in the very near future, before 2020 for sure according to the experts, there will be no ability to increase world production of crude oil. The chart shows the decrease in production to start about now, but it could shift to the right a few years before the decrease becomes noticeable. There are several reasons this shifting may occur. There will be increases in supply from more offshore deep drilling and the nontraditional sources such as tar sands and shale deposits and Arctic drilling; some demand may be suppressed due to price increases and a weak worldwide economy; and some demand will be met by alternative energy sources such as biofuels. In an ideal free market world, the alternative energy sources would pick up the slack and there would be no disruption in total production. Supply

[*] Kenneth D. Worth, *Peak Oil and the Second Great Depression (2010–2030)* (LaVergne, TN: The Outskirts Press, 2010).
[†] Christopher Steiner, *$20 per Gallon: How the Inevitable Rise in the Price of Gasoline Will Change Our Lives for the Better* (New York: Grand Central Publishing, 2009).

of energy would rise to meet demand, but with it lagging, prices would increase until some equilibrium point was again achieved.

Realistically, it is expected that there would be a constant increase in energy prices due to increases in costs of the energy sources and increasing demand due to increasing incomes and population growth. Wind, nuclear, solar, and biofuels are not competitive with oil at present prices, but as crude comes under production pressure, and price increases, the alternatives will start to become cost-competitive in some markets.

More important than the specific date for peak oil is the date that two things occur: (1) key users and policymakers realize that the peak has been in fact reached or is very close, and production is on a permanent decline; and (2) users realize there is no ready suite of alternatives to fill the gap between demand and supply in order to maintain growth. It will be a perfect storm for hyperventilating media and opportunistic politicians.

Opportunities

The opportunities abound in identifying and developing alternatives to oil in all industries, pharmaceutical, agriculture, plastics, heating, and the like. Similarly, there will be strong demand for techniques to extract the remaining oil from the ground, especially from wells that are currently categorized as depleted. There will be a stronger demand for these items as the supply and environmental constraints become more apparent to the general public. There are opportunities in transportation for alternatives that do not require gasoline or diesel fuels. Electric cars and a related infrastructure are expected to find a market and be competitive. Alternative fuels will be required for hybrid cars, trains, and buses. It is probable that future oil supplies will be dedicated to high-end usages, such as air travel, where alternatives are not readily available. Long-distance high-speed train systems are being constructed in China and they already exist in Europe. They have been proposed in the United States; however, it is unlikely that comparable systems will be implemented on an interstate highway scale, but shorter systems between large cities are probable. In passenger rail transportation, the demand follows the gravity rule: it is inversely proportional to the square of the distance between hubs. So, unless heavily subsidized both for capital and operating costs, high-speed rail on a large scale with today's technology is several decades away. The distance between hubs is much greater in the United States than in European countries and Japan, except in a few special corridors.

Threats

The major external threat to the future of the oil industry is geopolitical instability. The rate of depletion after the peak oil plateau will likely be delayed or postponed as demand is partially suppressed by an increase in prices, so the supply will remain relatively constant as prices increase and more expensive oil is extracted. The biggest near-term threat is geopolitical instability. With OPEC nations controlling more than half of the world's reserves and many of these nations either hostile to the United States or governed by weak or corrupt officials, or in the midst of internal upheavals, the security of the oil supply is really questionable. This may result in nations taking aggressive actions to protect or acquire a secure supply. It will also push the United States to continue to reduce dependence upon OPEC oil through increases in domestic production and use of unconventional oil sources.

A German study of the world supply situation after peak oil concludes, among other things, that the political and economic impacts of peak oil will result in nations that are importers of oil competing even more aggressively for favor with oil-producing nations. This would result in a more aggressive assertion of national interests on the part of the oil-producing nations. With an increase in the amount of oil traded through binational contracts, the freely accessible oil market will diminish. The laws of the free market will continue but in a restricted way as the unrestricted supply diminishes.[*]

Two segments of the market that will be impacted severely are transportation and industrial goods, as previously discussed. As the transportation of goods depends on crude oil, international trade could be subject to major price increases as the supply is constrained. In addition, since oil is used directly or indirectly in the production of 95% of all industrial goods, shortages in the supply of vital goods could arise. Price shocks could therefore be seen in almost any industry and throughout all stages of the industrial supply chain. A conceivable conclusion could be government rationing and the allocation of important goods or the setting of production schedules and other short-term coercive measures to replace market-based mechanisms. In the extreme, the industry could be nationalized to facilitate rationing.

---

[*] Stefan Schultz, "Military Study Warns of a Potentially Drastic Oil Crisis," Spiegel Online International, September 1, 2010, http://www.spiegel.de/international/germany/0,1518,715138,00.html (accessed September 10, 2010).

At a minimum it is possible that countries dependent on oil imports will be forced to show more pragmatism toward oil-producing states in their foreign as well as domestic policy due to the overriding concern of securing energy supplies. This is already evident in U.S. foreign policy regarding various OPEC nations. A sample risk matrix for liquid fuels is shown in Table 16.5.

TABLE 16.5

Liquid Fuels Sample Risk Matrix

No.	Risk Event	P1	P2	Px
1	Oil reaches a steady $120 per barrel by 2015	4	4	16
2	Mideast unrest causes serious disruption in oil supply	4	5	20
3	U.S. government nationalizes oil industry	1	2	2
4	Canada oil supply to United States disrupted	2	4	8
5	CAFÉ fuel economy standards relaxed	2	3	6
6	Alternate fuels production unable to increase significantly by 2020 and price instability ensues	3	5	15

Note: P1 = likelihood of risk event occurring; P2 = probable impact on the industry if P1 occurred; Px = product of P1 and P2 to assign ranking.

Overlay: Today, the world does not have a ready replacement for conventional forms of fuel such as crude oil and likely will not have one for some time as demand for energy grows worldwide. Cleaner energy alternatives, including natural gas, wind, solar, nuclear, and biofuel, have gained ground on oil, but there is still a long way to go before this inexpensive, efficient fuel source can be phased out.[*] Electric cars will take many years to become a significant share of the automobile market.

Oil accounted for approximately 34% of global energy consumption in 2010[†] and is expected to remain one of the dominant energy sources as the current focus is on replacing coal with gas and renewables. As the impacts of peak oil make their way onto the world stage, the result is unknown but likely to involve uncertainty and unrest. Higher oil prices are a certainty.

---

[*] Larry Greenemeier, "Crude Alternatives: Energy Industry Heavyweights Debate Fuels of the Future," *Scientific American*, Keynote panel featuring ExxonMobil and Shell at *Technology Review*'s Emerging Technologies (EmTech) conference in Cambridge, MA, http://www.scientificamerican.com/article.cfm?id=fuels-of-the-future&sc=CAT_ENGYSU.S._20100930 (accessed October 1, 2010).

[†] British Petroleum (BP) Statistical Review of World Energy. June 2011. See analysis on web page. http://www.bp.com/sectiongenericarticle800.do?categoryId=9037128&contentId=7068555. (Accessed February 29, 2012).

17

Natural Gas

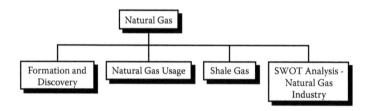

Chapter 17 outline.

Overlay: Because of the formation process, from fossils, there is a finite and therefore limited amount of gas available underground in the world. It is nonrenewable. However, recent technology—hydraulic fracturing—has greatly expanded the amount of gas potentially available to the United States from shale formations. As a result, the United States and the world now have large potential reserves for at least several generations.

The main ingredient in natural gas is methane, approximately 90%, and the remainder includes ethane, propane, and butane, and other complex hydrocarbons in smaller quantities. Methane (CH_4) consists of one molecule of carbon and four molecules of hydrogen, as indicated in the formula. When burned, the carbon is released as carbon dioxide and the hydrogen as water.

FORMATION AND DISCOVERY

> **Overlay:** The quantity of natural gas available has only recently become a concern due to the increasing reliance on it as a replacement for the more carbon-intensive coal power plants. However, the development of hydraulic fracturing technology has made extensive fields of natural gas trapped in shale now economical to extract and there appears to be a sufficient supply to the end of the century.

Natural gas is a product of decomposed algae and plankton, similar to oil. Ancient plants and animals, trapped in bogs and under water, broke down without the presence of oxygen. As they were covered with sediment, they became trapped. Pressure and heat and time changed this organic material into oil and/or gas.[*] Natural gas and oil are held in porous rocks, like sandstone, under a cap of impermeable rock. Natural gas is often found mixed in with oil, or floating on top of underground reservoirs of oil. When the cap is only partially impermeable, the gas leaks out so there is not always gas where there is oil.

Gas and oil are also trapped in another rock formation derived from layers of mud and sediment called *shale,* with one of the most interesting large formations located in the United States and referred to as the Marcellus shale.

Seismic methods are used to find rock formations most likely to contain oil and gas. Holes are then drilled and the gas and oil are extracted. Gas provides much of the natural pressure that drives oil to the surface. Natural gas is lighter than air, tasteless, odorless, and colorless. Mercaptan is added as an odorant for safety when it is used commercially.

NATURAL GAS USAGE

In the past, natural gas was not considered a useful product, and available transportation pipelines were not adequate to pipe it to markets. As a result, natural gas was simply burned off at the well, in huge flares. Since approximately 1950, a million miles of gas pipeline have been laid in the

---

[*] See discussion of formation at www.natgas.info/html/gasformation.html, and www.pge.com/microsite/pge_dgz/more/gas.html. (Accessed March 1, 2012.)

United States, with much of that in more recent years, to enable gas to be moved from the fields in the west to the markets on the east coast.

Carbon emissions from burning natural gas are much less than coal or oil, even though all are hydrocarbons and fossil fuels. Compared to coal, natural gas produces 43% fewer carbon emissions for each unit of energy produced and 30% less than oil. Gas also produces no solid waste, unlike the massive amounts of ash from a coal plant, and very little sulfur dioxide and particulate emissions. On the other hand, the combustion of natural gas produces nitrogen oxides, a cause of smog and acid rain. And while carbon emissions are lower, natural gas (methane) itself is a powerful greenhouse gas and is much more effective than carbon dioxide at trapping heat in the atmosphere, in fact, 58 times more effective on a pound-for-pound basis. Methane concentrations in the atmosphere have increased eight times faster than carbon dioxide, doubling since the beginning of the industrial age. Natural gas accounted for approximately 30% of the methane emitted in the United States in 2010 and overall approximately 3% of all greenhouse gas emissions.[*]

Natural gas requires limited processing to prepare it for end use. However, because of its gaseous form and low energy density, it has a disadvantage compared to other fossil fuels regarding transportation and storage. Natural gas for the most part must be delivered to the end user by pipeline, so delivery costs typically represent a relatively large component of the cost in the supply chain. Internationally, this creates potential supply security problems where a relatively inflexible supply pipeline structure exists, especially when the pipelines must cross many countries and the supplying or transit country has disputes with user countries. The development of liquefied natural gas (LNG) terminals provides some flexibility in the use of this commodity where seaports are available.

SHALE GAS

More recently, since approximately 2005, it has been determined that natural gas can be economically recovered from shale deposits. This

---

[*] Environmental Protection Agency (EPA), "Executive Summary," in *2011 U.S. Greenhouse Gas Inventory Report*, USEPA#430-R-11-005, April 2011, ES-5, http://www.epa.gov/climatechange/emissions/downloads11/US-GHG-Inventory-2011-Executive-Summary.pdf (accessed June 22, 2011).

has been a dramatic event since it effectively removes natural gas from its status as a rapidly diminishing resource, not unlike peak oil. Current EIA projections have between 40% and 50% of the natural gas used in the United States coming from shale gas.* Extraction requires a new hydraulic fracturing technology called *fracking*, which is discussed in more detail in upcoming text. Natural gas currently stands as an important source of energy that can replace coal and some petroleum applications in the movement to significantly reduce carbon emissions, and can be provided as a bridge until the technology of alternate fuels and infrastructure are developed to fully replace fossil fuel usage.

In the Barnett shale formation, near Fort Worth, Texas, oil and gas companies began to perfect the technology of horizontal or directional drilling in the late 1980s. As the technology evolved, tools became more reliable and affordable; these included directional mud motors and logging while drilling (LWD) equipment, which allows for the navigation of directional drilling assemblies. Now, horizontal drilling is being used in shale formations across the United States. This unconventional gas revolution has made natural gas one of the most affordable forms of energy. More discussion of shale extraction is included in the section titled "Weaknesses" in this chapter.

The Marcellus shale field stretches from southern New York through western Pennsylvania into the eastern half of Ohio and across West Virginia. Shale thickness runs from about 900 feet beneath New Jersey to around 40 feet across the border in Canada. In West Virginia, where much new drilling activity is located, the thickness is in the 200-foot range. Wells in the Marcellus formation are as deep as 9,000 feet and the productive zone is far below any water aquifers.

The Marcellus shale formation covers approximately 95,000 square miles and includes parts of Pennsylvania, southern New York, West Virginia, and eastern Ohio. The uniqueness is its proximity to the northeast consumer markets, which reduces transportation costs. Over 20,000 shale wells have been drilled in the United States in the last 10 years. Many of these are drilled in the northeastern states where the people are not familiar or comfortable with large-scale oil and gas development. The industry plans to drill some 30,000 wells by 2020. It is projected by the

---

* US. Department of Energy, *Report on the First Quadrennial Technology Review* (Washington, DC: DOE, September 2011), Figure 2, p. 11.

industry that shale gas will comprise over 20% of the total United States gas supply by that date—probably an optimistic projection. Natural gas from fracking would primarily supply electricity generators in the eastern half of the United States because of the expense of pipelines.[*]

The other big shale formations are the Barnett in east Texas, Haynesville in Louisiana, Fayetteville in Arkansas, and Woodford in Oklahoma.

Terry Engelder and SUNY Professor Gary Lash said the Marcellus shale conservatively contains 168 trillion cubic feet of natural gas in place, but the figure might be as high as 516 trillion cubic feet. The researchers said that America (United States, Canada, and Mexico) currently produces roughly 30 trillion cubic feet of gas annually. Engelder said the technology now exists to recover 50 trillion cubic feet of gas just from the Marcellus, making it a super-giant gas field."[†]

One major source of contention among environmental groups is the disposal of the quantity of chemicals pumped into the formation along with fracturing water and sand. Up to 50% of this fluid may remain in the ground; however, it may take millions of years for any of it to migrate upward to water-bearing zones. The other 50% therefore is contaminated water to be disposed of at the surface and this disposal is a problem.

Up until about 15 years ago, most oil and gas wells were drilled as vertical holes down through rock formations like the Marcellus. This technology worked fine for highly porous reservoirs made up of sandstone or fractured limestone. A vertical gas or oil well could drain an area of about 10 to 40 acres, on average, over a period of time. Shale, however, is a dense rock, which does not give up much fluid or gas from a vertical hole drilled through it. The Marcellus shale can be over 900 feet thick in some areas, but even this is not enough profile of the shale to release a significant amount of gas. What horizontal drilling accomplishes is a hole drilled up to several thousand feet horizontally across the shale. After horizontal drilling has been completed, hydraulic fracturing is performed in the newly drilled well. Because the technology is new and nontypical, gas from shale formations is referred to as *unconventional natural gas* in the Energy Information Administration (EIA) data.

[*] Joel Kirkland. "Big Money Drives Up the Betting on the Marcellus Shale," *ClimateWire*, July 8, 2010, http://www.nytimes.com/cwire/2010/07/08 (accessed March 1, 2012).

[†] Data from Dr. Terry Engelder's home page: http://www.geosc.psu.edu/~jte2/; Pennsylvania State University, quote dated January 17, 2010 (accessed December 8, 2010).

SWOT ANALYSIS: NATURAL GAS INDUSTRY

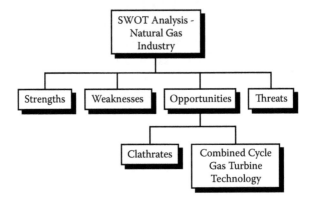

SWOT section outline.

Overlay: The use of hydraulic fracturing has given a new life to the natural gas industry. Environmental protections are likely to be legislated to preclude freshwater contamination and to provide for disposition of water used in the fracking process. Natural gas should be used to replace as many coal-burning power plants as possible, but be considered a short-term fix before being replaced in turn by carbon emissions–free energy sources. The reserves, including shale, are sufficient to meet our country's needs until the end of the century and beyond. Emissions reduction requirements will eventually require limited usage of natural gas unless methods of eliminating CO_2 are developed, such as carbon capture and storage (CCS).

The objective of the strengths, weaknesses, opportunities, and threats (SWOT) analysis is to evaluate the viability of the natural gas industry.

Strengths

There are five current strengths of natural gas as a supply of energy and future viability. The first is that it is available at a price that is close to being competitive with coal, and a long-term supply appears available. The second is that it releases much less carbon than coal when consumed and therefore is favored as a replacement for coal in new power plants. The new power plants do not need all the emissions control equipment that is required for coal plants. The third is the ability of gas-fired turbines to handle peak load situations and to also provide the necessary backup when much of the base load is provided by intermittent sources such as wind and solar. A gas turbine system is also more responsive to daily changes in demand. This enables gas turbines to replace coal-fired electricity generation and to operate more efficiently. The fourth strength is the ability to use natural gas as a bridge element in the replacement of oil and coal carbon-intensive fossil fuels until alternative, nonpolluting sources of energy are available in the quantities necessary to meet demand.

The fifth strength is its availability in liquid form as LNG, which means that while not currently competitive with gasoline on price or the ability to store energy, natural gas vehicles have been on the streets and highways for years and LNG can provide an alternative fuel for transportation.

Overlay: There is no world shortage of natural gas envisioned for the rest of this century. Its usage in the non-OECD countries is more dependent upon geopolitical considerations than resource shortage.

The world contains an abundant supply of natural gas that is and can continue to be developed and delivered at relatively low costs well into the next century. The biggest problem is that the sources of natural gas and the users are not always conveniently colocated.

Overlay: Natural gas usage worldwide is estimated by the EIA to remain approximately constant in the next decades even as it is under pressure to replace coal and meet other needs. However, as price drops, usage will increase in the United States.

The North American market for natural gas is the most mature in the world and has an effective infrastructure. Natural gas is able to be moved from the source—whether the gas reservoirs are in the west or Texas—to the markets in the east and north. At present, the United States has the flexibility to acquire gas entirely within the continental United States or import via LNG tanker depending on the relative economics. Since 2000 the United States has expanded its rated LNG capacity to approximately 35% of the average daily requirement. This occurred due to the concern over diminishing domestic supplies and the necessity to have reliable sources of energy. However, during the same time period, as discussed previously, the technology of accessing the shale gas evolved rapidly, which significantly altered the U.S. supply picture. The LNG import capacity is largely unused at present as we have returned to a period of supply surplus similar to what existed in the early 1990s.

> **Overlay:** Basically the United States is self-sufficient and secure regarding its natural gas supply. Unlike oil, it does not have to depend on supplies from other parts of the world. It has at least a 75-year supply at present usage rates and prices. Supply is a low-risk area.

A key factor of all fossil fuels is the amount still remaining in the ground. For gas, that is exceptionally difficult to determine since there has not been the extensive exploration for gas as has existed for oil. Globally, there are abundant supplies of natural gas, much of which can be developed at relatively low cost. The current mean projection of remaining recoverable resource is 16,200 trillion cubic feet (Tcf), 150 times the current annual global gas consumption according to an MIT study.[*]

Weaknesses

There are three significant weaknesses to the use of natural gas in the coming decades. One is that it is a fossil fuel and burning it has a negative environmental effect due to both the amount of unburned methane that escapes and the carbon that is emitted. While much less than coal or oil, it is still significant.

The second weakness is the potential negative environmental impact of the fracking process used to free the unconventional gas from the shale deposits. This arises from the potential to contaminate aquifers and the adequacy of the disposition of the *produced water*, which is the residue from the fracking process. There has also been a lack of transparency in the gas drilling industry regarding the chemical composition of the materials injected with the water, which has caused a large negative reaction in persons perceived to have been adversely affected.

---

[*] *The Future of Natural Gas: An Interdisciplinary MIT Study*, http://web.mit.edu/mitei/research/studies/natural-gas-2011.shtml, xii.

The third weakness is the entrenched coal interests that have the ability to stop any carbon regulation legislation and thereby keep coal the economic fuel of choice for power plants. Without a price on carbon or legislation that controls emissions, it is difficult for natural gas to replace coal in all but selected existing installations in the United States in the near future.

Overlay: Hydraulic fracturing, *fracking*, promises to eliminate United States dependence upon foreign natural gas sources. Large areas of shale deposits exist; however, planners need to be aware that problems with the fracking process itself and minimal regulation have resulted in strong local resistance. The lack of regulation has resulted in serious environmental problems in some areas and very bad publicity affecting public support. Proposed regulation will probably result in some increased costs and reduction in supply but, since the product is needed, the environmental problems will be resolved.

The process known as hydraulic fracturing is used by gas producers to stimulate wells and recover natural gas from sources such as coal beds and shale gas formations. It is also used for other applications, including oil recovery, and is being used to develop geothermal wells. Over the past few years, several key technical, economic, and energy policy developments have resulted in increased use of hydraulic fracturing for gas extraction from shale formations. However, the problem is the extraction process itself.

There are four primary environmental concerns:

1. Freshwater aquifer contamination by fracture fluids
2. Surface water contamination from process fluids, the produced water
3. Depletion of local water supply
4. Surface and local community disturbance

The process involves digging a well into the shale and subsequently pumping water and other chemicals into the shale under high pressure. This hydraulic fracturing releases the natural gas, which is then brought to the surface. The shale formations range approximately from 4,000 to 10,000 feet under the surface of the land and the freshwater aquifer depths range from 1,000 to 400 feet. Therefore, there is theoretically substantial vertical separation between the freshwater aquifers and the fracture zones created in the fracking process. The aquifers are protected from injected fracture fluids by a number of layers of casing and cement in the well. Unfortunately, a compromised casing in the system can potentially result in contamination of the freshwater aquifer.

The disposal of produced water is not a major difficulty in areas such as Texas, where the industry safely disposes of large volumes of produced water annually without difficulty and the communities are accustomed to living with this byproduct. In the Marcellus shale areas of the northeast, there is a much greater challenge in accommodating these fluids in populated areas composed of persons not comfortable with water–chemical mixes in their neighborhoods, especially when the disposal is into existing streambeds.

Every shale gas well that is developed by fracking requires between 1 and 8 million gallons of water.[*] These must either be trucked in or piped from the aquifer or a nearby stream. Put into context, this is comparable to the water drawn annually for the entire service area from the aquifer where I live in rural Virginia. And this is for the fracking of one well.

> My daughter was hiking in Pennsylvania in early 2011 and the streams she was used to relying on for fresh water (using purification tablets) were dry. When she asked about it she found out the reason was the water had been taken for fracking. It was another commons, per Chapter 4.

Finally, there is the issue of surface and local community disturbance, which includes the noise and dust from the many vehicles, the land disturbances during the drilling process, and the micro-earthquakes that are produced as part of the fracking process. The adverse actions should be mitigated by enforcement of state and local laws and regulations, but resources for enforcement are sometimes lacking. A *Vanity Fair* article in 2010 described the problems that can occur when best practices are not followed and regulations are not enforced.[†] It depicted the entire process as a local catastrophe. Federal law protects the drilling companies from any liability. In the Energy Policy Act of 2005, the fracking process was explicitly exempted from federal regulation, as it was also by the Safe Drinking Water Act of 1974, the Clean Water Act, and the Clean Air Act.[‡]

---

[*] Christopher Bateman, "A Colossal Fracking Mess," *Vanity Fair*, June 21, 2010, 5, http://www.vanity-fair.com/business/features/2010/06/fracking-in-pennsylvania-201006 (accessed June 22, 2010).

[†] Bateman, "A Colossal Fracking Mess," 5.

[‡] Bateman, "A Colossal Fracking Mess," 8.

Concern has been expressed in New York State that fracking may contaminate the aquifer that provides fresh drinking water for New York City. The EPA is in the process of performing a study of hydraulic fracturing and initial study results are to be available in late 2012.[*]

Opportunities

There is increasing pressure on the electric power industry to reduce carbon emissions. This will come in the form of regulatory measures to reduce emissions, which will encourage phase-out of existing coal-fired plants and increase the costs of coal plants by indirectly putting a price on carbon. The large amount of existing reserves of natural gas makes it an important, lower-carbon emission alternative to coal in electricity generation. It is likely that pressure will be reduced on the natural gas industry to reduce CO_2 emissions as the world realizes that it is needed to provide base-load power and complement the wind and solar industries rather than be replaced by them.

To the extent that CCS technologies are developed, natural gas will benefit further since carbon storage would extend the life of natural gas as an energy source in a reduced carbon emissions world.

Natural gas has had an impact on its competitors in the wind energy market. The dropping prices of natural gas combined with the large available reserves have resulted in a slowdown of production of wind turbines. Natural gas has become an environmentally friendly competitor to wind power with its lower costs.[†]

Clathrates: Methane Hydrate[‡]

Overlay: The technical and economic mining of clathrates to release methane is years away however, it is potentially an important energy source that needs R&D effort.

Methane hydrate is a cage-like lattice of ice inside which are trapped molecules of methane, the chief constituent of natural gas. These are

[*] Per EPA Hydraulic Fracturing web page at http://water.epa.gov/type/groundwater/uic/class2/hydraulicfracturing/index.cfm (accessed March 18, 2011).
[†] Dan Piller, "Natural Gas Takes Breeze from Wind Energy's Sails," *Des Moines Register*, May 27, 2010, http://mvwind.10.forumer.com/viewtopic.php?t=2304. (Accessed March 1, 2012).
[‡] Introductory material on methane hydrate derived from U.S. Department of Energy web site, http://fossil.energy.gov/programs/oilgas/hydrates/ (accessed September 28, 2010).

sometimes called *clathrates*. If methane hydrate is either warmed or depressurized, it will revert back to water and natural gas. Hydrate deposits may be several hundred meters thick and generally occur in two types of settings: under Arctic permafrost and beneath the ocean floor. Methane that forms hydrate can be both biogenic, created by biological activity in sediments, and thermogenic, created by geological processes deeper within the Earth. When brought to the Earth's surface, 1 cubic meter of clathrates releases 164 cubic meters of natural gas.

While global estimates vary considerably, the energy content of methane occurring in hydrate form is immense, possibly exceeding the combined energy content of all other known fossil fuels. However, future production volumes are speculative because methane production from hydrate has not been documented beyond small-scale field experiments. Clathrates are very unstable when brought to the surface, and the technology to handle clathrates is unproven. Because of their imported energy dependence, Japan has an active program to develop processes to use the clathrates to provide usable energy in their region of the world.

The U.S. R&D program is focused on the two major technical constraints to production: (1) the need to detect and quantify methane hydrate deposits prior to drilling, and (2) the demonstration of methane production from hydrate at commercial volumes.

In recent field tests, researchers have demonstrated the capability to predict the location and concentration of methane hydrate deposits using reprocessed conventional 3-D seismic data, and new techniques, including multicomponent seismic techniques, are being tested. Modeling of small-volume production tests in the United States and Canadian Arctic suggest that commercial production is possible using depressurization and thermal stimulation from conventional wellbores. Large-scale production tests are planned in these areas, but the dates are uncertain due to funding difficulties.

Demonstration of production from U.S. offshore deposits will lag behind Arctic studies by several years, because marine deposits are less well documented and marine sampling and well tests are significantly more expensive.

The development of new, cost-effective resources such as methane hydrate can play a major role in moderating price increases and ensuring adequate future supplies of natural gas for American consumers.

A committee from the National Academy of Sciences declared the following in 2010:*

> Research on methane hydrate to date has not revealed technical challenges that the committee believes are insurmountable in the goal to achieve commercial production of methane from methane hydrate in an economically and environmentally feasible manner.

Combined Cycle Gas Turbine Technology

Overlay: Combined cycle gas turbine technology (CCGT) is rapidly replacing coal power systems as a source of base-load electricity as the pressure increases to reduce emissions and as natural gas prices drop. CCGT plants can be built faster and are less expensive than coal power plants.

Current technology is enabling an increasing use by utilities of natural gas to generate electricity instead of coal in new installations. Gas turbines, similar to aircraft jet engines, use the natural gas as fuel to generate electricity directly, rather than using the heat to make steam, as in coal plants. Combined cycle gas turbines are the current most efficient designs and are two turbines connected together—one is a gas turbine and the second is a steam turbine. The hot gas exhausted by the jet engine turbine is used to boil water and produce steam, which then drives a steam turbine to generate more electricity. CCGT can be over 50% efficient at converting gas into electricity, compared to about 33% for single steam turbines. Because the same heat source is used by the gas turbine generator and the steam generator, their efficiencies are additive. A typical combination set has a gas turbine generating 400 megawatts (MW) and the steam turbine generating 200 MW for a total of 600 MW. Typical installations use two to six sets as the power plant.

Threats

There are two categories of threats the natural gas industry faces: threats to supply and threats to demand. Supply threats come primarily from

---

* National Academy of Sciences, *Realizing the Energy Potential of Methane Hydrate for the United States,* http://www.nap.edu/catalog/12831.html, 2010, Summary, p. 6.

the fact that it is a fossil fuel and a finite quantity of natural gas is available in the ground; and in the exploration and development of shale gas where the environmental damage may cause strong local opposition and restrictive legislation.

The demand threat comes primarily from the potential development and implementation of low-cost CO_2-free nuclear power generation. While not expected to come on line in major quantities in the next 10–20 years, the carbon-free nuclear alternative appears to be the primary competitor as development continues on small nuclear reactors. Wind and solar will contribute to the energy mix with increasing market penetration as their technologies mature, but at present the threat is small and the preferred backup system to renewables is gas-fired CCGT units.

A sample risk matrix for the natural gas industry is presented in Table 17.1.

TABLE 17.1

Natural Gas Industry Risk Matrix

No.	Risk Event	P1	P2	Px
1	Environmental problems will slow shale gas extraction process and thereby reduce production rate.	4	2	8
2	Environmental concerns about CO_2 will result in legislation that will increase costs of natural gas significantly.	2	2	4
3	Nuclear power will replace significant amounts of natural gas in the electricity market as concerns about carbon emissions and oil supplies increase.	1	2	2
4	Wind and solar power will replace natural gas in electricity market in significant quantity as storage problems are resolved.	2	2	4

Note: P1 = likelihood of risk event occurring; P2 = probable impact on the industry if P1 occurred; Px = product of P1 and P2 to assign ranking.

Overlay: The bottom line is that the United States has a secure supply of natural gas that will last well into the next century as long as the extraction from shale can be performed in an environmentally sound basis. Natural gas is a realistic bridging source of energy as the world shifts away from coal and moves to less carbon-intensive sources such as nuclear and renewables.

18

Nuclear Energy

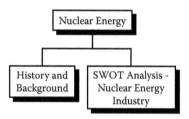

Chapter 18 outline.

I don't know the key to success, but the key to failure is to try to please everyone.

—Bill Cosby

HISTORY AND BACKGROUND

The history of nuclear energy starts with the discovery of uranium in 1789 by Martin Klaproth, a German chemist, who named it after the planet Uranus.* The science and technology of understanding and controlling radiation and nuclear fission were developed between 1895 and 1945, with most of it after 1939 focusing on the development of the atomic bomb. Subsequent to the bomb, the focus has been on harnessing and controlling this energy for naval propulsion and for making electricity. Since 1956 the prime focus has been on the technological evolution of reliable nuclear power plants.

From the late 1970s to about 2002, the nuclear power industry suffered general decline and stagnation in new development and innovative technology. Few new reactors were ordered; the number coming on line from

---

* Excerpted from "Outline History of Nuclear Energy," World Nuclear Organization, http://www. World-nuclear.org/info/inf54.html.

the mid-1980s little more than matched retirements, though capacity increased by nearly one third and output increased 60%. The share of nuclear energy in world electricity from the mid-1980s was fairly constant at 16–17%. By the late 1990s the first of the third-generation reactors was commissioned. This was a sign of the recovery to come.

Nuclear power plants are essentially base-load electric generators, running continuously. Individual plant power output cannot readily be ramped up and down on a daily and weekly basis, although some have control systems that do just that. In this respect they are similar to most coal-fired plants. (It is also uneconomic to run them at less than full capacity, since they are expensive to build but cheap to run.)

The next text box contains a summary list of the current types of nuclear power generators. The advantages and disadvantages of the specific technologies as well as more technical details are beyond the scope of this book. It is important to note there are many different technologies and different countries favor different technologies.

The United States is the leading producer of electric power from nuclear power plants, with 31% of the world total. France is second and produces 16% and Japan is third with 10%. The United States has the most installed capacity with 104 reactors and France and Japan follow with 63 and 49 reactors, respectively. However, France leads in the percentage of total domestic electricity generation with 78% and the Ukraine is second with 47%. The United States is in seventh place in dependence on nuclear power with approximately 20% of total electricity from nuclear.[*]

In 2007, the International Atomic Energy Agency (IAEA) reported there were 439 nuclear power reactors in operation in the world, operating in 31 countries. As of December 2010, the world had 441 reactors. Since commercial nuclear energy began in the mid-1950s, 2008 was the first year that no new nuclear power plant was connected to the grid, although two were connected in 2009.[†]

In the United States there are proposals for over 20 new reactors and the first 17 combined construction and operating licenses for these have been applied for. All are for late third-generation plants, and a further proposal is for two ABWR units. It is expected that 4 to 8 new reactors will be on line by 2020, a modest increase from the current 104 power plants.

---

[*] International Energy Agency, *Key World Energy Statistics 2009*, Paris, France, 17.
[†] International Energy Agency, Annual Reports, 2007 and 2010. Overview page 1. www.ieae.org. (Accessed March 1, 2012.)

SWOT ANALYSIS: NUCLEAR ENERGY

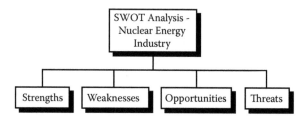

SWOT analysis section outline.

> **Overlay:** Nuclear energy is expected to be a significant component of the world's energy planning. R&D should continue to improve operating efficiency, plant producibility, and safety mechanisms. Offsite disposition of spent fuel needs to be actively pursued. Public concerns and fears about nuclear energy need to be addressed and resolved.

The objective of the strengths, weaknesses, opportunities, and threats (SWOT) analysis is to assess the viability of nuclear energy as a long-term power source.

Strengths

The performance of the 104 U.S. nuclear plants since 2003 has been reported to be excellent. The amount of electricity produced by the reactors has steadily increased and the fleet-averaged capacity factor has been maintained at about 90%.[*]

The primary strength of nuclear power is its ability to provide carbon-free base-load power with the emphasis on *carbon-free*. It also has been very reliable. Once the facility is up and running, the operating costs are very low.

In China and India in particular, nuclear power is important so that they utilize a carbon-free source of base-load electric power that can replace coal and at the same time meet the requirements of a growing population.[†]

When the cost of carbon emissions is taken into account, nuclear power has an advantage over its competitors natural gas and coal.

---

[*] John M. Deutch et al., *Update of the 2003 Future of Nuclear Power Study* (Cambridge MA, MIT Press 2009), 4.

[†] Hansen, *Storms of My Grandchildren,* 194, says nuclear will be their choice.

NUCLEAR REACTORS: CURRENT TECHNOLOGIES

Pressurized water reactors (PWR): These reactors use a pressure vessel to contain the nuclear fuel, control rods, moderator, and coolant. They are cooled and moderated by high-pressure liquid water. The hot radioactive water that leaves the pressure vessel is looped through a steam generator, which in turn heats a secondary (nonradioactive) loop of water to create steam that can run turbines. They are the majority of current reactors, and are generally considered the safest and most reliable technology currently in large-scale deployment.

Boiling water reactors (BWR): These reactors are like a PWR without the steam generator. A boiling water reactor is cooled and moderated by water like a PWR, but at a lower pressure, which allows the water to boil inside the pressure vessel, producing the steam that runs the turbines.

Pressurized heavy water reactors (PHWR): These reactors are heavy water cooled and moderated pressurized water reactors. Instead of using a single large pressure vessel as in a PWR, the fuel is contained in hundreds of pressure tubes.

Reaktor Bolshoy Moschnosti Kanalniy (high-power channel reactor) (RBMK): This reactor is a Soviet design, built to produce plutonium as well as power. RBMKs are water cooled with a graphite moderator; they are very unstable and large, making containment buildings for them expensive.

Gas-cooled reactors (GCR) and advanced gas-cooled reactor (AGR): These reactors are generally graphite moderated and CO_2 cooled. They can have a high thermal efficiency compared with PWRs due to higher operating temperatures.

Liquid metal fast breeder reactors (LMFBR): This reactor is cooled by liquid metal, totally unmoderated, and produces more fuel than it consumes. They are said to "breed" fuel, because they produce fissionable fuel during operation because of neutron capture. These reactors come in two types:

Lead cooled: Using lead as the liquid metal provides excellent radiation shielding, and allows for operation at very high temperatures.

Sodium cooled: Most LMFBRs are of this type. The sodium is relatively easy to obtain and work with, and it also manages to actually prevent corrosion on the various reactor parts immersed in it.

Pebble bed reactors (PBR): These reactors use fuel molded inside ceramic balls, and then circulate gas through the balls. The result is an efficient, low-maintenance, very safe reactor with inexpensive, standardized fuel.

Molten salt reactors: These reactors dissolve the fuels in fluoride salts, or use fluoride salts for coolant. These have many safety features, high efficiency, and a high power density suitable for vehicles.

Aqueous homogeneous reactors (AHR): These reactors use soluble nuclear salts dissolved in water and mixed with a coolant and a neutron moderator.

FUTURE AND DEVELOPING TECHNOLOGIES

Advanced reactors: More than a dozen advanced reactor designs are in various stages of development. Some are evolutionary from the PWR, BWR, and PHWR designs above; some are more radical departures.

Generation IV reactors: Generation IV reactors are a set of theoretical nuclear reactor designs currently in the research and development phase. These designs are generally not expected to be available for commercial construction before 2030. Current reactors in operation around the world are generally considered second- or third-generation systems, with the first-generation systems having been retired some time ago.

Fusion reactors: Controlled nuclear fusion could, in principle, be used in fusion power plants to produce power, but significant scientific and technical obstacles remain. Several fusion reactors have been built, but as yet none has developed more thermal energy than the electrical energy consumed. Despite research having started in the 1950s, no commercial fusion reactor is in sight.

Overlay: While the problems of the Fukushima plant in Japan have slowed the implementation of new nuclear power plants in some countries, there should only be a limited overall delay and these are for security reviews. The recent earthquake in Virginia has also caused a review of design criteria and safety systems and procedures. There will continue to be a strong market to replace coal and to meet growing demand for electricity.

The nuclear power industry has had limited growth in recent years. However, in the United States and throughout Europe, investment in research and in the nuclear fuel cycle has continued. The demand for nuclear power plants is logically expected to increase due to a combination of predicted electricity shortages, fossil fuel price increases, and emissions controls on fossil fuel use. New and improved technology, such as passively safe plants, and national energy security concerns will be the drivers.

According to the World Nuclear Association, globally during the 1980s one new nuclear reactor started up every 17 days on average, and by the year 2015 this rate could increase to one every 5 days if nontechnical barriers are removed or lowered. In this new century, several factors have combined to revive the prospects for nuclear power. First is realization of the scale of projected increased electricity demand worldwide, and particularly in rapidly developing countries. This is apparent from the forecast increase in population, as described in Chapter 3. Second is awareness of the importance of energy security to a country to have a long-term reliable supply, and third is the need to limit carbon emissions due to concern about climate change.

Weaknesses

There are four major weaknesses to the use of nuclear power. The first is public concern over safety—the perception that it is unsafe due to the existence of radioactive materials that might escape as at Chernobyl or Fukushima. Even though there were no significant releases from Three Mile Island, the likelihood of a similar event has people concerned and the recent problem in Japan reinforced the concern. This is an important consideration because even if the United States and other governments favor it, there is an extremely strong "not in my back yard" (NIMBY) effect when specific locations are being considered for new sites. Very strong local opposition may make it very difficult to significantly increase the number of nuclear plants in Western nations, or at least it will slow down the permitting and construction processes significantly.

Overlay: Security and potential vulnerability to various threats should not be a reason to exclude nuclear plants from the mix of energy options. Design criteria for new nuclear power plants are very stringent and thorough in this area.

The physical security of nuclear power plants and their vulnerability to deliberate acts of terrorism was elevated to a national security concern following the attacks of September 11, 2001. Since the attacks, Congress has repeatedly focused oversight and legislative attention on nuclear power plant security requirements established and enforced by the Nuclear Regulatory Commission (NRC).

Nuclear power plant vulnerability to deliberate aircraft crashes has been a continuing issue. After much consideration, the NRC published final rules on June 12, 2009, to require all *new* nuclear power plants to incorporate two major design features to reduce vulnerability. In the event of a crash by a large commercial aircraft the following would occur:

- First, the reactor core would remain cooled or the reactor containment would remain intact.
- Second, radioactive releases would not occur from encroachments into spent fuel storage pools.

The NRC has issued a specification for nuclear plant security design that is called the design basis threat (DBT), or the basic criteria that are to be used in the design of the plant. The DBT document describes general characteristics of adversaries that nuclear plants and nuclear fuel cycle facilities must defend against to prevent radiological sabotage and theft of strategic special nuclear material. Design engineers are used to using design and performance specifications as the basis for their designs and this document is simply an extension of the normal design documents to include consideration of terrorist threats. This document goes beyond normal engineering design criteria in that NRC licensees also use the DBT specification as the basis for implementing defensive strategies at specific nuclear plant sites through security plans, safeguards contingency plans, and guard training and qualification plans.

Nuclear power critics have called for retrofits of existing reactors as well, but it has been argued that this is a very expensive solution to a problem that may not exist. Existing reactors are protected by several feet of concrete just to contain radiation and they are in relatively small, low-profile facilities. The large cone-shaped structures are cooling towers and there is no benefit to terrorists to crash into them other than publicity since they are not part of the nuclear material cycle.

Nuclear plant security measures are designed to protect three primary areas of vulnerability: (1) controls on the nuclear chain reaction, (2) the cooling systems that prevent hot nuclear fuel from melting even after the chain reaction has stopped, and (3) storage facilities for highly radioactive spent nuclear fuel. These spent fuel pools hold highly radioactive nuclear fuel after its removal from the reactor and as a result are an attractive target since they are not normally as well protected physically.

Long-term management of spent nuclear fuel is a current unresolved security problem, but spent fuel stored at reactor sites is expected to be moved eventually to central storage, permanent disposal, or reprocessing facilities.* Large-scale transportation campaigns would increase public attention to NRC transportation security requirements and related security issues. The author spent some time working in the hazardous material transportation office of the Department of Transportation (DOT) and was amazed at the level of fear the media was able to arouse in the public over the transportation of hazardous materials. There is a significant innate or preternatural fear of nuclear radiation that is easily aroused.

The problems that Japan had with its reactor and the earthquake/tsunami incident will undoubtedly cause a review of the DBT to determine if the earthquake criteria are sufficiently stringent, including on the east coast. Recently it was shown that the seismic design criteria for east coast installations needs to be reviewed after the magnitude of the earthquake in Virginia exceeded expectations. And, for those power plants located near the coast where there is seismic activity, the risk of a tsunami needs to be evaluated as well to assure the DBT sufficiently addresses the issue. Recently it was shown that the design criteria for east coast installations needs to be reviewed after the earthquake in Virginia in 2011 was analyzed

---

* For details, see CRS Report RL33461, *Civilian Nuclear Waste Disposal*, by Mark Holt.

and shown to be equal to or slightly stronger than the seismic activity for which the nearest reactor was designed.

The second weakness is the problem of waste disposal; some persons would put this in first place. In the long term this is a major problem since no permanent storage sites have as yet gone operational. A waste disposal scheme is essential and urgent.

> **Overlay:** The need remains for a broad program that creates an understanding of the range of waste management options that is coupled with current technological advances, and provides a basis for robust long-term waste management policies. This is a central objective of an ongoing MIT nuclear fuel cycle study.* Current reactor technology and fuel cycle approaches all require the geological disposal of some radioactive waste.
>
> ---
> * Deutch et al. *Update of the 2003 Future of Nuclear Power Study,* 11.

The major problem of nuclear waste is simply what to do with it.* The biggest problem and potentially the single biggest expense of the nuclear power industry could eventually be the storage of nuclear waste. Currently there are several ways in which nuclear waste is stored. The four current approaches are as follows:

1. Store in on-site pools outside the containment area
2. Store in casks; 16-foot airtight steel canisters surrounded by concrete
3. Reprocess
4. Bury in transportable casks in dry, stable geological formations

Each of these methods has pros and cons. The spent fuel rods from a nuclear reactor are the most radioactive of all nuclear wastes and comprise 99% of all the radiation from nuclear waste. Fortunately, they have small volume, and therefore require relatively little storage area. There is, as of now, no permanent storage site for spent fuel rods in the United States. Temporary storage at the existing nuclear facilities is being used while a permanent site is searched for and prepared.

---
* See Oracle Education Foundation, http://library.thinkquest.org/17940/texts/nuclear_waste_storage/nuclear_waste_storage.html (accessed October 7, 2010).

When the spent fuel rods are removed from the reactor core, they are extremely hot and must be cooled down. Most nuclear power plants have a temporary storage pool next to the reactor that is filled with boric acid, which also helps to absorb some of the radiation given off by the radioactive nuclei inside the spent rods. The spent fuel rods are supposed to stay in the pool for only about 6 months, but because there is no permanent storage site, they often stay there for years. Many power plants have had to enlarge their pools to make room for more rods. Permanent disposal of the spent fuel is becoming more important as the pools become more and more crowded, which increases the risk of an accident. The second method is used after the waste has already spent about 5 years cooling in a pool. The casks are also usually located close to the reactor site.

The third problem is nuclear material proliferation concerns. There are several governments that would like to be able to join the nuclear club and the belief is that the more common is the existence of nuclear power facilities, the easier it will become to acquire or develop the military technology. This is especially the concern with the fast breeder reactor technology due to its ability to generate more fissionable materials. The United Nations is developing a program of establishing a common pool of nuclear power rods so industrial countries would not need to produce their own rods to support their nuclear power facilities.

Another weakness is the dependence upon the availability of uranium. There is no world uranium shortage; however, it is not always available where and when needed. Large amounts of uranium are required each year. Two major new Canadian uranium mine projects are coming into production in the next few years, and Australian, Namibian, and Kazakh mines are all expanding their operations. The United States is expected to follow suit.

Recent developments and forecast demand for uranium have increased the market price for the commodity to levels that make new mining ventures attractive. This has little effect on production costs for nuclear energy, but it has led to a renewed interest in uranium deposits that were not profitable to mine at price levels before 2003.

The fourth weakness is the high initial capital cost and related construction project management risks. This includes the very high initial capital cost and the worldwide history of massive cost overruns and schedule slippages. Related to this is the exceptionally long lead time from the initial application until construction is complete. No matter how good the program management is, if there are delays caused by external forces, there will be overruns. Especially difficult is the permitting process—to get all the necessary permits to build and operate the facility. This results in projects that are 10–20 years long. It is difficult to get investors interested with the large permitting risks and potential for delays that exist even prior to initial operation. It is obvious that if it is to take 10+ years before any revenue is generated to start to amortize the investment, it is difficult to get private sector investors interested.

There is also a local regulatory system weakness that sometimes impacts the ability to choose nuclear plants as the energy source of choice. The initial capital costs are very high for a nuclear power plant and the operating costs are relatively low. For competitive plants such as coal and gas turbines, the reverse is true. Some state regulatory agency policies may protect or hinder nuclear power plants depending on the rules for amortizing capital expenses and allowing invoicing of customers.

There is also sometimes a problem with "thermal pollution" where the cooling water drawn from a local water supply is returned at a much higher temperature and disturbs the local ecology.

Opportunities

There are three factors that drive the movement to building new nuclear facilities and all create opportunities for nuclear energy proponents or enterprise managers interested in this market.

Nuclear power provides stable, safe, and reliable base-load power. This will be needed to phase out fossil fuels or to take over as fossil fuels are exhausted or the seriousness of carbon emissions becomes a major concern.

The second is the lack of carbon emissions. This will become increasingly important as the world and the United States start to realize the magnitude of the warming problem. The construction lead times and the technology need serious improvement since it appears the demand will be there. As costs of fossil fuels increase and awareness that the various sources of renewable energy are insufficient, the overall economics of nuclear energy will continue to improve. The demand for base electricity will increase the demand for nuclear power plants.

As shown in Table 14.1, the price of advanced nuclear power plants on a total system basis is lower than coal with carbon capture and storage (CCS), lower than some natural gas power systems, and much lower than solar and offshore wind energy systems.

There are opportunities in the improvement of the technology to provide uranium *enrichment*. Efficient centrifuge technology is replacing the older energy-intensive diffusion technique and several plants are under construction in France and the United States. A new Australian process based on laser excitation is also under development by GE-Hitachi.

Many of the issues connected with nuclear power, such as safety issues, energy security, climate change, and nuclear nonproliferation, are global in dimension. Consequently, several initiatives have been taken to promote international cooperation in research and trade that provide opportunities.

A major difference from the boom in nuclear power during the 1960s and 1970s and the situation today is that major nuclear industry companies span several countries, giving much enhanced international collaboration. Also, countries with an established nuclear industry can, through formal international collaboration under IAEA auspices, assist developing countries to gain access to advanced technologies and fuel rods without the necessity of setting up their own uranium processing facilities. This helps to address energy needs without emissions of greenhouse gases.

Both France and Japan have set up joint government–industry schemes to enable the establishment of civil nuclear programs in countries wanting to develop them and will draw on all of those countries' expertise to assist.

The Generation IV International Forum (GIF) and the International Project on Innovative Nuclear Reactors and Fuel Cycles (INPRO) are two long-term research projects where leading scientists from a dozen countries join forces in the effort to develop future reactor designs.[*] The Forum looks at different types of reactors that will improve plant safety and economics and at the same time reduce proliferation risk. INPRO is focused more on assessment methodology for the needs of developing countries.

There are already examples of the globalization of the nuclear industry.

At the commercial level, by the end of 2006 three major Western–Japanese alliances had formed to dominate much of the world reactor supply market:

- Areva with Mitsubishi Heavy Industries
- General Electric with Hitachi
- Westinghouse had become a 77% subsidiary of Toshiba

Several of China's existing and planned reactors will use technology from Canada, Russia, France, and the United States, while China itself assists countries like Pakistan and Bangladesh to develop their nuclear power programs.

---

[*] From World Nuclear Association, http://www.world-nuclear.org/info/inf104.html.

Threats

The first external threat is the general public reaction to any nuclear facilities due to an emotional fear of the unknown, of potential radiation. This fear lurks always over the horizon and any safety problem that becomes public is a source of major concern and anxiety. NIMBY in the case of nuclear power is a real threat. The recent problem in Japan and the media response only exacerbate this concern.

The second threat is the inability to find suitable disposal sites for expended fuel rods and other nuclear wastes. This is used commonly as a basis for rejecting nuclear power as a viable source of clean energy. This makes the finding of a permanent solution of the disposal problem of utmost importance to the industry.

The third threat is the problem of financing of the initial capital cost. The initial estimated cost combined with a history of overruns makes the financing initial cost a high-risk item. Related is the inconsistency across states of regulatory rules regarding the ability to amortize the initial costs across the bill-paying public. Also, the lead time for construction (especially in the United States) and the permitting process are fraught with reasons for causing delays in approvals.

There is a possible impediment to production of new nuclear power plants as only a few companies worldwide have the capacity to forge single-piece reactor pressure vessels, which are necessary in most current reactor designs. Utilities across the world are submitting orders years in advance of any actual need for these vessels and this complicates construction planning. Manufacturers are examining various options, including making the component themselves, or finding ways to make a similar item using alternate methods. Other solutions include using designs that do not require single-piece forged pressure vessels.

A final threat is discussed in the MIT Update Report. While there is a lot of motivation to use nuclear power because of its ability to provide carbon-free base-load capacity, perceived negatives are even greater. These perceived negatives by the public are predicted by MIT to push nuclear power out of the picture as a timely and practical option for deployment on a scale that would contribute materially to any climate change risk mitigation program.[*]

Table 18.1 is a sample risk matrix for the nuclear power plant industry.

---

[*] Deutch, Update of the 2003 Future of Nuclear Power Study, 4.

TABLE 18.1

Nuclear Power Plant Risk Matrix

No.	Risk Event	P1	P2	Px
1	Inability to get suitable locations for new plants near the sources of demand	3	5	15
2	Long-term spent fuel disposal site away from plant site not available	3	3	9
3	Private financing not available due to construction overrun risk and delays in permitting	2	3	6
4	Government guarantees for loans not available	1	4	4
5	Lead times for critical components delay construction	3	2	6

Note: P1 = likelihood of risk event occurring; P2 = probable impact on the industry if P1 occurred; Px = Product of P1 and P2 to assign ranking.

Overlay: The bottom line appears to be that nuclear power is unlikely to increase its market share of the world's electric power generation over at least the next 25 years in the United States because of its long lead times for new plants and an ingrained fear of nuclear energy by the public. In time, concerns over carbon emissions and a lack of an alternative are expected to override concerns over nuclear energy. Most increases in the United States will be after 2035.

19

Renewable Energy Sources

A wise man will make more opportunities than he finds.

—Sir Francis Bacon

The diagram on page 258 presents the outline of this and the next six chapters. They all address various renewable energy sources.

INTRODUCTION

Renewable energy sources or simply *renewables* include solar and wind power, geothermal, biomass, and conventional hydroelectric power. Biomass in turn includes wood, wood waste, biogenic municipal waste, landfill gas, corn, sugar cane, switch grass, and other biomass. By definition, these represent resources that are relatively inexhaustible or are replaceable by new growth, with the caveat that hydropower is dependent on the availability of water.

> **Overlay:** Renewables are important energy sources, but each has its preferred application niche and limitations. At present they provide a limited percentage of the world's energy needs but are necessary to ultimately provide relatively CO_2-free energy for a growing population. Current growth in renewables is impressive but maintaining that growth rate is problematic.

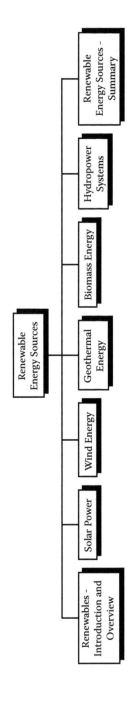

Outline for renewable energy chapters.

OVERVIEW

Renewable energy in total is currently a serious component of the global energy supply. Renewables comprise fully one quarter of global power capacity from all sources. They were responsible for 18% of global electricity supply in 2009.[*]

These are some highlights of the growth of renewable energy power capacity:[†]

- In recent years, investment in new renewable power capacity represented over half of total global investment in new power generation.
- Grid-connected solar photovoltaic (PV) has grown by an average of 60 percent *every year* for the past *decade*, increasing 100-fold since 2000.
- During the past 5 years, wind power capacity grew an average of 27 percent annually, solar hot water by 19 percent annually, and ethanol production by 20 percent annually.
- By early 2010 more than 100 countries had enacted some type of policy target and/or promotion policy establishing renewable energy standards (RES), most calling for shares of energy or electricity from renewables in the 15–25 percent range by 2020.
- Globally, there are an estimated 3 million direct jobs in renewable energy industries, about half of them in the biofuels industry.

The establishment of RES is especially important since this establishes a firm market for renewables so they do not have to compete on price. This is necessary because in most cases, renewables are not economically competitive with fossil fuels unless the cost of carbon emissions is taken into account. This was illustrated in Chapter 14, Table 14.1.

The International Energy Agency (IEA) projects global energy demand to increase by 53% over the period from 2005 to 2035.[‡] As that happens, use of modern renewable energy sources, excluding nuclear, will triple as their share of total primary energy demand increases from a current 8% to a forecast 14% as total demand increases as well.

---

[*] REN21. *Renewables 2010 Global Status Report* (Paris: REN21 Secretariat, 2010) Executive Summary, 9.

[†] REN21. *Renewables*, Executive Summary, 9.

[‡] EIA, International Energy Outlook 2011, Report Number DOE/EIA.0484 (2011) Sept. 19, 2011. Page 1 of *Highlights*. (Accessed March 1, 2012.)

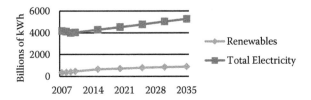

FIGURE 19.1

Total electricity generation. (From Energy Information Agency (EIA) Annual Energy Outlook 2010 Report, Table 8, "Electricity Supply, Disposition, Prices, and Emissions." www.eia.gov/oiaf/aeo

According to current government commitments and policies, the IEA projects that government intervention in support of renewables (electricity from renewables and biofuels) may result in an increase from $57 billion in 2009 to $205 billion (in 2009 dollars) by 2035 depending on the degree of government budget deficits and the Congressional response.

The driving force behind supporting renewables is the necessity to mitigate climate change by reducing CO_2 emissions, reducing dependence upon foreign energy sources, and to be in accordance with international agreements.

To keep temperatures from rising more than 3.6°F (2°C), which is the international target, as discussed in Part 2 of this book, the share of renewables among total energy use must reach close to 40% by 2035, a very ambitious goal. Governments need to end their subsidies on fossil fuels, and global demand for fossil fuels of coal, oil, and natural gas must plateau before 2020. Although meeting these goals currently seems impossible or impractical, governments are expected to continue to work toward them, creating opportunities for renewable energy sources.

Figure 19.1 shows the forecast of renewables as estimated by the Energy Information Administration (EIA). It is about half of what is needed to meet emissions goals. The figure illustrates the expected growth of renewable power supplies to approach between 15% and 20% of the total electricity generation by 2035. Renewables are expected to supply more than half of the increase of the total expected growth in energy demand.[*] The next six chapters discuss each of the renewables in turn.

Figure 19.2 puts the renewable usage in the United States in context. At present, renewables provide only 8% of our energy consumption. Within

---

[*] Energy Information Administration (EIA), Annual Energy Outlook 2010 with Projections, Executive Summary, 2.

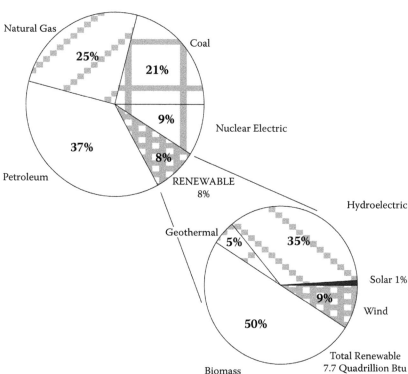

TOTAL U.S. 94.8 Quadrillion Btu

FIGURE 19.2

Energy consumption in the United States, 2009. (From U.S. Energy Information Administration, Office of Coal, Nuclear and Alternate Fuels, U.S. Department of Energy, Washington, DC, *Renewable Energy Consumption and Electricity, Preliminary Statistics 2009*, August 2010, 1, http://www.eia.gov/fuelrenewable.html.)

that, hydroelectric and biomass provide the bulk of the renewable energy. Items such as solar and wind receive a lot of support and publicity, but they only provide a small fraction of the total power needs of the United States.

The U.S. use of renewables is presented in Figure 19.3 along with the estimates of the EIA out to 2035. The major players are hydropower, biomass, and wind, as shown on the chart, with biomass projected to have the largest growth between today and 2035. Keep in mind that Figure 19.3 indicates that renewables are only 8% of the total energy consumption.

An important concept is *grid parity*. This is the price point where the cost of renewables matches the cost of electricity from the primary competitors of natural gas, coal, and nuclear.

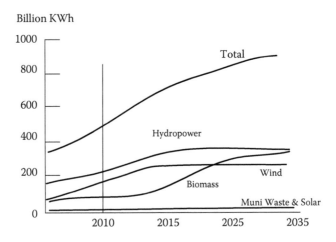

FIGURE 19.3
Renewables electricity generation. (Data from EIA Annual Energy Outlook 2010, December 2009. Reference case, Table 16 of Excel data file aeo2010r.d111809a. http://www.eia.gov/oaif/archive/ae010/aeoref_tab.html. Figure designed by author based on data in tables.)

From Table 14.1 (Chapter 14), it appears that legislated subsidization of most renewables is necessary until grid parity is reached. The competing fossil fuel energy sources have been heavily subsidized in various ways or have costs that are not reflected in the prices, such as environmental and health impacts.

20

Solar Power

Every hour, the Sun provides the Earth with as much energy as all of human civilization uses in an entire year.[*]

—Krump and Horn

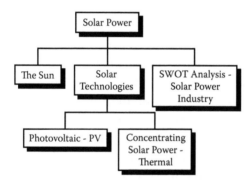

Chapter 20 outline.

Overlay: Even though solar power is currently a miniscule portion of the overall energy equation, it potentially could be significant in the future simply because of the immense amount of energy coming from the sun each day. It appears that R&D to pursue technologies to develop solar power systems is essential for the future. At present, the life-cycle costs of solar power are double most other forms of energy. There are currently two technologies that utilize solar power. A third technology, yet to be invented, is needed.

---

[*] Fred Krupp and Miriam Horn, *Earth: The Sequel* (New York: W.W. Norton & Company, 2008), 15.

In this section we will discuss the Sun and its energy, the two current leading technologies used to take advantage of the Sun's energy and will present the strengths, weaknesses, opportunities, and threats (SWOT) analyses.

THE SUN

Overlay: The sun provides a tremendous source of energy and we convert very little of it into the usable form of electricity or heat. We are not taking advantage of what we are being given.

The sun is the major source of energy for Earth's oceans, land, and biosphere. Life on Earth is supported by the sun, which produces an amazing amount of energy. Only a very small percentage of this energy strikes the Earth. The sun is a ball of fire 93 million miles away emitting energy in all directions. Part of this strikes our small 7,900-mile-diameter Earth. That is still enough to provide all our needs. A nearly constant 1,366 kilowatts per square meter (the solar constant) of solar radiant power impinges on the Earth's outer atmosphere. This is not exactly a constant; it varies by 0.0002 kilowatts per square meter over a typical 11-year cycle. This almost constant value translates to continuously providing 180 quadrillion watts of energy to the outer atmosphere of the Earth, 14,000 times our requirements for generating power to support the current world's needs.[*]

This is a tremendous amount of energy—44 quadrillion (4.4×10^{16}) watts of power. As a comparison, a large electric power plant produces about 1 billion (1×10^9) watts of power. It would take 44 million such power plants to equal the energy coming from the sun.[†]

The Earth receives a total amount of radiation determined simply by its cross section, as if you cut it in half like an orange, but as it rotates, this energy is distributed across the entire surface area. Hence the average

---

[*] Brian Palmer, "Solar Energy Offers a Vast Supply of Power but Harnessing It Is a Challenge," *Washington Post*, June 22, 2010, http://www.washingtonpost.com/wp-dyn/content/article/2010/06/ (accessed June 22, 2010).

[†] National Aeronautics and Space Agency, NASA Facts, *The Balance of Power in the Earth-Sun System*, Report FS-2005-9-074-GSFC, 1, http://eospso.gsfc.nasa.gov/ftp_docs/NASA-Facts-EnergyBalance.pdf/.

incoming solar radiation, taking into account the angle at which the rays strike and that at any one moment half the planet does not receive any solar radiation, is one-fourth the solar constant (approximately 342 W/m²) measured at the top of the atmosphere, approximately 60 miles above the surface of the Earth and averaged over the entire year. At any given moment, the amount of solar radiation received at a location on the Earth's surface depends on the state of the atmosphere and the location's latitude. The important scientific concept of radiative forcing is discussed in the sidebar.

Radiative forcing is a measure of how the energy balance of the Earth–atmosphere system is influenced when factors that affect climate are altered. The word *radiative* signifies that the factors affect the balance between incoming solar radiation and outgoing infrared radiation. Positive forcing tends to warm the surface while negative forcing tends to cool it. Forcing values are expressed in watts per square meter (W/m²).

When net radiative forcing is positive, the energy of the Earth–atmosphere system will ultimately increase, leading to a warming of the system as it moves toward equilibrium.

When in equilibrium, the net radiative forcing is zero. Examples of radiative forcing are the reflection of sunshine off the ice in the arctic, or the impact of aerosols or smog in the atmosphere or the impact of ozone or CO_2 in the atmosphere.

Of the 342 watts per square meter striking the Earth, 31% is reflected back to space and only 69% is absorbed (20% absorbed in the atmosphere and 49% on the surface), so this means 236 watts per square meter are absorbed by the Earth (obtained by multiplying 342 times 0.69).

The 236 watts per square meter absorbed by the Earth from the sun is an average over all locations of the Earth. This takes into account that during the night, there is no solar energy being absorbed. And during the day, the amount of solar power depends on the angle of incidence of the sunlight. For the point of the Earth in which the sun is directly overhead, the power absorbed can be as much as 1,000 watts per square meter. The fraction of sunlight energy absorbed (the 69% is only an average) varies a lot over the Earth at any given time depending on cloud cover, latitude, or angle of incidence of the sunlight, and the reflective properties of the surface.

On any given day, the solar radiation varies continuously from sunup to sundown and depends on cloud cover, sun position, and content and turbidity (haziness) of the atmosphere. The maximum irradiance is available at solar noon, which is defined as the midpoint, in time, between sunrise and sunset. Irradiance is the amount of solar power striking a given area and is a measure of the intensity of the sunshine. Photovoltaic engineers also use units of watts (or kilowatts) per square meter (W/m^2) for irradiance. Insolation (now commonly referred as irradiation) differs from irradiance because of the inclusion of time. Insolation is the amount of solar energy received on a given area over time measured in kilowatt-hours per square meter (kWh/m^2). Insolation varies seasonally because of the changing relation of the Earth to the sun. This change, both daily and annually, is the reason some solar energy systems use tracking arrays to keep the array pointed at the sun. For any location on Earth, the sun's elevation will change about 47 degrees from winter solstice to summer solstice.[*]

[*] U.S. Department of Energy, Solar Energy Technologies Program, "Solar FAQs: Photovoltaics—The Basics," http://diy-solar-green.com/articles/the-basics (accessed September 8, 2010).

SOLAR TECHNOLOGIES

Solar power is generated on Earth by the conversion of sunlight to electricity or heat. Sunlight can: be converted (1) directly using photovoltaics (PV) or (2) indirectly by concentrating solar power (CSP) in a form to focus the sun's energy on a receptor to provide a high heat, which is then used to provide power. Technologies using a modern steam engine are used to power an electric generator.

Overlay: At present there are two solar technologies—photovoltaic (PV) and concentrating solar thermal (CST). The CST technology has been proposed as having the ability to provide a significant portion of grid power.[*]

[*] Up to 60% of the grid power of Australia by 2020.

Neither one is a real breakthrough in using the power from the sun. What is needed is a new technology that can utilize a much greater share of the energy reaching the Earth from the sun, which is currently simply being redirected or reflected back into space. Until a breakthrough occurs harnessing the sun's radiation, there is no real alternative to fossil fuels and all the problems they entail.

Solar—Photovoltaic Systems

Overlay: Although the use of PV systems is expanding, most applications are off the grid. That means they only supply electricity to a local installation like a home or a Walmart or a water heater. They are not yet sufficiently efficient to be utilized as major power sources, although the technology is moving in that direction.

When semiconducting materials, such as certain kinds of silicon, are exposed to sunlight, they release small amounts of electricity—the photoelectric effect. This is the basic physical process in a solar electric or photovoltaic (PV) cell. Sunlight is made up of photons, or particles of solar energy. Photons contain various amounts of energy, corresponding to the different wavelengths of the solar spectrum. When photons strike a PV cell, they may be reflected or absorbed, or they may pass right through. Only the absorbed photons generate electricity. When this happens, the energy of the photon is transferred to an electron in an atom of the PV cell (which is actually a semiconductor).

With its additional energy, the electron escapes from its normal position in an atom of the semiconductor material and becomes part of the direct current in an electrical circuit. Special electrical properties of the PV cell—a built-in electric field—provide the pressure or voltage needed to drive the current through an external load (such as a light bulb).

A PV system is made up of different components. Typically these include PV modules (groups of PV cells), which are commonly assembled into PV panels, one or more batteries, a charge regulator or controller for a stand-alone system, an inverter for a utility grid-connected system when alternating current (AC) rather than direct current (DC) is required, wiring, and mounting hardware or a framework.

There is a smaller market for off-grid power for remote dwellings, boats, recreational vehicles, electric cars, roadside emergency telephones, remote sensing, yard lights, and cathodic protection of pipelines.

Although the selling price of modules is still too high to compete directly with grid electricity in most places, significant financial incentives in Japan and then Germany, Italy, and France triggered a huge growth in demand, followed quickly by production. As the PV technology improves, more specialty applications will evolve.

The grid-connected solar PV industry has recently seen price declines and rapidly changing economic conditions and changing technology as thin-film PV has increased market share. There are now several utility-scale plants providing electricity to the grid.[*]

As of 2010, solar photovoltaic units generate electricity in almost every country in the world, and while yet comprising a tiny fraction of the 4,800 GW total global power-generating capacity from all sources, it is the fastest growing power-generation technology in the world. Between 2004 and 2009, grid-connected PV capacity increased at an annual average rate of 60%, to some 21 GW. Off-grid PV accounts for an additional 3–4 GW. With PV prices dropping consistently by 22% each time the cumulated global production doubles, PV prices have dropped by 40% over the last 2 years and are expected to decrease up to 60% in 2020.

The three leading countries (Germany, Japan, and the United States) represent nearly 89% of the total worldwide PV installed capacity. Notably, the manufacture of solar cells and modules has expanded in recent years.

The German PV industry is reported to generate over 10,000 jobs in production, distribution, and installation.

Concentrating Solar Thermal (CST) Power Systems

Overlay: CST systems combined with molten salt as a storage source are the predominant solar technology and are used in most new systems. When renewable energy mandates exist and when the appropriate land area and amount of sunlight exists, this is the technology of choice.

---

[*] Overview contains data from REN21. *2010* in *Renewables Global Status Report* (Paris: REN21 Secretariat), 5. http://www.ren21.net/Portals/97documents/GSR/Ren21_GSR_2010_Full_revised%20Sept2010.pdf.

Concentrating solar thermal (CST) systems use lenses or mirrors and sun-tracking systems to focus a large area of sunlight into a small beam to provide a concentrated heat source. In all of these systems, a working fluid is heated by the concentrated sunlight, and then is used for power generation or energy storage. A typical working fluid may be water or molten salt. A wide range of concentrating technologies exists; the most developed are the parabolic trough, the concentrating linear Fresnel reflector, the Stirling engine dish, and the solar power tower. Various techniques are used to track the sun. In mid-2010, the world's first molten salt-based solar thermal power plant opened in Sicily; it provides 5 megawatts of power, enough for 5,000 homes.[*]

The system operates as follows:[†] mirrors called *heliostats* track the sun and focus sunlight onto a central "power tower." This energy is stored in molten salt as heat, warming the salt to 565°C. This energy storage has an efficiency of up to 93%. To produce electricity, the hot salt is pumped into a generator, where the heat is transferred to steam, which drives a turbine. Once the salt is cooled to 290°C (still warm enough to be molten), it returns to the tank to be reheated. The sun doesn't shine at night, but the advanced solar thermal plants have a store of energy ready to go at any time in the molten salt. CST can produce power around the clock. An Australian report describes it as "better-than-baseload" because it is more flexible. CST works well in combination with wind power, because the stored solar energy can be used when there is not enough wind.

The CST power approach is potentially a significant new power source, especially with large-scale installations in the U.S. southwest and Spain, with construction or planning under way for much more capacity in many more countries, including Australia. Please note that in Figures 19.3 and 19.4 of the previous chapter, the projections of market share are not encouraging for the near term.

Another small percentage of solar power goes to solar hot water collectors where China dominates the world market with some 70% of the existing global capacity. Europe is a distant second with 12%. Virtually all installations in China are for hot water only. But there is a trend in Europe toward larger "combi" systems that provide both water and space heating; such systems there now account for half of the annual market.

[*] Lemonick, Michael D. A Solar-power first, *Climate Central*. July 27, 2010. http://www.climate-central.org/blogs/a-solor-power-first. (Accessed March 2, 2012.)

[†] Adapted from "Zero Carbon Australia: We Can Do It," Skeptical Science, http://www.skepticalscience.com/Zero-Carbon-Australia-2020.html (accessed March 22, 2011).

The European Union is backing projects to turn the plentiful sunlight in the Sahara desert into electricity for Europe. The largest one is priced at $495 billion and is designed to help the European Union meet its target of deriving 20% of its energy from renewable sources in 2020.[*]

> **Overlay:** Worldwide the use of solar energy systems is growing rapidly, although it still has a very small proportion of the energy market.

The U.S. outlook on solar power is a mixed bag. At present the United States is the world's largest user of solar power, but because of the size of its population, it is well down the list as a percentage of the total electric power usage within a country. As shown in Figure 19.3, solar is only 1% of the total U.S. renewable energy and renewables are only 8% of the total energy usage. It is easy to see that 1% of 8% is not a very large number (0.08%).

It is expected that the falling costs of photovoltaics and solar heat systems will meet the rising costs of the competition within 10 years, and governmental requirements for a percentage of renewable power (RES) such as exists in Europe will provide a near-term market.

At present there are approximately 33 concentrating solar thermal power projects in the United States; most of these are in California, with others in Arizona, Colorado, Florida, Nevada, and Hawaii.[†]

SWOT ANALYSIS: SOLAR POWER

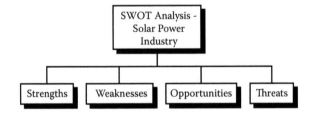

SWOT analysis section outline.

---

[*] The Joint Venture is Solartec.

[†] National Renewable Energy Laboratory List, http://www.nrel.gov/csp/solarpaces/by_country_detail.cfm/country=U.S.?print (accessed March 22, 2011).

Overlay: The primary energy source in the far future after fossil fuels are depleted will be some variation of solar power. At present two methods, photovoltaic and solar arrays, are the sole variants. These need to be pursued and installations made wherever feasible. Improvements in linkages to the grid to accommodate their periodicity are needed as well as improved energy storage systems. A breakthrough is needed to develop new systems to convert the energy of the sun to usable energy.

The objective of this SWOT analysis is to evaluate the status of the solar power industry.

Strengths

The amount of sunlight reaching the Earth's surface is plentiful—almost 6,000 times more than the 15 terawatts equivalent of power consumed by humans.

PV installations are emissions-free during operation and can operate for many years with little maintenance or intervention after their initial setup. After the initial capital cost of building any solar power installation, total operating and maintenance costs are low compared to most existing alternate electric power technologies.

Solar electric generation is economically superior where grid connection or fuel transport is difficult, costly, or impossible, such as on a satellite, on island communities, and remote locations.

When grid-connected, solar electric generation replaces some or all of the highest-cost electricity otherwise used during times of peak demand (in most climatic regions); the grid, in effect, is operating as a virtual reservoir. Conceptually, the fuels not used during sunshine hours when the solar system is operating (coal, gas, or hydro) are storage mechanisms for the solar energy after dark. The newer CST systems using molten salt storage can provide continuous power for the grid.

As stated at the beginning of this section, a new breakthrough solar power technology is needed to take advantage of the tremendous energy output of the sun. The PV and CST technologies continue to improve, and with technological improvements they can potentially provide a significant portion of the world's energy needs by the end of the century.

Weaknesses

There are five weaknesses of solar power systems:

- Siting restrictions
- Initial cost
- Dependence on the sun
- Access to market (primarily CSP)
- Surface area requirements

The location of solar power plants of current designs is an issue as more plants are built or planned. Locating a large solar power plant in a pristine location such as the Mohave Desert raises objections. More acceptable is use of farmland taken out of production due to salinization or lack of water, or other contaminated locations such as reclaimed landfills or surface coal mines. When located near residences, sometimes noise, such as that caused by hundreds of Sterling engines in a CSP field, is another issue. There are other esthetic concerns that include the overall visual impact on the state or region. Industrial-scale solar power is thought to "eat up precious farmland and be an eyesore for tourists."[*] An alternative is to have smaller distributed solar farms that serve communities, complemented by individually owned solar panels on roofs.

Solar electricity is seen to be expensive; the initial costs of CSP or PV are high and it takes many years to recover the investment without subsidization or other incentives. This is illustrated clearly in Table 14.1 in the column labeled "Levelized Capital Cost."

Photovoltaics are costly to install in a home situation. While the modules are often warranted for upward of 20 years, much of the investment in a home-mounted system may be lost if the homeowner moves and the buyer puts less value on the system than the seller. Of course the reverse can be true and a buyer may put a high value on a system that provides a reduced monthly electric bill. The initial cost becomes hidden in the property sale price. However, this is just one home, and what is needed is millions of homes and solar farms to make a significant impact. Also, PV cells produce *direct current* which must be converted to *alternating current* (using an inverter) when used in existing distribution grids. This incurs an energy loss of 4–12%.

---

[*] National Renewable Energy Laboratory List, 2.

Solar electricity is not produced at night and is much reduced in cloudy conditions. Therefore, a storage or complementary power system is required. Solar electricity production depends on the power density of the location's insolation (the rate of delivery of solar energy to the surface of the Earth). This varies with season and latitude. For example, Europe on average being at higher latitude than the United States receives less solar energy.

An obvious consideration in planning large solar power farms is the delivery mechanism to get the electricity to market. Large solar farms require high-voltage transmission lines to connect to the national grid. These new transmission lines often receive strong opposition from land owners, which delays or adds uncertainty to the project. The same problem is faced by wind farms. These higher costs are also reflected in Table 14.1 in the column labeled "Transmission Investment."

In 2010 in southern Colorado in Alamosa County a new 17-megawatt solar farm was under construction, but there was uncertainty about this and other projects since there were problems with local opposition to the proposed new high-voltage transmission line. The county has approved three large solar-power developments and had six applications pending.[*] Another 30-megawatt large-scale plant is proceeding, anticipating the transmission problems will be solved. These add to the investor risk.

Opportunities

There are many competing solar power technologies, including at least 14 types of photovoltaic cells, such as thin film, monocrystalline silicon, polycrystalline silicon, and amorphous cells, as well as multiple types of concentrating solar power. It is too early to know which technology or technologies will become dominant, including perhaps a new technology not yet developed.

Currently there is a wide range of solar panel efficiencies in different types of solar panels as measured by the energy conversion ratio.[†] The current market average is around 12–18% but others have claimed efficiencies of double this using special manufacturing technology. Laboratory work is continuing both by manufacturers and academia.

---

[*] Kirk Siegler (2010-06-23), San Luis Valley, CO (KUNC) "Regional/Uncertainty of Transmission Puts Solar in Limbo." http://www.publicbroadcasting.net/kunc/news.newsmain/article/1/0/1666373/ (accessed June 23, 2010).

[†] See Glossary.

Compared to fossil and nuclear energy sources, very little research money has been invested in development of solar cells, so there is potentially considerable room for improvement.

Solar power has four significant advantages. The first is rapidly improving technology in materials and in manufacturing processes, which are driving costs down. This is partly because of increased production in China, where the price of photovoltaic equipment has dropped sharply; but in addition, manufacturing techniques have improved and volumes have increased to meet growing demand. European companies are establishing large facilities in Singapore and Malaysia.

Second is the geographically localized nature of many applications on rooftops and in back yards, which allows for the use of net metering, a system that lets consumers feed excess energy back into the electricity grid. The nature of solar panels is that they do not have to transfer power to the grid. They can provide power directly to the user so they compete at the retail level.

Third is the creative payment approaches being used, such as a power purchase agreement where energy services companies install solar panels on the roofs of large factories or big-box retail stores such as Walmart and they own and operate the technology, selling electricity to the building owner at prices that are lower than those offered by the local utility. The building owner has no capital investment or maintenance costs and can lock in rates for a certain period of time. This also becomes a physical hedge against rising electricity prices.

Finally, the fourth is the recognition worldwide that government incentives or other form of government intervention are currently necessary for solar power to achieve net parity, or at least a competitive price, or to provide a guaranteed market. At present, discussion of grid parity relates to the retail level, not the wholesale level of pricing. The more mature markets for solar power tend to be found where subsidies have been most generous: in U.S. states such as California and countries such as Germany and Spain and parts of Japan. Table 14.1 clearly illustrates the cost situation.

But while experts and analysts acknowledge the importance of policy decisions on energy, most agree that solar power is likely to continue to increase its market share even if governments sometimes must reduce the subsidy due to cost considerations.[*]

---

[*] Sarah Murray, "Solar Power: Photovoltaic Panels Make Strides in the Drive for a Sunnier Future," *Financial Times*, September 12, 2010, 45, http://www.ft.com/cms/s/0/b47242b4-bc71-11df-a42b-00144feab49a.html (accessed September 13, 2010).

Research work is ongoing to use solar power for other purposes such as the conversion of CO_2 directly into fuels. This is exactly what photosynthetic organisms have been doing for billions of years, although their fuels tend to be foods, like sugars. Now humans are trying to store the energy from sunlight by making a liquid fuel from CO_2 and hydrogen—a prospect that could recycle CO_2 emissions and slow down the rapid buildup of such greenhouse gases in the atmosphere. The process consists basically of using an electrochemical cell that employs a semiconducting material used in photovoltaic solar cells for one of its electrodes, thereby succeeding in tapping sunlight to transform CO_2 into the basic fuel.[*]

As fossil fuel resources are replaced or we run out, we may be returning to prehistoric days where survival depended on the heat from the sun. But this looks like very long term—after mid-2100.

This author believes that technology will eventually learn how to take advantage of this input from the sun and be able to convert this energy to electricity many times more efficiently than today.

This is important because of the first sentence in this section on solar power: "Every hour, the sun provides the earth with as much energy as all of human civilization uses in an entire year."[†]

Threats

Long term, there are no real threats to the use of solar power, other than the relative cost of the technology. One way or another we are going to have to rely on solar power, directly or indirectly, for much of our energy needs as fossil fuels are phased out and the resources are depleted unless there is a significant breakthrough in nuclear power generation or some new energy source. In the near term—to 2050—the use of solar power is estimated to tend to level out at some low percentage of our electrical needs, limited by the hours and amount of sunshine and by technology.

At present the primary threat to development of solar power is the availability and low cost of coal and the worldwide economic slowdown, which limits funding for R&D in the United States. In addition, at present natural gas, nuclear energy, and oil are also much more economical than solar at the wholesale level for power generation. Only a small fraction of

---

[*] David Biello, "Reverse Combustion: Can CO_2 Be Turned Back into Fuel?" *Scientific American*, September 23, 2010, http://www.scientificamerican.com/article.cfm?id=turning-carbon-dioxide-back-into-fuel&sc=CAT_ENGYSU.S._20100923 (accessed September 25, 2010).

[†] Krupp and Horn, *Earth: The Sequel*, 15.

TABLE 20.1

PV Solar Power Risk Matrix: Typical Project

No.	Risk Event	P1	P2	Px
1	Availability of sufficient land	3	5	15
2	Access to the grid	2	5	4
3	Design phase delays due to technical problems	2	3	6
4	Cost overrun of implementation of construction phase of the project	2	2	4
5	Schedule delays due to permitting or legal challenges	3	2	6
6	Promised state subsidy is withdrawn	2	4	8

Note: P1 = likelihood of risk event occurring; P2 = probable impact on the program if P1 occurred; Px = product of P1 and P2 to assign ranking.

this nation and the world's energy needs are currently derived from solar power. It is simply a problem of economics. The high initial costs of solar systems, including the cost of efficient storage systems to operate when the sun is not available, currently appear to preclude widespread application without significant government subsidy. At present there are only two industry risks: will government subsidies continue and will the government continue Renewable Energy Standards at a level that would encourage solar energy system implementation?

If we assume we are going to implement a typical CST solar power project, the initial risk matrix could be as illustrated in Table 20.1.

21

Wind Energy

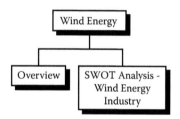

Chapter 21 outline.

In this chapter we provide a comprehensive overview followed by a strengths, weaknesses, opportunities, and threats (SWOT) analysis of the industry.

OVERVIEW

Overlay: Major trends in wind energy include new growth in off-shore development and the growing popularity of distributed, small-scale grid-connected turbines. The new wind projects are in a much wider variety of geographical locations around the world and within countries. Firms continue to increase average turbine sizes and improve technologies. Increasing, however, is local resistance to wind farms adjacent to residential areas or near offshore where the view is involved.

Coal, natural gas, and nuclear are all competitors of wind energy in the near term. The current economics of wind energy utilization requires some form of subsidy or guaranteed market. In the long term all types of energy sources will be needed to meet the expected increases in energy demand as the population and income grows. As the environmental problems of coal cause restrictions in the usage of coal for energy, wind energy will become a much needed and utilized component of the world's energy supply.

Since early recorded history, people have been using the energy of the wind. Wind energy propelled boats along the Nile River as early as 5000 BC. By 200 BC, simple windmills in China were pumping water, while vertical-axis windmills with woven reed sails were grinding grain in Persia and the Middle East.

New ways of using the energy of the wind eventually spread around the world. By the eleventh century, people in the Middle East were using windmills extensively for food production; returning merchants and crusaders carried this idea back to Europe. The Dutch refined the windmill and adapted it for draining lakes and marshes in the Rhine River Delta.

American colonists used windmills to grind wheat and corn, to pump water, and to cut wood at sawmills. Some six million mechanical windmills were in operation from in the late 1880s up until about 1935, helping homesteaders and farmers to settle the West. Mechanical wind energy is most commonly used today for pumping water in rural or remote locations.*

Today the primary use of wind energy is for electricity generation, replacing pumping water, grinding grain, and other classic uses of windmills. Wind turbines, activated by the wind, generate electricity for homes, businesses, and for sale to utilities. Wind energy, however, provides only 9% of our renewable energy and less than 1% of our total energy usage, as illustrated in Figure 19.2 in Chapter 19.

Most of the wind power plants in the world are located in Europe and in the United States where government programs have helped support its development. As of 2008, the United States ranked first in the world in wind power capacity, followed by Germany, Spain, and China. China moved up to second by the end of 2009. Denmark ranks ninth in the world in wind power capacity, but generates about 20% of its electricity from wind. Major offshore wind farms are being planned and implemented in Europe and in the United States.

---

* InternationalEnergyAgency(IEA),http://www.eia.doe.gov/kids/energy.cfm?page=wind_home-basics.

The most common windmills today are horizontal-axis wind turbines. The wind blows through blades, which converts the wind's energy into rotational shaft energy. The blades are mounted atop a high tower to a drive train, usually with a gearbox, that uses the rotational energy from the blades to spin magnets in the generator and convert that energy directly into electrical current. The shaft, drive train, and generator are covered by a protective nacelle. Electronic and electrical equipment, including controls, electrical cables, ground support equipment, and interconnection equipment, control the turbine and transmit the electrical current. Today's utility-scale turbines can be 100 meters (over 300 feet) high or more.

Figure 21.1 is a sample work breakdown structure (WBS) for a wind turbine project. The output of a wind turbine depends on the turbine's size or power rating and the wind's speed through the rotor. Wind turbines being manufactured now have power ratings ranging from 250 watts (for simple battery charging) to 10 kW (which can generate about 15,000 kWh annually, more than enough to power a typical household) to giant 7-megawatt (MW) machines or more.

Worldwide, wind is the fastest-growing energy source. Installed generating capacity in the United States increased by an average 39% annually from 2004 to 2009, but the rate of increase slowed in 2010.* Its use is expanding because modern technology has reduced the cost by more than 80% since the first commercial wind turbines were installed in California in the 1970s (many of those wind turbines still work today and can be seen in Palm Springs and Tehachapi in Southern California, and in the Altamont Pass outside San Francisco). In areas with an excellent wind resource, it can sometimes be more affordable to get new power by building a wind farm than by building a fossil fuel or other type of power plant.

The U.S. wind industry got its start in California when the oil shortage increased the price of electricity generated from oil. The California wind industry benefited from federal and state investment tax credits as well as state-mandated standard utility contracts that guaranteed a satisfactory market price for wind power. By 1986, California had installed more than 1.2 GW of wind power, representing nearly 90% of the global installations at that time.

Expiration of the federal investment tax credit (ITC) in 1985 and the California incentive in 1986 brought the growth of the U.S. wind energy

* Global Wind Energy Council, *Global Wind 2009 Report* (Brussels, Belgium: Renewable Energy House, March 2010), 62, and *Global Wind, 2nd Report*, Annual Market Update, 2010. Renewable Energy House, April 2011. 66. http://GWEC.net/index.php?id=8.

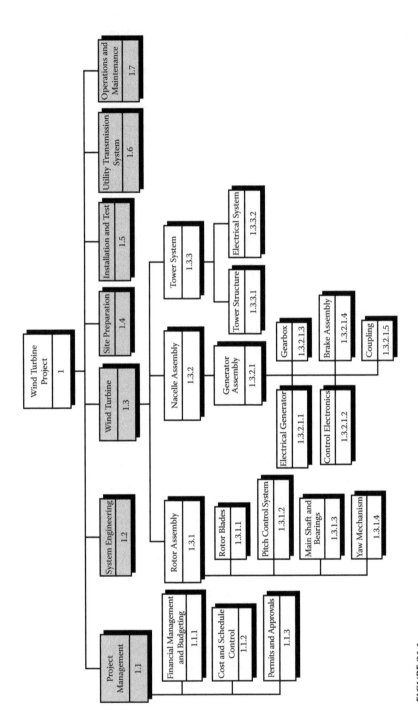

FIGURE 21.1
Wind turbine project WBS.

industry to an abrupt halt in the mid-1980s. Europe then took the lead in wind energy, propelled by aggressive renewable energy policies enacted between 1974 and 1985. As the global industry continued to grow into the 1990s, technological advances led to significant increases in turbine power and productivity. Turbines installed in 1998 had an average capacity 7 to 10 times greater than that of the 1980s turbines, and the price of wind-generated electricity dropped by nearly 80%. By 2000, Europe had more than 12,000 MW of installed wind power, versus only 2,500 MW in the United States, and Germany became the new international leader.[*]

After a decade of trailing Germany and Spain, the United States reestablished itself as the world leader in new wind energy in 2005. This resurgence is attributed to increasingly supportive government policies, growing interest in renewable energy, and continued improvements in wind technology and performance. The United States added just over 10 GW of wind power capacity in 2009, enabling it to maintain its lead in existing capacity with a total of 35 GW. As of the end of 2009, 14 U.S. states had more than 1 GW each of installed capacity. Texas remained the leader with nearly 10 GW of cumulative capacity, enabling the state to reach its 2025 renewable energy target 15 years early.

The United States has lost its leadership of wind development today to China but, because of its natural large wind resources, is likely to remain a major force in the highly competitive wind markets of the future.

Large wind turbines generated electricity in 34 different states in 2008. The top five states with the most wind production were Texas, California, Minnesota, Iowa, and Washington.

> **Overlay:** Overall, it is expected that the percentage of electric power provided by wind energy will continue to increase worldwide as technology improves, costs are reduced, and demand for nonpolluting renewable energy increases.
>
> The energy plan of every country must include reliance on renewables such as wind energy and be able to accommodate the variability of the wind within the grid operating system.

---

[*] U.S. Department of Energy, Office of Scientific and Technical Information, *20% Wind Energy by 2030*, report number DOE/GO-102008-2567, July 2008. See A brief history of the U.S. wind industry, p. 6. http://www.nrel.gov/docs/fy08osti/41869.pdf.

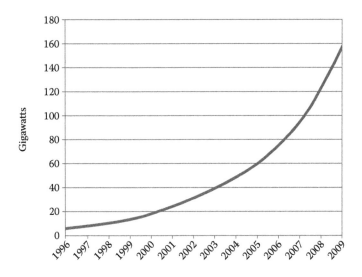

FIGURE 21.2

World wind power capacity, 1995–2015. (Data from A. Pullen and S. Sawyer, eds, *Global Wind Report: Annual Market Update 2010* (Brussels, Belgium: Global Wind Energy Council, April 2011), 4, http://www.gwec.net/index.php?id=180 (accessed October 29, 2011).

Despite the 2009 global economic crisis, new wind power capacity installations in 2009 reached a record high of 38 GW. This represented a 41% increase over 2008 and brought the global total to 159 GW. This same amount of growth continued into 2010, bringing the total installed capacity to 197 GW. The investment in 2010 was worth $71.8 billion,[*] China now being the largest market, adding 18.9 GW of new capacity.

Figure 21.2 illustrates the growth in global wind capacity. Eleven countries had offshore wind farms at the end of 2009. The vast majority of capacity remains in Europe, where the United Kingdom (883 MW) and Denmark (639 MW) retained the lead. (The United Kingdom surpassed the 1 GW mark in April 2010 after two additional wind farms went on line.)

As shown in Table 14.1, the cost of land-based wind power is close to competitive with coal but well behind natural gas. It is less expensive than nuclear. However, the offshore wind projects are very expensive due to the very high capital cost and the cost of investment in transmission lines to connect to the grid.

---

[*] A. Pullen and S. Sawyer, eds, *Global Wind Report: Annual Market Update 2010* (Brussels, Belgium: Global Wind Energy Council, April 2011), 10, http://www.gwec.net/index.php?id=180 (accessed October 29, 2011).

To promote renewable energy systems, many states began requiring electricity suppliers to obtain a small percentage of their supply from renewable energy sources, with percentages typically increasing over time. With Iowa and Texas leading the way, more than 20 states have followed suit with Renewable Portfolio Standards (RPSs), creating an environment for stable growth.

The current rate of increase in growth is not expected to continue past approximately 2013, as shown by the EIA projections. The principal reason is uncertainty regarding government policies that subsidize wind energy and state and federal RPS (Renewable Portfolio Standard) policies and programs. These programs need market certainty such as a requirement for a level of minimum percentage of renewables by certain dates.[*]

> **Overlay:** Although current Energy Information Administration (EIA) projections indicate little growth after 2013, it is likely that concerns about emissions will be a stimulus to the industry and the government will again realize some incentives are important. Therefore, U.S. growth would likely exceed current estimates.

SWOT ANALYSIS: WIND POWER

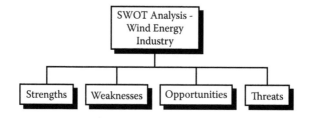

SWOT wind analysis.

The objective of this SWOT analysis is to evaluate the near- and long-term viability of the wind power industry.

---

[*] Ryan Wiser, Mark Bolimer, NREL. *2009 Wind Technologies Market Report*, p. 68. August 2010, DOE/60-102010-3107.

Overlay: Wind farms should be located wherever feasible on land considering the prevailing winds and local conditions. They should be built offshore where practical from the point of water depth and access to the grid. R&D should continue on increasing system efficiency and the ability to operate in the hostile climate offshore. Problems of energy storage, grid access, and variable input to the grid should continue to be addressed. The economics are expected to continue to improve with improving technology.

Strengths

The strengths of the use of wind energy production for electricity lie in the relatively mature technology and the inexhaustible supply of wind energy. The costs of constructing and operating a wind turbine or a wind farm can be estimated fairly accurately, at least insofar as onshore farms. The costs and therefore the economics of offshore installations are still subject to a fair amount of uncertainty due to the inhospitable water environment and related construction and operating costs. This is evidenced in the data in Table 14.1.

Wind farms have almost no associated carbon emissions, and the fuel—the wind—is free and in unlimited supply. Locations for wind farms, especially offshore, are relatively unlimited. Continuing R&D will result in constant improvements in wind turbine technology.

Weaknesses

The basic weaknesses are as follows:

1. The inherent problems of storage of wind energy for use when the wind is not blowing.
2. The current electrical grid is not always located where the output from proposed wind farms can be readily connected, so the grid needs to be extended and this may be a costly investment.
3. The output from the wind farm is variable and does not always match the demand pattern of the grid, which causes balance problems.
4. "Not in my back yard" (NIMBY) and view impairment objections from local citizens and organizations are problematic.

Wind power is renewable and the wind is free. However, currently, except in combination with hydropower or some other base source, wind-generated electricity cannot be stored in large quantities. The power companies have to provide electricity at the moment you need to use it. This does not always match the availability of energy from the wind due to its relative unpredictability and uncontrollability.

The grid transmission problem is resolved by negotiations between the wind farm supplier and the grid manager. When they are the same organization, it becomes an issue of economics and regulations. The issue is whether and how the individual utility can pass on the cost of the new interconnector system to its customers.

The resolution of the variable output problem is a function of the flexibility built into the basic power system. Some of the time, the wind does not blow at the right speeds to generate electricity, and even when it does, that is often at times when little electricity is needed, such as in the middle of the night. If there are requirements that a high percentage of energy come from renewable sources such as wind, this means that the electric grid operation needs a mechanism to be able to adapt to the variability of the energy source. According to the American Wind Energy Association:

> [A] tremendous amount of flexibility is already built into the power system. Demand for electricity can vary by a factor of three or more depending on the time of day and year and the current system has the flexibility to accommodate this variation in demand using spinning and non-spinning reserves. ... The amount of energy a grid can accommodate depends on the flexibility and the amount of storage available for wind energy that is generated in periods of low demand. While continuing advances in energy storage technology can make it more economically competitive as a provider of grid flexibility, it is important to remember that resources like wind energy can already be cost-effectively and reliably integrated with the electric grid without energy storage.[*]

Current estimates are that at about 20% market penetration by wind power, the inherent flexibility in a typical grid may be fully utilized.

---

[*] American Wind Energy Association Fact Sheet, Michael Goggin, *Wind Power and Energy Storage*, undated, http://www.awea.org/learnabout/publications/upload/Energy-Storage-Factsheet_WP11.pdf. (Accessed March 2, 2012.)

It would be expected that as time goes on R&D work or redesign of grids would allow this number to be increased.

The fourth threat is mitigated by developing offshore sites. These currently are very expensive due to the harsh environment, but it is expected that improvements in technology and demand for clean energy power will resolve these problems in time.

Opportunities

Worldwide there is an increasing market for energy and therefore a market for wind energy. Europe in 2010 was in the midst of a wind energy boom, with the continent installing more wind power capacity than any other form of energy.[*]

Today, only approximately 5% of Europe's electricity comes from wind, but that will not be the case for long. For the past 2 years, 40% of all new electricity generating capacity in Europe came from wind turbines. From Spain to Sweden, so many new turbines are being erected that Europe is on target to produce 15% of its electricity from wind by 2020.

The European Union recently adopted legislation that mandates that each member state have a specific target for its share of renewable energy in the energy mix by 2020 and it has also indicated that it believes that wind energy could contribute up to 20% of European electricity in 2020. Northern Europe has ambitious plans for adding offshore wind power. The United Kingdom, Denmark, the Netherlands, Belgium, and other northern European neighbors are gearing up to add giant wind farms up to 120 miles off their coasts.

The move is part of their efforts to shift to renewable power sources to meet tough European Union climate-change targets for 2020 and to reduce the region's dependence on imported supplies of natural gas. This will require a serious effort in terms of changing the way they operate their grids, including developing an offshore grid for utilizing the offshore wind energy. In the United States an offshore very large wind farm is proposed for Rhode Island Sound and would be connected to both Rhode Island and to Long Island, New York, by cables.[†] This would link the grids of New York and New England.

[*] Fen Montaigne, Yale Environment 360, September 9, 2010, http://e360.yale.edu/feature/steady_growth_of_wind_industry_moves_eu_closer_to_green_goals/2314/. (accessed March 2, 2012).

[†] Matthew L Wald, "Wind Farm Would Link Northeastern Grids," *New York Times*, Green Blog, December 9, 2010, http://nytimes.com.

The reason that wind will be the main contributor to reaching these renewable energy targets is that onshore wind is the cheapest of the new renewables, as shown in Table 14.1. So the majority of the target will be met by wind turbines on land. Offshore is still much more expensive, but it is expected to play an increasing role as well. But in terms of wind versus solar energy sources, wind is significantly lower cost in terms of producing a kilowatt-hour of electricity.

There appears to be a good market for wind power technology and construction.

While energy storage technologies may currently have difficulty competing economically with conventional sources of flexibility—especially over the time frame most relevant for wind integration—continuing advances in energy storage technology can make wind energy storage more competitive and to overcome this primary weakness of wind as a source of energy.

Threats

The inherent long-term threat to wind power development and expansion is the availability of economically suitable sites. Wind power should be a component of every country's energy plan. Because of the current economic problems, the investments in wind energy in the United States have slowed and the U.S. government policies regarding renewables are not clear. The extent of the U.S. government investment in R&D and subsidies is very unstable, especially when compared to other countries such as China. It cannot be predicted more than 1 or 2 years ahead. This is not the case elsewhere in the world. The threat currently is that the important manufacturing side of the U.S. wind industry will be overtaken by investments and new technology and manufacturing capability from overseas—Europe and China.

Driven by rapidly growing energy demands and strong policy support, China more than doubled its capacity in 2009 and has become the world's second largest wind power market.[*] It is expected to lead the world in annual wind power capacity additions in the coming years. Industrial policy and market conditions have also resulted in the growing dominance of Chinese wind turbine manufacturers within the Chinese market, and those manufacturers are beginning to explore export strategies.

---

[*] Global Wind Energy Council, *Global Wind 2009 Report*, 8.

TABLE 21.1

Wind Farm Risk Matrix

No.	Risk Event	P1	P2	Px
1	Availability of suitable site	2	5	10
2	Grid access costs excessive	2	3	6
3	Variability of wind and input to grid acceptable to grid operator	2	4	8
4	Excessive bird kills requiring special sensors to shut down when large flocks approach	2	2	4
5	Project meeting construction cost goals	2	3	6

Note: P1 = likelihood of risk event occurring; P2 = probable impact on the program if P1 occurred; Px = product of P1 and P2 to assign ranking.

U.S. manufacturing of turbines and components is also expected to continue to grow, as already-announced manufacturing facilities come on line, as existing facilities reach full capacity and expand, and as new announcements and investments are made. In part as a result, and in a continuation of recent trends, the historically dominant wind turbine suppliers in the United States market will face growing competition from new entrants that may be getting subsidies from their governments in order to compete.

Table 21.1 is a wind power risk matrix for a project to set up a wind farm in a rural area.

22

Geothermal Energy

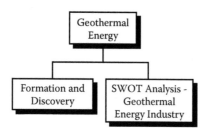

Chapter 22 outline.

This chapter provides a description of the formation and discovery of geothermal energy, followed by a strengths, weaknesses, opportunities, and threats (SWOT) analysis of the industry.

Overlay: Conventional geothermal systems that rely on heat exchange with surface or close-to-surface heat sources have limited expansion capacity since all the good sites are already taken. Engineered geothermal energy systems that rely on hydraulic fracturing have the potential for providing large amounts of electrical generating capacity. However, at present the technologies for sustainable heat mining from large volumes of accessible hot rock are in preliminary developmental phases. Many attributes of geothermal energy, namely, its widespread availability, base-load dispatchability without storage, small footprint, and low emissions, are desirable for reaching a sustainable energy future for the United States.

Current weaknesses in geology knowledge, water requirements, well reliability, scaling in components, and local environmental impacts seriously hamper advance of engineered systems based on fracking technology.

Lack of a current aggressive R&D program anywhere in the world puts the likelihood of progress in this technology well into the future.

FORMATION AND DISCOVERY

Geothermal energy systems use the heat located below the surface of the Earth as their source of energy. In somewhat of an oversimplification, there are two types of geothermal systems. The first is conventional geothermal systems that depend on water or other fluid circulation in areas near the surface of the Earth where subsurface magma or other tectonic or volcanic processes elevate the temperatures. This involves simply pumping water in pipes through areas like Yellowstone National Park where natural heat sources are near the surface of the Earth. Most of these locations in the world are already developed and are providing steady geothermal energy. Reykjavik, Iceland, receives much of its energy from geothermal sources.

The second type is the enhanced (or engineered) geothermal systems (EGS), which use underground fracture generation similar to the fracking process used to extract natural gas from shale. This is performed in permeable rock where drilling technology permits depths to be achieved where sufficiently high temperatures are encountered.

Engineering is required to develop or enhance the permeability of the subsurface rock area necessary for the circulation of water and the recovery of heat in the form of steam or superheated water for the electrical power generation.

The basic engineering of an EGS is to drill two wells and manipulate an underground rock mass to enhance permeability so that cooled water can be injected into one well and steam or hot water is returned from other well(s), all at an acceptable cost.

Temperatures from the Earth's hot core are moderated normally from reaching the surface by the blanketing effect of layers of sedimentary geology (volcanic activity is a notable exception). Temperatures from the surface downward increase at an average rate of approximately 52° to 90°F/mi. (So 3 miles could result in 150–270°F.)

Hot igneous rocks (formed by the cooling and solidification of molten magma) can be located at considerable depths in the Earth's crust and are not at the same depth in all areas. Reaching them with conventional drilling equipment is costly and difficult. In the United States, the favorable areas where the heat is closer to the surface are all west of the Mississippi River.

There are several steps to the process.

- First, there needs to be exploration to locate high-temperature rocks within an achievable drilling distance.

- Second, the rocks need to be sufficiently fractured or demonstrate potential for artificial fracturing to allow water to be circulated and hot water produced at sufficiently high rates to drive a steam turbine.
- Third, the EGS technology involves drilling two or more wells several hundred yards apart down 1.5 to 3+ miles into a rock system that has the right characteristics to be manipulated to produce superheated water at the surface.
- Fourth, water is pumped down into the injection well and returns through the production well(s), heated up via the artificially created heat exchanger in the rocks at the bottom of the pipes.
- Fifth, at the surface, the hot water (270+°F) is used to drive a conventional steam turbine, with each two-well module generating between 3 and 6 MW.

The main parameters that determine the heat energy that is exploited are the size of the reservoir in the rock, the rate at which water circulates through the reservoir, the distance between the faults through which the water flows, and distribution of the flow within the reservoir.

The key to the technology is the skill in identifying and enhancing the fracture permeability in the rock through which the water travels in order to be heated up. The work breakdown structure (WBS) for an EGS is illustrated in Figure 22.1.

The most important conclusion from the work around the world regarding the development of EGS as a power-producing technology is that we can probably form an EGS reservoir at any depth and anywhere in the world that has both a temperature high enough for energy conversion and sufficient far-field connectivity through existing natural fractures.* In other words, the technology exists to develop a workable EGS wherever we want. But it most likely would be uneconomic to do so in most places at today's cost structure.

The first set of problems is at the bottom of the wells. Uncertainties exist in knowledge of the natural state of stress and rock properties, even within well-characterized geologic regions. Most important, the required properties for stimulation by shear failure and creation of the underground reservoir are fundamentally different than normal practice in oil- and gas-bearing formations and require different fracking technologies. Other aspects of the underground reservoir structure may cause operational problems and

* MIT Report, *The Future of Geothermal Energy, Impact of Enhanced Geothermal Systems (EGS) on the United States in the 21st Century*, (Idaho Falls, ID: Idaho National Laboratory, 2006), http://geothermal.inel.gov/publications/future_of_geothermal_energy.pdf. (Accessed March 3, 2012), 4–6.

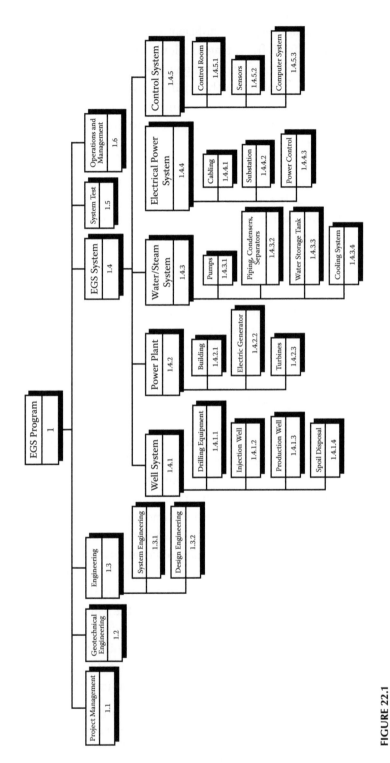

FIGURE 22.1

Enhanced Geothermal System Project WBS.

because of a limited understanding of the subsurface strata of the reservoir, the long-term effect of injecting water into the reservoir is unknown.

The second set of problems relates to scaling—the hard mineral coating that forms on the inside surface of containers in which water with dissolved minerals is repeatedly heated. The injected water heats and dissolves the minerals in the bedrock, which is beneficial since it tends to keep the fractures open, but once the water starts to cool precipitation takes place. Since these are silicate minerals, it is a serious problem for all elements in the water/steam system illustrated in the WBS 1.4.3 element of Figure 22.1.

Many features associated with the technical feasibility of EGS technology have been demonstrated at more than one site in the past 30 years. However, the major shortcoming of the field testing, so far, is that circulation rates through the stimulated regions have been below commercially viable rates and scaling has seriously increased maintenance costs.

While a given stimulation method may not provide for efficient, cost-effective heat mining at today's energy prices, it still extracts net energy. Field efforts have repeatedly demonstrated that EGS wells can be drilled; preexisting, sealed fractures at depth can be stimulated; and a connection can be made between wells. Fluid can be circulated through the network and heated to economic temperatures, and we can maintain the circulation and use the heat from the produced fluid directly—or use it to generate electricity.

There is a third type of geothermal that is a combination of the first two called a single-well engineered geothermal system (SWEGS).[*] It is a closed-loop system that uses the geothermal heat from hot, dry rock. It uses a proprietary heat exchanger underground and the heat transfer fluid is pumped down the hole through the heat exchanger and back to the surface where it is converted into electricity.

SWOT ANALYSIS: GEOTHERMAL ENERGY

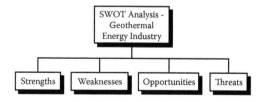

SWOT analysis outline.

---

[*] See GTherm, http://www.gtherm.net/gtherminnovation/gtherm-swegs/ (accessed March 22, 2011).

Overlay: There are two geothermal energy communities: one is the shallow system where heat is provided near the surface, such as in Iceland or Yellowstone or places in California. These should be utilized to the maximum feasible since they involve no technical risk and are economic. The second is the enhanced geothermal system or EGS, which uses fracking technology to create a "boiler" deep underground. This latter is generally feasible west of the Mississippi River since the magma is closer to the surface in that region. At present almost all aspects of the technology other than the turbines and generators need development and there appears to be little interest from private sector investors. However, EGS technology should be pursued and developed and especially in coordination with other countries who are experimenting with the technology and currently leading in investment. The United States cannot let any possible technology go undeveloped in view of the energy shortages likely in the near future.

A combination of the two systems, a single-well closed system, is used in households at relatively shallow depths for home hot water and at larger depths for commercial application and electricity generation. The technology for this currently exists but the economics are not quite competitive yet.

This section contains the SWOT analysis of the geothermal power industry.

Strengths

Geothermal resources span a wide range of heat sources from the Earth, including not only the more easily developed, currently economic hydrothermal resources, but also the Earth's deeper, stored thermal energy, which is present anywhere.

Although conventional hydrothermal resources are used effectively for both electric and nonelectric applications in the United States, they are limited in their location and ultimate potential for supplying electricity.

There is an opportunity to develop technologies for sustainable heat mining from large volumes of accessible hot rock anywhere in the United States. Many attributes of geothermal energy, namely, its widespread distribution, base-load dispatch ability without storage, small footprint, and low emissions, are desirable for reaching a sustainable energy future for the United States.

EGS methods have been tested at a number of sites around the world and the processes and technology and geotechnical knowledge have been improving steadily.

Weaknesses

The Department of Energy has identified what they see as "Program Challenges" for EGS; these are the perceived institutional and economic barriers, challenges, and obstacles to market penetration.* These include the following:

- Lack of available and reliable resource information
- High exploration risks and high up-front costs
- Complicated siting, leasing, and permitting issues
- High local impact on the environment
- Limited access to transmission infrastructure
- Absence of national policy

Each of these is discussed in turn.

Lack of Available and Reliable Resource Information

Poor availability of accurate and reliable resource data and information is a significant deterrent to potential geothermal investors. Recent attempts at organizing existing data on geothermal resources in the United States, specifically across western states, have done little to improve information quality, since most of the existing information regarding geothermal resources comes from private lands while federal lands make up a great proportion of the identified resource. The Department of Energy (DOE) is taking steps to develop a National Geothermal Database to assist in identifying and assessing sites with the best geothermal potential.

High Exploration Risks and High Up-Front Costs

EGS has significant up-front costs that must be incurred prior to determining the viability of a selected site. This investment requirement raises the stakes for investors who must commit capital without assurance of a positive return. The high probability of loss in the early stages of development makes supporting geothermal development very challenging.

---

* Department of Energy, Geothermal Technologies Program, Multi-Year Research, Development and Demonstration Plan, Washington, DC, Draft, 2009.

EGS must be cost-competitive in order for industry to accept the technology as commercially viable. Drilling the deep wells necessary to access the resource is currently not economically feasible. In order for the technology to succeed, costs of drilling deep wells must be reduced, and the probability of the site being viable, and plant efficiency and resistance to scaling must increase. Technology and innovation must show significant improvement throughout the industry.

Siting, Leasing, and Permitting Issues

Most of the geothermal energy facilities in the United States are located on federal lands. The Bureau of Land Management (BLM) has the responsibility for issuing geothermal leases on federal lands and reviews permit applications for geothermal development. Although the BLM has the primary authority over leasing, the concurrence of the U.S. Forest Service (FS) is required for leases on lands it manages.

Geothermal projects on state or private lands are under the jurisdiction of state and local regulatory agencies. States are not consistent in how they define geothermal resources or in how siting and permitting are handled. Mineral rights, water use rights, and environmental laws vary by state. Some states grant power plant siting authority to a public utility commission or siting board. A few of these boards coordinate environmental review and permitting; others leave this in the hands of the developer.

High Local Impact on the Environment[*]

One major limitation of EGS power generation is that it requires very large quantities of water to serve the needs of the injection well in an EGS well system. In those areas where sufficient water is available, a problem arises due to the ultimate pollution of that water due to the minerals, salts, and other toxic elements injection well water concentrates as it moves through the EGS cycle.

In addition to the pollution of injection well water, hydrofracking of subsurface hot rock associated with EGS power generation to create an underground reservoir can adversely affect land stability in the surrounding region; cause gaseous emissions; cause noise pollution; induce seismic activity (several plants have been decommissioned due to tremors); induce

---

[*] GTherm, *Geothermal Basics/Current Limitations of Enhanced Geothermal Systems*, http://www.gtherm.net/geothermal-basics/current-limitations-of-egs/ (accessed March 22, 2011).

landslides, potential aquifer contamination, and cause disturbance of natural hydrothermal manifestations. In areas like Southern California, where there is already seismic activity and earthquake sensitivity, injection of water for EGS has been shown to increase seismic activity.*

Access to Transmission Infrastructure

Like many of the renewable resource options, the ability to transmit electricity from the source to the power grid represents one barrier to expanding the development and deployment of EGS. Geothermal resources are generally remote from load centers, requiring investment in transmission infrastructure, which can lead to high delivery costs that are not competitive with conventional technologies. A large amount of capital is required for transmission expansion, providing a disincentive for utilities to build infrastructure to reach remote geothermal sources.

Absence of National Policy

The largest current problem facing the geothermal industry is the lack of a federal policy of promoting and supporting geothermal development. The economic viability of most geothermal electricity production projects continues to be dependent on the financial support created by national and state energy policy. Policy-based support will be necessary to produce any level of investment in all but a select group of fringe projects.

Opportunities

Under the assumption of continued successful development and implementation of EGS technology, models for the extension of geothermal energy recovery techniques into regions of hot but low permeability crust yield an estimated mean electric power resource on private and accessible public land of up to approximately half of the current installed electric power generating capacity in the United States and an order of magnitude larger than the conventional geothermal resource.†

An important opportunity exists to develop and implement EGS. An MIT study includes the following conclusions: "Analysis suggests that,

---

* Op. cit. MIT Report.
† Colin F. Williams, Marshall J. Reed, Robert H. Mariner, Jacob DeAngelo, S. Peter Galanis Jr., 2008, "Assessment of Moderate- and High-Temperature Geothermal Resources of the United States," *U.S. Geological Survey Fact Sheet* (2008): 2008–3082, 3.

with significant initial investment, installed capacity of EGS could reach 100,000 MWe within 50 years, with levelized energy costs at parity with market prices after 11 years. In this period, we expect that the development of new EGS resources will occur at a critical time when grid stabilization with base-load power will be needed to avoid redirecting expensive natural gas facilities when they are most in demand worldwide."[*]

A comprehensive research and demonstration effort should begin moving toward the period when replacement of retiring fossil and nuclear units and new capacity growth will most affect the U.S. electrical supply.

Threats

The biggest threat is that little or no governmental development funding is being provided and the technology development is lagging. EGS power needs further R&D funding support to solve the existing technical problems and to demonstrate its capability to provide electricity at competitive prices. Although there have been some demonstration wells, the overall concept is lagging seriously in development interest and funding. At present the risks are too high for a totally private sector investment.

An EGS geothermal power risk matrix is presented in Table 22.1.

TABLE 22.1

Geothermal Power Station Risk Matrix

No.	Risk Event	P1	P2	Px
1	Chosen site has unsuitable geology	2	5	10
2	Permitting and licensing are delayed	3	2	6
3	Fracking process is unsuccessful—cannot create permeable rock reservoir	2	5	10
4	Producer wells are not providing suitable flow and temperatures	3	5	15
5	Waste water disposal solution inadequate	2	4	8
6	Life of well insufficient to amortize unsubsidized costs	2	3	6

Note: P1 = likelihood of risk event occurring; P2 = probable impact on the industry if P1 occurred; Px = product of P1 and P2 to assign ranking.

---

[*] Op. cit. MIT Report, 9–43, 44.

23

Biomass Energy

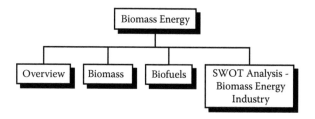

Chapter 23 outline.

OVERVIEW

In this section we provide an overview and description of the two major types of biomass energy, the solids and the liquids, followed by a strengths, weaknesses, opportunities, and threats (SWOT) analysis of the industry.

> **Overlay:** It is expected that biomass will have a long-term role to play in meeting the world's energy needs. Biomass has two customers: one is the electric power industry and the other is transportation in the form of biofuels. Biofuels will become increasingly important after peak oil and shortages start to arise. Biofuels are under intense R&D by the Department of Defense as the backup fuel for transportation.

Biomass is a generic term used to describe fuel generated from plant or animal matter. Its importance is that it is a renewable resource. Approximately 4% of our energy comes from biomass—the largest amount of any renewable source, as illustrated in Figure 19.3 in Chapter 19. Much of this energy originates from recycling garbage or waste material. Some of it is used for electricity generation, some for heating, and some for biofuel production.

Biofuel is a subset of biomass and is also a generic term that includes ethanol, methanol, biodiesel, and other fuels derived from plant or animal matter. Biofuels can be generated from any organic source, but in the United States virtually all biofuels come from corn grown for ethanol, and to lesser extent from soybeans. Current research efforts also include algae, camelina (a relative of mustard), and switchgrass. Brazil has an extensive and effective biofuel program based on sugar cane biomass, which has more inherent energy than corn and therefore is preferable from an engineering standpoint. U.S. protective tariffs currently preclude the import of the less expensive, more efficient Brazilian ethanol.

BIOMASS

The world has used biomass energy since people began burning wood to cook food and keep warm. Wood is still the largest biomass energy resource today, but other sources of biomass include food crops, grassy and woody plants, residues from agriculture or forestry, paper mill residue, lumber mill scrap, oil-rich algae, and the organic component of municipal and industrial wastes. Even the fumes from landfills (which are methane, a natural gas) are used as a biomass energy source.[*]

The important use of biomass is its ability to replace oil because biofuels are currently the only renewable liquid transportation fuel available that has reasonable economics. Fuel made from coal is currently also available but at much higher cost.

Biomass power plant size is driven by the biomass availability in close proximity as transport costs of the (bulky) fuel play a key factor in a plant's economics. Rail and especially shipping on waterways can reduce transport costs significantly, which has led to a global biomass market.

Biomass power plants exist in over 50 countries around the world and supply a growing share of electricity. Several European countries are expanding their total share of power from biomass, including Austria (7%), Finland (20%), and Germany (5%).

---

[*] Introductory material derived from the learning pages of the National Renewable Energy Laboratory, a component of the U.S. Department of Energy. See http://www.nrel.gov/.

The Biomass Power Association (BPA) describes the role of biomass as one of reducing greenhouse gases.* The BPA states that using biomass to create usable energy actually reduces greenhouse gases. They say the use of biomass power removes over 30 million tons of carbon dioxide annually. It accomplishes this feat both by replacing fossil fuels and by preventing the release of greenhouse gases from organic waste that would otherwise decompose in the open.

The Environmental Protection Agency's (EPA's) basic premise is that burning biomass for energy is considered to be carbon-neutral when considered in the context of natural carbon cycling. Although the burning of biomass produces CO_2, it is considered to be part of the natural carbon cycle of the Earth. The plants take up carbon dioxide from the air while they are growing and then return it to the air when they are burned, thereby causing no net increase. However, whether or not it is carbon-neutral depends on the time frame. If the time frame is only a few years, net carbon is released to the atmosphere since a mature forest takes nearly a century to develop. The carbon-neutral argument is only valid over a century time period.

Biomass contains much less sulfur and nitrogen than coal; therefore, when biomass is co-fired with coal, sulfur dioxide and nitrogen oxide emissions are lower than when coal is burned alone.

The biomass-is-carbon-neutral theory as discussed previously was put forward in the early 1990s. However, it does not apply to harvesting forestland. More recent science recognizes that mature, intact forests sequester carbon more effectively than cut-over areas. Since the goal should be to reduce emissions, not stay equal, the justification of biomass as carbon-neutral appears strained.

The existing biomass power generating industry in the United States produces about 1.4% of the U.S. electricity supply. It consists of approximately 11,000 MW of summer operating capacity actively supplying power to the grid.

BIOFUELS

Unlike other renewable energy sources, biomass can be converted directly into liquid fuels, called *biofuels,* to help meet transportation fuel

* See Biomass Power Association, http://www.usabiomass.org/pages/facts.php for more information and documented studies.

needs. The two most common types of biofuels in use today are ethanol and biodiesel.

For biofuels, the most common feed stocks used today are corn grain (for ethanol) and soybeans (for biodiesel). Corn accounts for more than half of global ethanol production, and sugar cane for more than one-third. The United States and Brazil account for almost 90% of global ethanol production.

Ethanol is an alcohol, the same as in beer and wine (although ethanol used as a fuel is modified to make it undrinkable). It is most commonly made by fermenting any biomass high in carbohydrates through a process similar to beer brewing. Today, ethanol is made from starches and sugars, but scientists are working on technology to allow it to be made from cellulose and hemicellulose, the fibrous material that makes up the bulk of most plant matter.

Ethanol can also be produced by a process called *gasification*. Gasification systems use high temperatures and a low-oxygen environment to convert biomass into synthesis gas, a mixture of hydrogen and carbon monoxide. The synthesis gas, or *syngas*, can then be chemically converted into ethanol and other fuels.

Ethanol is mostly used as blending agent with gasoline to increase octane and cut down carbon monoxide and other smog-causing emissions, and of course to reduce gasoline consumption. Some vehicles, called Flexible Fuel Vehicles, are designed to run on E85, an alternative fuel with much higher ethanol content than regular gasoline.

Unfortunately, ethanol stores less energy per gallon than gasoline, tends to absorb water, and is corrosive to some materials; people will use it only if it is cheap or if you force them to through mandatory blending. In Brazil, which turned to biofuels after the 1970s oil shocks, the price of ethanol eventually became low enough for the fuel to find a market, thanks to highly productive sugar plantations and distilleries powered by the pulp left when that sugar was extracted from its cane. As a result Brazil is now a biofuels superpower. North American ethanol is mostly made from corn (maize), which is less efficient, and often produced in distilleries powered by coal; it is thus neither as cheap nor as environmentally benign. But American agribusiness, "which knows a good thing when it sees one, used its political clout to arrange subsidies and tariffs that made corn-ethanol profitable and that kept out the lower cost alternative from Brazil."[*]

---

[*] *The Economist*, "The Post-Alcohol World: Biofuels Are Back. This Time They May Even Work," October 28, 2010, http://www.economist.com/node/17358802/print (accessed November 1, 2010).

There is strong evidence that growing corn, soybeans, and other food crops to produce ethanol takes a heavy toll on the environment due to increased greenhouse gas emissions as well as heavy applications of nitrogen fertilizer. It also has a requirement for massive amounts of water for irrigation and processing, and is hurting the world's poor through significantly higher food prices. It also increases the costs of meat due to the higher costs of corn. Environmentally and economically there is little justification for the subsidization of corn-based ethanol.

In 2010, more than one third of the United States corn harvest of 335 million metric tons was used to produce corn ethanol. Within 5 years, fully 50% of the U.S. corn crop is expected to wind up as biofuels.[*] Analyses indicate that to replace only 10% of the gasoline in the United States with ethanol and biodiesel would require 43% of the current U.S. cropland.

The year 2009 was a record year for ethanol production, with 200 biorefineries producing 10.6 billion gallons of renewable ethanol in the United States. Efficiency enhancements and innovations in production combined with improved farming techniques allowed the U.S. ethanol industry to achieve this record with existing corn acreage and reduced process water.[†]

Biodiesel is made by combining alcohol (usually methanol) with vegetable oil, animal fat, or recycled cooking grease. It can be used as an additive (typically 20%) to reduce vehicle emissions or in its pure form as a renewable alternative fuel for diesel engines.

SWOT ANALYSIS: BIOMASS

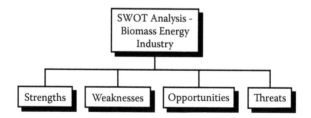

SWOT analysis outline.

[*] C. Ford Runge, The Case against Biofuels: Probing Ethanol's Hidden Costs, Environment 360, March 11, 2010, http://e360.yale.edu/feature/the_case_against_biofuels_probing_ethanols_hidden_costs/2251/ (accessed June 23, 2011).

[†] Renewable Fuels Association Resource Center, http://www.ethanolrfa.org/pages/ethanol-facts (accessed September 25, 2010).

Overlay: Biomass is an important source of electricity and of fuel. The use of biomass needs to be encouraged and additional R&D supported—with one caveat. The use of corn to make ethanol should be scaled back. It is a misuse of farmland. Elimination of the restrictive tariffs on Brazilian ethanol makes sense as a source of less-expensive, more energetic ethanol. Biofuels will be essential to complement and replace jet fuel as oil wells are depleted and oil prices move upward dramatically.

Strengths

Congress passed energy legislation, known as the Energy Independence and Security Act of 2007, which raises standards for vehicle fuel economy and mandates that U.S. transportation fuel include 21 billion gallons of advanced biofuels by 2022 and 2 billion gallons as soon as 2012. The legislation further requires that these advanced biofuels must achieve at least a 50% reduction in life-cycle greenhouse gas emissions.

National security concerns have made a strong market for biofuels.[*] The Navy has established a goal of using alternative energy for half of its power at sea and on shore by 2020. That would require more than 300 million gallons of biofuels a year for blending with conventional fuels. The Air Force plans to fly on a 50–50 blend of biofuels and conventional fuel by 2016, an annual requirement of 400 million gallons. The military goal also includes the requirement that their biofuels do not displace food, do not use up fresh water, emit less greenhouse gases than conventional fuels, and cost the same. The first two criteria effectively eliminate ethanol from corn. The cost of the current biofuels is over $30 per gallon or 10 times the cost of conventional jet fuel. Camelina, one of the leading candidates as a source of raw material for biofuels, has been grown on Montana wheat fields that would otherwise lay fallow.

Biofuels are currently the only proven source of alternatives to petroleum in transportation. This means that as petroleum prices rise, as is anticipated happening, the economics of biofuels as a replacement or complement to gasoline and diesel fuel improve. In the worst case, such as a cutoff of or drastic reduction in supply of petroleum, it becomes the only alternative.

---

[*] Renee Schoof, "Air Force, Navy Set Goals for Cutting Fossil-Fuel Use," *Richmond Times-Dispatch*, July 3, 2011, A2.

The use of biomass for heating and generating electricity will continue based on the availability of feed stock and new power plants will be required. The assumption that there is no net carbon release helps provide an attractive justification for using this source of energy as an important supplement to fossil fuels.

Weaknesses

While incentives and policies may promote biomass electric plant construction, the pace and penetration of biomass power plants are controlled most significantly by the raw fuel supply; it is such a large portion of the cost of operations that it is looked at very carefully by investors.[*] (See also Table 14.1 in Chapter 14.)

The availability of sustainable resources used as fuel is a constraining factor and determines the number of biomass facilities that a particular area can support assuming feed stock is not shipped in from outside the area. When timberlands are considered as resources, the amount of wood supplied from private lands will increase as the supply prices increase. A key input factor in an analysis of the amount of biomass that can be harvested from private lands is the amount of land that should be excluded from potential harvesting due to biophysical constraint or lack of landowner interest in timber production.[†] Also, a consideration is the share that would be drawn into production at various price levels.

According to the online *Wall Street Journal*, the author, Jim Carlton, indicated that "unless the U.S. adopts a national renewable-energy standard (RES), requiring utilities to obtain a certain percentage of their power from renewable sources such as biomass, the industry will continue to struggle."[‡]

Increased use of biofuels puts increasing pressure on water resources in at least two ways: water use for the irrigation of crops used as feed stocks and water use in the production of biofuels in refineries, mostly for boiling and cooling. In many parts of the world, supplemental or full irrigation

---

[*] Manomet Center for Conservation Sciences, *Massachusetts Biomass Sustainability and Carbon Policy Study: Report to the Commonwealth of Massachusetts Department of Energy Resources*. Edited by T. Walker. Contributors: Cardellichio, P., Colnes, A., Gunn, J., Kittler, B., Perschel, R., Recchia, C., Saah, D., and Walker, T. Natural Capital Initiative Report NCI-2010-03. Brunswick, Maine, 24.

[†] Manomet Center, *Massachusetts Biomass Sustainability*, 45.

[‡] Jim Carlton, "Mass Confusion: High Costs and Environmental Concerns Have Pushed Biomass Power to the Sidelines in the U.S." *Wall Street Journal*, October 18, 2010 (http://online.wsj.com/).

is needed to grow feed stocks. For example, if in the production of corn (maize) half the water needs of crops are met through irrigation and the other half through rainfall, about 3,500 gallons of water are needed to produce 1 gallon of ethanol. In the United States only 5–15% of the water required for corn comes from irrigation, while the other 85–95% comes from natural rainfall.

Large-scale farming is necessary to produce ethanol and this requires substantial amounts of cultivated land. This means growing corn for ethanol competes with using the land for food. University of Minnesota researchers report that if all corn grown in the United States were used to make ethanol, it would displace only 12% of current U.S. gasoline consumption. There are claims that land for ethanol production is acquired through deforestation, while others have observed that areas currently supporting forests are usually not suitable for growing crops. In any case, corn farming for ethanol may involve a decline in soil fertility due to reduction of organic matter, a decrease in water availability and quality, an increase in the use of pesticides and fertilizers, and potential dislocation of local communities. The primary beneficiaries of the current requirement to use ethanol are the large agribusinesses with strong lobbying organizations.

Opportunities

Using corn limits the size of the industry in the United States and pits it against the interests of people all over the world who need food. It is believed that cellulose could become a substitute for the starch in corn if suitably treated. Both starch and cellulose consist of sugar molecules, linked together in different ways, and fermentation feeds on sugar. But economic cellulosic biofuel has so far been a poor investment. Currently, only a handful of factories around the world produce biofuel from cellulose and that fuel is still ethanol.

Companies working on a new generation of biofuels want to change from making ethanol to making hydrocarbons, molecules chemically much more similar to those that already power planes, trains, and automobiles. These will be "drop-in" fuels, any quantity of which can be put into the appropriate fuel tanks and pipelines with no chemical conflict whatsoever. For that reason alone, they are worth more than ethanol. Research in this area is being heavily sponsored by the Department of Defense, the Navy, and the Departments of Agriculture and Energy.

There are several emerging technologies for using biomass that have the potential to change the demand for low-grade wood over time. Most of these are transportation sector related. The U.S. Department of Energy has invested hundreds of millions of dollars over the last decade to augment the ethanol production of agricultural crops (corn primarily) with ethanol derived from woody biomass sources (cellulosic ethanol). It has sponsored both research and development, funding six pilot-scale plants throughout the country.[*]

It is expected that ongoing R&D will improve the conversion of nonfood crops (such as switchgrass and a variety of woody crops) to biofuels. In addition, agricultural residues such as corn stover (the stalks, leaves, and husks of the plant) and wheat straw may also be used. Long-term plans include growing and using dedicated energy crops, such as fast-growing trees and grasses, camelina, and algae. These feed stocks can grow sustainably on land that will not support intensive food crops. With the threat of increasing prices of petroleum due to shortage of supply, there will be more activity in finding economic replacements to support transportation needs.

The reason for the large R&D effort has been government mandates: America's Renewable Fuel Standard (RFS-2)[†] and its European equivalent. On pain of fines, but with the carrot of subsidies, these regulations require that a certain amount of renewable fuel be blended into petroleum-based fuels over the next decade or so. RFS-2 calls for a 10% blend of cellulosic fuel by 2022.[‡]

The targets in RFS-2 mandated that only 6 million gallons be produced in 2010. The industry in fact has a capacity of about 17 million gallons per year today, according to the Biotechnology Industry Organization (BIO), an American lobby group. Compare this to the combined Air Force and Navy requirement of 700 million gallons per year by 2016.

The low expectations reflect the fact that making fuel out of cellulose is hard and costly. Today's cellulosic ethanol is competitive with the gasoline it is supposed to displace only when the price of crude oil reaches and remains at $120 a barrel. The price was at $80–$85 per barrel in 2011.

---

[*] Manomet Center, *Massachusetts Biomass Sustainability*, 43.

[†] See the 2007 Energy Independence and Security Act (EISA). Title II, Subtitle A. Available at http://frwebgate.access.gpo.gov/cgi-bin/getdoc.cgi?dbname=110_Cong_bills&docid=f:h6enr.txt.pdf. (Accessed March 3, 2012.)

[‡] See Clayton McMartin and Graham Noyes, "America Advances to Performance-Based Biofuels, the Advanced Fuel Standard/RFS/2," White Paper, February 26, 2010, RINSTAR, Renewable Fuels Registry, Clean Fuels Clearinghouse, http://www.CFCH.com.

A study carried out in 2009 by Sandia National Laboratories suggests that, in theory, 1.8 billion barrels of cellulosic biofuel a year could be extracted from the country's agriculture and forestry industries. This compares to American oil imports of 4.3 billion barrels in 2009.

A consideration in forecasting biofuels growth as a gasoline or oil substitute is the suggestion of recent studies that some biofuels may not be as effective in reducing greenhouse gas emissions as previously thought. From a portfolio perspective, biofuels projects may have some carbon emissions concerns and corn ethanol may see some reduction in financial support from governments, but since liquids are necessary for the transportation and military sector and oil prices are expected to rise, a market for biofuels will surely exist.

Threats

As with most other alternatives to coal, oil, or natural gas, biomass energy currently has an economic problem that can only presently be addressed via government subsidy or usage standard. Three events that can mitigate this are: (1) substantial increases in the wholesale rates of electricity, or (2) a barrel of oil, or (3) the policy direction for renewables is maintained as an increasing requirement. There is currently a federal government subsidy of $0.46 per gallon for ethanol and a $1.00 per gallon tax credit for biodiesel. Any reduction in subsidy is a threat in the current civilian market.

Achieving a larger share of the transportation energy market depends on cars continuing to be powered by liquid fuels, which is the most likely situation. A large shift to electric cars would threaten the biofuel market as currently conceived by most of its supporters since this additional power demand would be provided by a different energy source. However, such a transition would take a generation or more. The goal of reducing emissions needs low-carbon generators to power the grid the electric cars require, but air transportation and the military fighting vehicles will require liquid fuels.

Table 23.1 presents a risk matrix for a new biofuel plant in the Midwest.

TABLE 23.1

Biofuel Power Risk Matrix

No.	Risk Event	P1	P2	Px
1	Increase in price of corn	2	4	8
2	Increase in energy cost to power the distillery	2	2	4
3	Strong market for electric cars to weaken biofuels market	1	3	4
4	Significant reduction in government subsidy	3	4	12
5	Abolishment of tariff on Brazilian ethanol	2	4	8
6	Shortage of land to produce feed stock	3	3	9

Note: P1 = likelihood of risk event occurring; P2 = probable impact on the industry if P1 occurred; Px = product of P1 and P2 to assign ranking.

24

Hydropower Systems

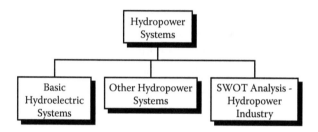

Chapter 24 outline.

In this section we provide an overview and description of the basic hydropower systems followed by a discussion of alternate hydropower systems and a strengths, weaknesses, opportunities, and threats (SWOT) analysis of the industry.

> **Overlay:** Most suitable sites for dams to produce hydropower in the United States are already developed. The undeveloped areas of Asia, Africa, and South America have the greatest opportunity and need for hydropower.

BASIC HYDROELECTRIC SYSTEMS

Hydroelectricity is the term referring to electricity generated by hydropower, the production of electrical power through the use of the gravitational force of falling or flowing water. It is the most widely used form of renewable energy. Once a hydroelectric complex is constructed, the project produces no direct waste, and has almost no carbon emissions. Worldwide, the installed capacity is approximately 20% of the world's electricity, and accounts for about 88% of electricity from renewable sources. In the United States, as shown in Figure 19.3 in Chapter 19, it comprises 35% of the renewable energy and approximately 3% of the total energy.

Hydropower has been used since ancient times to grind flour and perform others tasks. In the mid-1770s, hydraulic machines were developed and by the late 1800s, the electrical generator was developed that could be coupled with hydraulics. The old Schoelkopf Power Station No. 1 near Niagara Falls on the U.S. side began to produce electricity in 1881. By 1886 there were about 45 hydroelectric power plants in the United States and Canada, and by 1889 there were 200 in the United States alone.

Hydroelectric power plants were built at a fast pace and continued to become physically larger throughout the twentieth century. Soon after the Hoover Dam's initial 1,345-MW power plant became the world's largest hydroelectric power plant in 1936, it was eclipsed by the 6,809-MW Grand Coulee Dam in 1942. Brazil's and Paraguay's Itaipu Dam opened in 1984 as the largest, producing 14,000 MW, but was surpassed in 2008 by the Three Gorges Dam in China, with a production capacity of 22,500 MW. Hydroelectricity supplies countries like Norway, Democratic Republic of the Congo, Paraguay, and Brazil with over 85% of their electricity. The United States currently has over 2,000 hydroelectric power plants.

In non-OECD (Organization for Economic Cooperation and Development) countries, hydroelectric power is expected to be the predominant source of renewable electricity growth. Strong growth in hydroelectric generation, primarily from mid- to large-scale power plants, is expected in China, India, Brazil, and a number of nations in Southeast Asia, including Malaysia and Vietnam.

Figure 24.1 presents the world net renewable electricity sources and their trends. Geothermal, solar, and other types were not plotted since their overall amounts are very low, as indicated in the table. These are more important in selected local areas.

To put these numbers in context, the United States generated over 4,000 billion kilowatt-hours of electricity in 2010 and hydropower is fourth after coal, natural gas, and nuclear power as the leading renewable energy source used by electric utilities to generate electric power in the United States.[*]

---

[*] Energy Information Administration (EIA), *International Energy Outlook 2010*, Figures 72 and 73, 82.

World Net Renewable Electricity Generation Sources

	2007	2015	2020	2025	2030	2035
					Total	
					Hydropower	
				Wind		
Hydropower	2,999	3,689	4,166	4,591	5,034	5,418
Wind	165	682	902	1,115	1,234	1,355
Geothermal	57	96	108	119	142	160
Solar	6	95	126	140	153	165
Other	235	394	515	653	773	874
Total World	3,462	4,968	5,817	6,618	7,336	7,972

(Y-axis: Billion Kilowatt-hours, 1,000 to 8,000)

International Energy Outlook 2010 Table 12, p. 81.

FIGURE 24.1
World net renewable electricity sources.

Hydroelectric plants operate where suitable waterways are available; many of the best of these sites have already been developed. Hydropower can be controlled readily and can provide reliable base-load power for a grid. Like other energy sources, the use of water for electricity generation has limitations, including environmental impacts caused by damming rivers and streams, which affects the habitats of the local plant, fish, and animal life.[*]

OTHER HYDROPOWER SYSTEMS

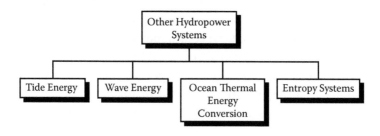

Other Hydropower Systems section outline.

---

[*] See Fred Pearce, *When the Rivers Run Dry*, for a thorough discussion of the problems of siting of dams.

> **Overlay:** At present these systems are all in early development or conceptual phases. They are areas for continuing R&D to possibly develop into practical and economic sources of energy.

There are several other systems that take advantage of current water flows. These are briefly discussed in upcoming text.

Tide Energy Systems

Tide energy systems use the tidal flow to drive large turbines. They are located underwater such as in the East River in New York. A company is planning on installing 30 turbines there to take advantage of the strong tidal flows. Elsewhere, the *New York Times* reported that the "world's largest tidal power turbine" is to be installed in 2010 in northern Scotland to provide power for a computer data center at the European Marine Energy Center.* This turbine, the AK1000, delivers 1 megawatt, weighs 1,430 tons, is nearly 75 feet tall, and has six 60-foot-diameter blades that can produce enough electricity to supply several hundred homes.

There are existing systems in France and Canada that use a barrage system to trap water at high tide then direct it down through a turbine.

Wave Energy Systems

Wave energy systems take advantage of the vertical motion of the waves to generate electricity. Floating buoys have been developed that can generate energy from the bobbing or pitching motion caused by the waves. In some buoy-type systems, the buoy uses a simple mechanical system to turn a crankshaft one revolution for every wave. Using a gear box and a generator, the current is produced continuously.

Vertical cylindrical buoys can also be used in a similar manner to move a piston, which contains a permanent magnet, up and down. The magnet is surrounded by a copper wire coil. As the magnet moves back and forth through the coil, an electric current is automatically generated. One of the

---

* John Collins Rudolf, "Prince of Tides: a Mammoth Turbine," *New York Times*, August 13, 2010, http://green.blogs.nytimes.com/2010/08/13/the-prince-of-tides-a-mammoth-turbine/ (accessed August 13, 2010).

advantages of this approach is that the current is produced directly without the need of a generator.

A horizontal buoy uses semisubmerged cylinders linked by hinged joints. (They are reported to look like sea snakes.) Inside each cylinder there is a hydraulic ram that pumps high-pressure oil through hydraulic motors. The hydraulic motors in turn drive electrical generators inside the cylinder. Many of these cylinders can be combined and then the energy is fed to an underground sea cable and back to shore.

Another approach to generating electricity using wave energy is to use a water-filled column in which the rise and fall of the water in the column moves air or fluid, which in turn spins an electrical generator mounted at the top of the column.

Water, by its very nature, is capable of transferring a great deal of kinetic energy as compared to wind energy systems.* Consequently, even small wave-energy devices are capable of producing a great deal of energy. Also, wave-energy devices are usually low profile and so do not provide much of a visual distraction if placed offshore. However, their problems are multiple: locating a suitable site and then engineering the system at scale to stand the rigors of the oceans, to be economic in operation, and to be profitable. Few meet these criteria.

Ocean Thermal Energy Conversion (OTEC)

Ocean thermal energy conversion systems take advantage of the temperature differences at the surface versus deep water. The greater the temperature difference, the greater the potential efficiency. Because the temperature difference generally increases with decreasing latitude, the preferred locations for OTEC facilities are near the equator, in the tropics where there is warm surface water.

The Earth's oceans are continually heated by the sun and cover over 70% of the Earth's surface; this temperature difference contains a vast amount of solar energy, which can potentially be harnessed for human use. If this extraction could be made cost effective on a large scale, it could provide a source of renewable energy needed to deal with energy shortages and other energy problems. The total energy available is one or two orders of magnitude higher than other ocean energy options such as *wave power*,

---

* Kinetic energy is provided by motion.

but the small magnitude of the temperature difference makes energy extraction comparatively difficult and expensive, due to low thermal efficiency. Early OTEC systems had an overall efficiency of only 1% to 3% (the theoretical maximum efficiency lies between 6% and 7%). Current designs under review will operate closer to the theoretical maximum efficiency. The energy carrier, seawater, is free, though it has an access cost associated with the pumping materials and pump energy costs. An OTEC plant can be configured to operate continuously as a base-load power generation system.

Closed-cycle systems use fluid with a low boiling point, such as ammonia, to rotate a turbine to generate electricity. Warm surface seawater is pumped through a heat exchanger where the low-boiling-point fluid is vaporized. The expanding vapor turns the turbogenerator. Then, cold, deep water—pumped through a second heat exchanger—condenses the vapor back into a liquid, which is then recycled through the system.

In 1979, the Natural Energy Laboratory and several private-sector partners developed a mini-OTEC experiment, which achieved the first successful at-sea production of net electrical power from closed-cycle OTEC. The mini-OTEC vessel was moored 1.5 miles (2.4 km) off the Hawaiian coast and produced enough net electricity to illuminate the ship's light bulbs and run its computers and televisions.

Then, the Natural Energy Laboratory in 1999 tested a 250-kW pilot closed-cycle plant, the largest of its kind ever put into operation. Since then, there have been no tests of OTEC technology in the United States, largely because the poor economics of energy production today have delayed the financing of a permanent, continuously operating plant.

Entropy Systems

Entropy systems are based on the phenomenon that electricity is generated from salinity differences between fresh water and salt water. One process is known as capacitor double-layer expansion (CDLE). There are variations of this process known under similar complex names being developed. In general they involve the use of porous carbon electrodes which, when immersed in salt solutions, store an electric charge similar to capacitors. These ideas have yet to move out of the laboratory.

The problems with all of these ongoing schemes and test beds are the hostile environment in the sea. Wave heights and surges during storms can destroy the installations. Saltwater corrosion, expensive equipment, and expensive power transmission lines combine to keep the capital and operating costs noncompetitive by a wide margin. This doesn't mean that the development work and testing shouldn't go on, only that it may be many years before the economics make any of them viable and there is a payoff or grid parity. There is a tremendous amount of energy in the sea; harnessing it is very difficult but a breakthrough technology may yet exist.

SWOT ANALYSIS: HYDROPOWER

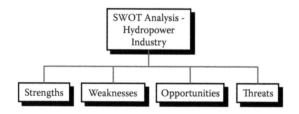

SWOT analysis section outline.

Overlay: Hydropower is an important source of renewable electricity. However, expansion is limited in the United States and OECD-Europe since all the good sites are already taken. Many of the remaining sites face serious environmental concerns. Support should be given for the considerable expansion of hydropower from dams in the less-developed countries over the next 25 years.

The objective of this SWOT analysis of hydropower systems is to evaluate the future availability of additional energy sources from this area.

Strengths

An important advantage of hydroelectric dams for power production is that electricity generation patterns can be easily controlled and the water release pattern can be made to fit the daily or seasonal changing levels of demand for electricity. In a typical daily generating cycle in the summer, the highest demand comes at midday and afternoon because of the need for air conditioning. Like a yo-yo, the river level goes down and up as water is dumped fast in a high electricity demand period and held back during low demand periods.

Compared to wind farms, hydroelectric power plants have a much more predictable load factor. Wind projects really need energy storage reservoirs of some type so electricity can be dispatched to generate power when needed. Hydroelectric plants can be easily regulated to follow variations in power demand and the reservoir is the storage system.

The major advantage of hydroelectricity is economic, with the elimination of the cost of fuel. The cost of operating a hydroelectric plant is nearly immune to increases in the cost of fossil fuels such as oil, natural gas, or coal, and no imports are needed. Hydroelectric plants also tend to have longer economic lives than fuel-fired generation, with some plants now in service that were built 50 to 100 years ago, as described in the opening paragraphs of this section. Operating labor cost is also usually low, as plants are automated and have few personnel on site during normal operation. Where a dam serves multiple purposes, a hydroelectric plant may be added with relatively low construction cost, providing a useful revenue stream to offset the costs of dam operation. Since hydroelectric dams do not burn fossil fuels, they do not directly produce carbon dioxide. While some carbon dioxide is produced during manufacture and construction of the project, this is a tiny fraction of the operating emissions of equivalent fossil-fuel electricity generation.

Reservoirs created by hydroelectric schemes often provide facilities for water sports and become tourist attractions themselves. In some countries, aquaculture in reservoirs is common. Multiuse dams installed for irrigation support agriculture with a relatively constant water supply. Large hydro dams can control floods, which would otherwise affect people living downstream of the project.

Weaknesses

There is a series of weaknesses or side effects that are unique to hydroelectric. These are illustrated in Figure 24.2. Ironically, once constructed,

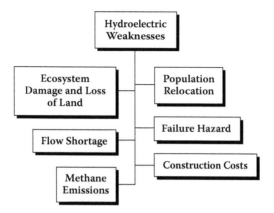

FIGURE 24.2
Hydroelectric weaknesses.

the hydroelectric systems are usually the safest and most reliable clean energy producers in existence.

Each of the major weaknesses of hydroelectric power generation is discussed in the following text.

Ecosystem Damage and Loss of Land

Large reservoirs required for the operation of hydroelectric power stations result in submersion of extensive areas upstream of the dams, often destroying biologically rich and productive lowland and riverine valley forests, marshland, and grasslands. The loss of land is often exacerbated by the fact that reservoirs cause habitat fragmentation of surrounding areas.

Hydroelectric projects can be disruptive to surrounding aquatic ecosystems both upstream and downstream of the plant site. Obvious problems occur in the prevention of access to spawning grounds of fish when they are upstream of the dam.

Generation of hydroelectric power changes the downstream river environment. Water exiting a turbine usually contains very little suspended sediment, which can lead to scouring of river beds and loss of riverbanks. Since turbine gates are often opened intermittently, rapid or even daily fluctuations in river flow occur. Depending on the location, water exiting from turbines is typically much warmer than the pre-dam water, which can change aquatic faunal populations, including endangered species, and prevent natural freezing processes from occurring. Another important issue is the displacement of human beings from their land and their proper resettlement.

Flow Shortage

Changes in the amount of river flow will correlate with the amount of energy produced by a dam. Lower river flows, because of natural cyclical drought, or semipermanent changes due to climate change, or upstream dams and diversions will reduce the amount of live storage in a reservoir, therefore reducing the amount of water that can be used for hydroelectricity. The result of diminished river flow can be power shortages in areas that depend heavily on hydroelectric power.

Methane Emissions (from Reservoirs)

The reservoirs of power plants in tropical regions may produce substantial amounts of methane due to plant material in flooded areas decaying in an anaerobic environment and forming methane, a very potent greenhouse gas. According to the World Commission on Dams report, where the reservoir is large compared to the generating capacity (less than 100 watts per square meter of surface area) and no clearing of the forests in the area was undertaken prior to impoundment of the reservoir, greenhouse gas emissions from the reservoir may be higher than those of a conventional oil-fired thermal generation plant. Although these emissions represent carbon already in the biosphere, not fossil deposits that had been sequestered from the carbon cycle, it can be argued that this factor is carbon-neutral. However, there is a greater amount of methane due to anaerobic decay, causing greater damage than would otherwise have occurred had the forest decayed naturally.

Population Relocation

Another disadvantage of hydroelectric dams is the need to relocate the people living where the reservoirs are planned. In February 2008, it was estimated that 40–80 million people worldwide had been physically displaced as a direct result of dam construction. In many cases, no amount of compensation can replace ancestral and cultural attachments to places that have spiritual value to the displaced population. Additionally, historically and culturally important sites can be flooded and lost.

Such problems arose at the Aswan Dam in Egypt between 1960 and 1980, and at the Three Gorges Dam in China, the Clyde Dam in New Zealand, and the Ilisu Dam in Turkey.

Failure Hazard

Because large conventional dammed hydro facilities hold back large volumes of water, a failure due to poor construction, terrorism, or other causes can be catastrophic to downriver settlements and infrastructure. Dam failures have been some of the largest man-made disasters in history. Also, good design and construction are not an adequate guarantee of safety. Dams are tempting industrial targets for wartime attack, sabotage, and terrorism.

Many dams are constructed with the promise that not only will electricity be generated that will benefit the people in the area, but they will control the disastrous floods that occur occasionally. However, controlling floods requires the reservoir to be relatively low when major storms, heavy snow melt, or monsoons arrive. Because of the demand for electricity, dam operators usually maintain full reservoirs with little spare capacity. As a result, the excess water is released via flood gates to protect the dam, with disastrous results for the downstream residents.* These incidents make river users very wary of promises when dams are proposed upstream of them.

Construction Costs and Schedules

Unlike fossil-fueled combustion turbines, construction of a hydroelectric plant requires a long lead time for site studies, hydrological studies, and design engineering. Hydrological data up to 50 years or more is usually required to determine the best sites and operating regimes for a large hydroelectric plant in the United States. Unlike plants operated by fuel, such as fossil or nuclear energy, the number of sites that can be economically developed for hydroelectric production is very limited; in many areas the most cost-effective sites have already been exploited. New hydro sites tend to be far from population centers and require extensive transmission lines. Hydroelectric generation depends on rainfall in the watershed and may be significantly reduced in years of low rainfall or snowmelt. Long-term energy yield may be affected by climate change because of the impact of changing rainfall amounts and timing. Utilities that primarily use

---

* Fred Pearce, *When the Rivers Run Dry* (Boston: Beacon Press, 2006), 147.

hydroelectric power may need to spend additional capital to build extra capacity to ensure sufficient power is available in low water years.

Opportunities

The total amount of power obtained worldwide from the hydroelectric power plants increased by about 18% in the 10 years from 1995 to 2005. The overall increase in power production from various sources throughout the world during the same period was 37%.

The total hydropower that has the potential to be converted into hydroelectricity is about 14,000 TWh, which is five times the hydroelectricity being exploited today. Of the total potential hydroelectricity available in various parts of the world, 25% is each in Asia, South America, and the former Soviet Union. North America and Europe utilize about half of their potential hydroelectricity, but Asia exploits only 11%, the former Soviet Union 7%, and Africa only 4%. Significant growth in hydropower is expected in Africa, non-OECD Europe, and Asia.

A Department of Energy (DOE) hydropower resource assessment team completed a preliminary assessment of potential hydropower resources in the United States in February 1990.[*] Considering the environmental, legal, and institutional constraints, it has identified 5,677 sites that have a total undeveloped capacity of about 30,000 megawatts or about 1.5 Three Gorges Dams.

Threats

Apart from the various land issues in the development of a hydroelectric power plant, one of the major hindrances is funding of the project. With the rising costs of cement, steel, and iron, the construction of hydroelectric power plants has become very expensive.

If the issues of the environment, ecology, and human displacement and resettlement are not addressed right in the beginning of the project, few private organizations are willing to invest in these types of projects. This is the problem faced by developing countries without the resources in the government to fund the projects. Currently private investors prefer to invest in the thermal projects rather than hydro projects because

---

[*] Allison Conner, James Francfort, and Ben Rinehart, *U.S. Hydropower Resource Assessment Final Report*, U.S. Department of Energy Report DOE/ID-10430.2, Idaho National Engineering and Environmental Laboratory (Idaho Falls, ID: Idaho National Engineering and Environmental Laboratory, December 1998).

of previous bad experiences of improper planning of the project, not handling the resettlement issues, projects getting delayed, project costs becoming over budget, and so on.

The second major threat in developed countries is the lack of suitable sites. All the good sites without problems are taken in the United States and OECD-Europe countries, so the expansion is virtually all overseas. China has a very ambitious program of dam construction to provide hydropower and is able to shortcut many of the environmental and social constraints that exist elsewhere.

A third threat is climate change. As indicated earlier, dams are built to last for many years. The Hoover dam is 75 years old. For new dams, the climate change overlay analysis of Section 2 needs to be done to assess and plan for the likely impacts of climate change on the specific watershed several decades in the future. It is to be expected that the stream flow time profile will be quite different from today.

Table 24.1 is a sample risk matrix for a new hydropower dam project, assuming a site has been located.

TABLE 24.1

Conventional Hydropower Risk Matrix

No.	Risk Event	P1	P2	Px
1	Geology shows site is unacceptable	2	5	10
2	Environmental impact exceeds expected levels	2	4	8
3	Movement of people more complex than planned	3	3	9
4	Construction cost and schedule control	4	2	8
5	Drought—reservoir not filling up	1	4	4

Note: P1 = likelihood of risk event occurring; P2 = probable impact on the industry if P1 occurred; Px = product of P1 and P2 to assign ranking.

25

Renewable Energy Sources Summary

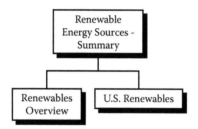

Chapter 25 outline.

RENEWABLES OVERVIEW

In the last century, the countries that had the energy resources or otherwise used the energy resources of coal, petroleum, and natural gas to improve the standards of living of their peoples were the leading countries of the world. Some countries with extensive resources only used them to enrich the ruling class, as is seen in the Middle East.

Overlay: The International Panel on Climate Change (IPCC) Working Group III released a special report on renewable energy sources and climate change mitigation in May 2011 that presented an assessment from the literature on the scientific, technological, environmental, economic, and social aspects of the contribution of six renewable energy sources to the mitigation of climate change. It is intended to provide policy-relevant information to governments, intergovernmental processes, and other interested parties. It is recommended that planners acquire this report and use it as a complement to this book in the area of the interaction of renewables and climate change.* The conclusions are consistent with our recommended overlays.

---

* Available at IPCC, "Special Report on Renewable Energy Sources and Climate Change Mitigation," http://srren.ipcc-wg3.de/report. (Accessed March 3, 2012.)

With the possible limits of production, as discussed earlier regarding peak oil, the costs of petroleum fuels in the next decade and beyond is really an unknown. The nature of the competition for oil resources is also an unknown. In addition, the concern about carbon emissions places a cloud over the long-term future of coal. Some believe that in this century the energy competitions are going to be won by those who understand how to develop new technology, deploy new technology, and get the benefits of exporting that technology to the rest of the world.* The emphasis will be on renewable energy sources that are the result of continuing technological progress. Renewables are needed to replace fossil fuels.

It would be nice if it were that clear to all, but that is not the situation. The United States appears to have a government still solving the last century's problems by assuming oil and coal are unlimited resources that still need subsidization and that there is no hurry to develop renewable technology. "There is plenty of oil in the ground and only government regulations are preventing us from accessing it" is a common theme. Of course this is the result of a strong and effective lobbying effort on the part of the oil and coal interests. And the development of fracking and new technologies to enable access to the oil locked in oil sands lends some credence to this mantra. China is rapidly developing renewable technology and Europe is moving forward aggressively toward a target of 100% renewable electricity by 2050. At present, approximately two thirds of new electricity capacity is from renewables and it is expected that by 2020 all new capacity will be renewables. Continuing that policy would mean all of Europe's electric power by 2050 would be renewable or nuclear since between now

---

* Christian Kjaer, the European Wind Energy Association's CEO. Yale e360, posted on September 9, 2010, "Topic: Business & Innovation," http://e360.yale.edu/content/topic.msp?id=55; "Topic: Energy," http://e360.yale.edu/content/topic.msp?id=15; "Topic: Policy & Politics," http://e360.yale.edu/content/topic.msp?id=247; and "Topic: Europe," http://e360.yale.edu/content/region.msp?id=35.

and 2050 all existing fossil fuel power plants would be retired. Also, with Germany backing off from nuclear power, this adds more incentive to change the European power transmission infrastructure to accommodate the changes.

U.S. RENEWABLES

An overlay and summary status of renewables in the United States is as follows:[*]

> Solar and wind energy have significant potential for the United States and are likely to be deployed in increasing amounts. They alone cannot meet the entire demand but together may be able to meet the increases in demand that accompany population increase and standard of living increase. Solar and wind energy are inherently intermittent and cannot provide 24-hour-a-day base load without an associated energy storage system. Concentrating solar power (CSP) with salt storage provides an option for increased base-load capacity in the southwest, where demand is growing.
>
> Economic deep engineered geothermal systems are still far in the future due to (1) the uncertainties inherent in the geology and (2) the fracking process providing a permeable reservoir at the bottom of the drilled holes.
>
> Biomass can be used as a renewable fuel to provide electricity using existing heat-to-power technology. However, its value to the United States as a feed stock for biofuels for transportation may be much higher, given the increasing prices of oil and the future beyond peak oil.
>
> There is considerable opportunity for capacity expansion of U.S. hydropower potential using existing dams and impoundments. All the good sites are being utilized. But outside of a few pumped storage projects, hydropower growth has been constrained by reductions in capacity imposed by the Federal Energy Regulatory Commission (FERC) as a result of environmental concerns.

---

[*] Extracted from MIT report. The Future. See page 29, bottom, for complete reference.

Clearly, we need to increase energy efficiency in all end-use sectors, but even aggressive efforts cannot eliminate the substantial replacement and new capacity additions that will be needed to avoid reductions in the services or increases in costs and to provide for an expanding population.

26

Program Planning in an Energy Constrained and Uncertain World

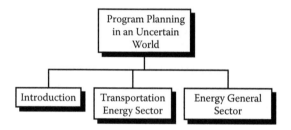

Chapter 26 outline.

INTRODUCTION

My parents and grandparents lived through the twentieth century and there was absolutely no way someone born in the early 1900s could have predicted either the wonders of the world in the year 2000 or the amazing increase in the standards of living of the people in the Western world. However, we have a big advantage over the citizens of 1910: our knowledge base is almost infinitely larger and so some predictions can be made with a fair amount of certainty—at least to mid-century.

The energy pillar of the triple constraint is very complex and composed of many components. We have seen how the population is growing—from 7 billion today to over 9 billion in the world by 2050, or in the United States we go from 308 million today to over 400 million by 2050. These people need to be fed, housed, provided with jobs, educated, and cared for. And they all want an increased standard of living. This requires energy. The demand exists and the issue is whether the supply of energy will match the demand. We will need more barrels of oil, more coal, more natural gas, more nuclear power, and more renewables—at least 30% more on a worldwide basis by 2035 just to keep the per capita supply even with today's per capita usage. But, as we discussed earlier, controlling world-wide emissions to levels needed to mitigate climate change would mean in China and India the increases in standard of living would have to stop and there would be little hope for many in Africa of moving out of their current difficult living conditions.

The two energy demand drivers are energy for powering transportation and energy for powering everything else. Transportation is different because we have to carry our energy sources with us except in the case of electric trains and trolley buses. These we will lump with the other forms of energy because they depend on electric power.

For this discussion, we will generally ignore the big elephant in the room called *emissions* and CO_2, and look at problems of energy production. The elephant and its impact were discussed earlier.

TRANSPORTATION ENERGY SECTOR

Overlay: Transportation relies on oil. It is the major operating cost. As supplies dwindle, major changes will occur due to price increases, especially in air travel, where fuel is a larger share of operating costs. These changes are predictable, although the timing is somewhat vague. Transportation cost changes will impact choices of living and commuting. Planning should consider that globalization may reverse as air transportation and energy costs rise, resulting in domestic production again becoming competitive. And as ground transportation costs increase, locally produced goods and services will become preferable.

The principal driver in the energy sector is the availability and price of oil. At present there appears to be no supply shortage due to the impact of the recession. However, we have seen the price of a barrel of oil increase in the past 4 years from $40 to $80 per barrel to over $100 and back to $80 in 2011, so there are some supply problems or constraints. Although there may be a larger number of electric vehicles running around our streets and highways in the next few years, it will take 2–3 decades until the numbers really become significant. (Maybe sooner if driven by shortages of oil.)

More biofuels and synfuels will be produced and higher ethanol percentages are likely to be allowed in fuel mixes. There will also be some natural gas–powered vehicles, especially buses and trucks where there are fleet quantities involved and the necessary refueling infrastructure. The use of hydrogen in fuel cells will continue to be researched and developed and some few may eventually go into production. But, all in all, in the next several decades and beyond we will be dependent upon oil for our major transportation needs.

Because of the supply and production constraints, the price of a barrel of oil will increase significantly and probably in a series of spikes and drops, as indicated earlier. But it will be a steady and relentless increase. In the book *$20 Per Gallon*, Christopher Steiner presents a chapter-by-chapter, step-by-step, dollar-by-dollar description of the impact of this constant rise; it is scary. What the book does not do is provide a timetable or indication of the rate of the increases, although it does predict an increase to $10 per gallon within a decade.[*] (Based on when his book was written, his forecast should probably be measured as the decade after the recession ends.) Petroleum will be available for transportation, especially air transportation, many years into the future. Free market pricing will ensure that, or rationing if the market fails. The incidence of peak oil does not mean that the world runs out immediately, only that the relentless process of decline is underway. We are still finding oil in the United States even though peak oil occurred in 1972. We are just not finding it and extracting it fast enough to match the depletion rate. Additional oil will be found in expensive locations such as deep water offshore and various rationing schemes may arise. (The politics will be ferocious.)

It is easy to visualize what will happen to the transportation sector as petroleum fuel costs rise significantly. Trains and automobiles will move toward electric; train travel will replace air travel for certain short-haul air routes in the United States (where the tracks exist). The future of long-haul train service in the United States is very uncertain even with the

---

[*] Christopher Steiner, *$20 per Gallon* (New York: Grand Central Publishing, 2009), 89.

multibillion dollar stimulus proposed by President Obama. The author was the program manager for the upgrade of the rail system in the Northeast Corridor. It is very depressing to see how few persons can actually be moved by train, considering the cost of the infrastructure and maintenance. A national high-speed rail network would be great and some planning is currently underway, but the capital and operating and maintenance costs are daunting and the benefits are very small—unless air travel becomes inordinately expensive and the price of gasoline moves toward $14 to $18 per gallon.* The rationale for the upgrade of the Northeast Corridor rail passenger service was that the program provided a needed service to the area and not energy savings or economics. It was a social program. It could barely support the operating costs and was unable to amortize any capital investment costs. This is the situation in high-speed rail worldwide. But if airline tickets need to be at Concorde price levels due to fuel costs to fly from New York to Chicago, then high-speed rail, subsidized by the government, becomes attractive for some links between major cities.

Globalization will slow down or may even be reversed when transportation costs make foreign products uneconomic compared to domestic production. Large cargo ships will eventually go nuclear and this will be expensive. All of this will take time to come about, maybe not significantly until after 2050, but it will happen and you will need to watch the signals and plan accordingly if you are involved in transportation or rely on transportation as part of your supply chain. One of the main signals is production from Organization of the Petroleum Exporting Companies (OPEC): Is it able to increase production to meet increasing demand and rising prices? The Energy Information Administration (EIA) estimates assume a significant increase in Middle East oil production to meet the energy requirements of 2035. Many doubt this capability. Further, it is unlikely that significant production will occur from offshore and Alaskan sources as compared to the demand. These sources may delay a serious oil production slowdown for a few years, but even the optimistic forecasts do not show another Saudi Arabia hidden anywhere in the world.

Another factor is our military—it runs on oil—tanks, planes, ships, and so on. Perhaps the National Petroleum Reserve will be turned over to the Department of Defense (DOD) at some point in the future.

---

* Steiner, *$20 per Gallon*, 198.

ENERGY GENERAL SECTOR

Overlay: It is important to shift from a business-as-usual mind-set toward one concerned about the availability of energy and the impact of emissions of CO_2. Coal and natural gas are in relatively abundant supply and it will be difficult to replace them as energy sources. However, since these are fossil fuels, the supply will only be available for a few generations and will eventually be superseded by emissions-free fuels.

The trends in the nontransportation sector are also relatively easy to predict if we assume business as usual. The timing, however, is not easy. It is expected that coal will continue to be a dominant source of energy throughout the world for the foreseeable future, at least to 2035. While the U.S. usage will remain flat or may even decline, the non-OECD (Organization for Economic Cooperation and Development) areas of Asia will see a major increase since the coal is available and cheap and rising incomes and population will demand higher standards of living and that requires energy. Beyond 2035, the usage of coal may depend upon carbon capture and storage (CCS) technology as the significant climate changes force a change from a business-as-usual philosophy.

Since there do not appear to be any constraints on the supply of natural gas, other than adding to the extraction and distribution infrastructure in the shale fields and adjusting for some environmental impact, it will tend to replace coal in power plants in the United States due to concerns over CO_2 and also where it is more economic. Natural gas–powered plants are also easier to justify and faster to construct.

But this will only partially mitigate CO_2 concerns since natural gas is itself a fossil fuel and gives off CO_2. In the longer term, when it becomes impossible to avoid taking action to mitigate CO_2, nuclear power or renewables using some new technology will be needed to replace both coal and natural gas.

Note that I said, "When it becomes impossible to avoid taking action." As discussed in the climate change section of Chapter 4, the actions necessary to get governments to act, especially the U.S. government, are indeterminate at this time. For scientists, the time occurred some years ago, as documented in Appendix A.

In all of this, renewables will become more important to take an increasing percentage of the load and any breakthroughs will be very welcome. Renewables must increase their share of the energy market.

Section IV

Supporting Appendices

Four supporting Appendices are included to expand on certain topics. These are illustrated in the figure below.

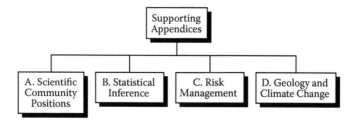

Supporting Appendices outline.

Appendix A: The Scientific Community Positions on Climate Change and Global Warming*

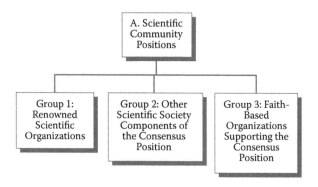

Appendix A outline.

GROUP 1: RENOWNED SCIENTIFIC ORGANIZATIONS AND THEIR CONCLUSIONS ON CLIMATE CHANGE

- **Intergovernmental Panel on Climate Change (IPCC):** This group is made up of hundreds of scientists and was commissioned by the World Meteorological Organization and the United Nations Environmental Program to provide the most authoritative, up-to-date, objective information on climate change. They assessed the findings of thousands of scientific studies conducted across the globe. The IPCC recently shared the 2007 Nobel Peace Prize for their work on climate change. "Warming of the climate system is unequivocal, as is now

---

* Group 1 Compiled by Dr. Peter Gleick, President, Pacific Institute : http://www.sfgate.com/cgi-bin/blogs/gleick/detail?entry_id=59226#ixzz15prAsTaB (last accessed March 24, 2011).

evident from observations of increases in global average air and ocean temperatures, widespread melting of snow and ice, and rising global average sea level. ... The understanding of anthropogenic warming and cooling influences on climate has improved since the Third Assessment Report, leading to very high confidence that the global average net effect of human activities since 1750 has been one of warming." (IPCC4 2007 Physical Science Basis, Summary for Policymakers, http://www.ipcc.ch/ipccreports/ar4-wg1.htm)

- **National Research Council of the National Academy of Sciences:** The NAS is a private, non-profit organization established in 1863, that advises the government on scientific matters and conducts scientific research to further the general welfare of society. "Climate change is occurring, is very likely caused by human activities, and poses significant risks for a broad range of human and natural systems. Each additional ton of greenhouse gases emitted commits us to further change and greater risks. In the judgment of the Committee on America's Climate Choices, the environmental, economic, and humanitarian risks of climate change indicate a pressing need for substantial action to limit the magnitude of climate change and to prepare to adapt to its impacts.*"

- **U.S. Climate Change Science Program:** This program was established by President Bush in 2002 and is a federal program sponsored by 13 federal agencies, including the National Aeronautics and Space Administration (NASA), the National Oceanic and Atmospheric Association (NOAA), and the Environmental Protection Agency (EPA). "Studies to detect climate change and attribute its causes using patterns of observed temperature change in space and time show clear evidence of human influences on the climate system (due to changes in greenhouse gases, aerosols, and stratospheric ozone). The observed patterns of change over the past 50 years cannot be explained by natural processes alone, nor by the effects of short-lived atmospheric constituents (such as aerosols and tropospheric ozone) alone." (http://www.climatescience.gov/Library/sap/sap1-1/finalreport/sap1-1-final-execsum.pdf, p. 2)

- **American Association for the Advancement of Science:** This is the largest and one of the most prestigious scientific organizations. It

---

* (Reference: National Academy of Sciences, America's Climate Choices, 2011. http://www.nap.edu/catalog/12781.html. Summary Page 1. (Accessed February 27, 2012.)

publishes the most widely circulated peer-reviewed journal, *Science*. "The scientific evidence is clear: global climate change caused by human activities is occurring now, and it is a growing threat to society. ... It is time to muster the political will for concerted action. Stronger leadership at all levels is needed. The time is now. We must rise to the challenge. We owe this to future generations." (http://www.aaas.org/news/press_room/climate_change/mtg_200702/aaas_climate_statement.pdf)

- **American Meteorological Society:** This group was founded in 1919 and has more than 11,000 members. It is one of the most trusted and well-respected organizations that deal with atmospheric sciences. "Human activities have become a major source of environmental change. Of great urgency are the climate consequences of the increasing atmospheric abundance of greenhouse gases and other trace constituents resulting primarily from energy use, agriculture, and land clearing. ... Because greenhouse gases continue to increase, we are, in effect, conducting a global climate experiment, neither planned nor controlled, the results of which may present unprecedented challenges to our wisdom and foresight as well as have significant impacts on our natural and societal systems. It is a long-term problem that requires a long-term perspective." (http://www.ametsoc.org/policy/climatechangeresearch_2003.html)

- **Geological Society of America:** This group was established in 1888, and with over 20,500 members, is the leading professional organization in the field of geology. "The Geological Society of America (GSA) supports the scientific conclusions that Earth's climate is changing; the climate changes are due in part to human activities; and the probable consequences of the climate changes will be significant and blind to geopolitical boundaries. Furthermore, the potential implications of global climate change and the time scale over which such changes will likely occur require active, effective, long-term planning." (http://www.geosociety.org/positions/position10.htm)

- **American Chemical Society:** This group was founded in 1876 and is the world's largest scientific society representing professionals in all fields of chemistry. "Careful and comprehensive scientific assessments have clearly demonstrated that the Earth's climate system is changing rapidly in response to growing atmospheric burdens of greenhouse gases and absorbing aerosol particles (IPCC, 2007). There is very little room for doubt that observed climate trends are due to human activities. The threats are serious and action is urgently needed to mitigate the risks of climate change." See Google as "ACS Global Climate Change Position Statement. http://portal.acs.org/portal/acs/corg/content?_nfpb=true&pageLabel=PP_SUPERARTICLE&node_id=1907&use_sec=false&sec_url_var=region1&uuid=0d5fe2fc-8048-42dd-a461-3dbf6436921b.

- **American Geophysical Union:** This is a worldwide scientific society with over 50,000 members that seeks to promote scientific advances in the understanding of the Earth and space. Its statement on climate change was endorsed by the American Institute of Physics and the American Astronomical Society. "Human activities are increasingly altering the Earth's climate. These effects add to natural influences that have been present over Earth's history. Scientific evidence strongly indicates that natural influences cannot explain the rapid increase in global near-surface temperatures observed during the second half of the 20th century." (http://www.agu.org/sci_soc/policy)

GROUP 2: OTHER SCIENTIFIC SOCIETY COMPONENTS OF THE CONSENSUS POSITION

The following statements were compiled by Peter Gleick, president, Pacific Institute and published on his SFGate.com web posting at http://blog.sfgate.com/gleick/2010/03/15/cimat-change-deniers-versus-the-scientific-communities-of-the-world-who-should-we-listen-to/#ixzz15prAsTaB

National Science Academies of the G8+5 Nations (Brazil, Canada, China, France, Germany, Italy, India, Japan, Mexico, Russia, South Africa, the United Kingdom, and the United States)

It is unequivocal that the climate is changing, and it is very likely that this is predominantly caused by the increasing human interference with the atmosphere. These changes will transform the environmental conditions on Earth unless counter-measures are taken.

Ecological Society of America

The Earth is warming—average global temperatures have increased by 0.74 deg. C (1.3 deg. F) in the past 100 years. The scientific community agrees that catastrophic and possibly irreversible environmental change will occur if average global temperatures rise an additional 2 deg. C. Warming to date has already had significant impacts on the Earth and its ecosystems. Most warming seen since the mid 1900s is very likely due to greenhouse gas emissions from human activities.

American Physical Society

Emissions of greenhouse gases from human activities are changing the atmosphere in ways that affect the Earth's climate. The evidence is incontrovertible: Global warming is occurring. If no mitigating actions are taken, significant disruptions in the Earth's physical and ecological systems, social systems, security and human health are likely to occur. We must reduce emissions of greenhouse gases beginning now.

International Council of Academies of Engineering and Technological Sciences (CAETS)

[M]ost of the observed global warming since the mid-20th century is very likely due to human-produced emission of greenhouse gases and this warming will continue unabated if present anthropogenic emissions continue or, worse, expand without control. CAETS, therefore, endorses the many recent calls to decrease and control greenhouse gas emissions to an acceptable level as quickly as possible.

Network of African Science Academies

The 13 signatories were the science academies of Cameroon, Ghana, Kenya, Madagascar, Nigeria, Senegal, South Africa, Sudan, Tanzania, Uganda, Zambia, Zimbabwe, as well as the African Academy of Sciences.

A consensus, based on current evidence, now exists within the global scientific community that human activities are the main source of climate change and that the burning of fossil fuels is largely responsible for driving this change. The IPCC should be congratulated for the contribution it has made to public understanding of the nexus that exists between energy, climate, and sustainability.

European Physical Society

The emission of anthropogenic greenhouse gases, among which carbon dioxide is the main contributor, has amplified the natural greenhouse effect and led to global warming. The main contribution stems from burning fossil fuels. A further increase will have decisive effects on life on earth. An energy cycle with the lowest possible CO_2 emission is called for wherever possible to combat climate change.

European Science Foundation Position Paper

There is now convincing evidence that since the industrial revolution, human activities, resulting in increasing concentrations of greenhouse gases, have become a major agent of climate change. These greenhouse gases affect the global climate by retaining heat in the troposphere, thus raising the average temperature of the planet and altering global atmospheric circulation and precipitation patterns. On-going and increased efforts to mitigate climate change through reduction in greenhouse gases are therefore crucial.

Federation of Australian Scientific and Technological Societies Policy Statement

Global climate change is real and measurable. The spatial and temporal fingerprint of warming can be traced to increasing greenhouse gas concentrations in the atmosphere, which are a direct result of burning fossil fuels, broad-scale deforestation and other human activity.

European Federation of Geologists Position Paper

The EFG recognizes the work of the IPCC and other organizations, and subscribes to the major findings that climate change is happening, is predominantly caused by anthropogenic emissions of CO_2, and poses a significant threat to human civilization. It is clear that major efforts are necessary to quickly and strongly reduce CO_2 emissions.

Geological Society of Australia Position Statement

Human activities have increasing impact on Earth's environments. Of particular concern are the well-documented loading of carbon dioxide (CO_2) to the atmosphere, which has been linked unequivocally to burning of fossil fuels, and the corresponding increase in average global temperature. Risks associated with these large-scale perturbations of the Earth's fundamental life-support systems include rising sea level, harmful shifts in the acid balance of the oceans and long-term changes in local and regional climate and extreme weather events. GSA therefore recommends ... strong action be taken at all levels, including government, industry, and individuals to substantially reduce the current levels of greenhouse gas emissions and mitigate the likely social and environmental effects of increasing atmospheric CO_2.

International Union of Geodesy and Geophysics (IUGG) Resolution

The IUGG concurs with the "comprehensive and widely accepted and endorsed scientific assessments carried out by the Intergovernmental Panel on Climate Change and regional and national bodies, which have firmly established, on the basis of scientific evidence, that human activities are the primary cause of recent climate change.

Royal Meteorological Society (UK)

The Fourth Assessment Report (AR4) of the Inter-Governmental Panel on Climate Change (IPCC) is unequivocal in its conclusion that climate change is happening and that humans are contributing significantly to these changes. The evidence, from not just one source but a number of different measurements, is now far greater and the tools we have to model climate change contain much more of our scientific knowledge within them. The world's best climate scientists are telling us it's time to do something about it.

American Public Health Association Policy Statement

The long-term threat of global climate change to global health is extremely serious and the fourth IPCC report and other scientific literature demonstrate convincingly that anthropogenic GHG [greenhouse gas] emissions are primarily responsible for this threat. U.S. policy makers should immediately take necessary steps to reduce U.S. emissions of GHGs, including carbon dioxide, to avert dangerous climate change.

Australian Medical Association

The world's climate—our life-support system—is being altered in ways that are likely to pose significant direct and indirect challenges to health. While "climate change" can be due to natural forces or human activity, there is now substantial evidence to indicate that human activity—and specifically increased greenhouse gas (GHGs) emissions—is a key factor in the pace and extent of global temperature increases.

Read more at SFGate, Peter Gleick, "Climate-Change Deniers versus the Scientific Societies of the World: Who Should We Listen To?" http://www.sfgate.com/cgi-bin/blogs/gleick/detail?entry_id=59226#ixzz15prAsTaB.

GROUP 3: FAITH-BASED ORGANIZATIONS SUPPORTING THE CONSENSUS POSITION

Pontifical Academy of Sciences, Vatican, Rome, May 11, 2011[*]

> We call on all people and nations to recognize the serious and potentially irreversible impacts of global warming caused by the anthropogenic emissions of greenhouse gases and other pollutants, and by changes in forests, wetlands, grasslands, and other land uses. We appeal to all nations to develop and implement, without delay, effective and fair policies to reduce the causes and impacts of climate change on communities and ecosystems, including mountain glaciers and their watersheds, aware that we all live in the same home. By acting now, in the spirit of common but differentiated responsibility, we accept our duty to one another and to the stewardship of a planet blessed with the gift of life.
>
> We are committed to ensuring that all inhabitants of this planet receive their daily bread, fresh air to breathe and clean water to drink, as we are aware that, if we want justice and peace, we must protect the habitat that sustains us.
>
> The believers among us ask God to grant us this wish.

Society of Friends Statement on Global Climate Change

At the June 2000 session of Interim Meeting, Philadelphia Yearly Meeting approved these minutes on the responsibility to address global climate change[†]:

> Protecting God's Earth and its fullness of life is of fundamental religious concern to the Society of Friends. The links between human activity, the dramatic rise in atmospheric greenhouse gas concentrations, and the rise of average global temperatures are now of sufficient concern to lead us to action.

---

[*] Ajai, L. B., et al. Working Group Commissioned by the Pontifical Academy of Sciences, *Fate of Mountain Glaciers in the Anthropocene* (Vatican, Rome: Pontifical Academy of Sciences, May 11, 2011), 1, "Declaration," http://www.vatican.va/roman_curia/pontifical_academies/acdscien/2011/PAS_Glacier_110511_final.pdf (accessed May 12, 2011).

[†] http://www.webofcreation.org/ncc/statements/sof.html.

Climate change is apt to affect everyone and everything: food, water, air quality, biodiversity, forests, public health, social order, and world peace. It is therefore an issue of great importance for ecological sustainability, social and economic justice, and international diplomacy.

Because the United States uses much more energy per capita than any other nation, our policies to curtail greenhouse gas emissions will be crucial. We must consider not only the kind of fuels used directly but also the energy embodied in all material goods we use. Our nation has long set a standard for others with consequences of past and current behavior.

Involvement by religious communities in education and advocacy will be needed if policies to address global warming are to succeed in politics or in practice in the United States. We unite in urging individual Friends, monthly meetings, and other Friends organizations to seek Divine Guidance in understanding how to

- reduce our own use of energy and material resources;
- support strong international agreements for reducing greenhouse gas emissions;
- promote national policies for assuring energy and resource conservation;
- participating in a transition to less damaging technologies in our industries, agriculture, buildings and transportation.

These are essential steps to protect life on Earth as God creates and sustains it.

American Baptist Churches[*]

The original of the American Baptist Resolution on Global Warming is a four-page resolution; a portion follows:

Global warming affects hunger, access to clean water, environmental stewardship, health and peace. Addressing global warming will make it more possible for all to live the life of possibility that God intends. Therefore, based on our faith in the Creator God who makes us a part of a unified creation, the General Board of the American Baptist Churches USA calls on national boards, regions, American Baptist institutions, congregations and individuals to: …

C. Address the causes and reverse the consequences of global warming by:
   1. Advocating the passage of legislation at all appropriate levels to reduce carbon dioxide output and to set reduction targets for other greenhouse gases.

---

[*] See http://www.abc-usa.org/LinkClick.aspx?fileticket=0JpsQst6Agw%3D&tabid=199.

2. Supporting the passage of mandatory higher fuel efficiency for new vehicles and phasing out of older, less efficient vehicles.
3. Supporting rail and other means of increased transportation efficiency including subsidies for public transportation.
4. Combating deforestation domestically and internationally through programs of preservation and reforestation and through responsible consumption.
5. Sponsoring and supporting shareholder resolutions to corporations on issues like reduction of carbon dioxide and other greenhouse gases, phasing out of CFC's, increased energy efficiency and fuel conservation, environmental cost accounting, and other issues affecting global warming.
6. Calling for an international treaty such as the Kyoto Protocols on global warming with specific targets for the reduction of greenhouse gases.
7. Working to implement just intra- and inter-national trade and economic relationships (based on principles like the transfer of technical and economic resources, self-reliance, sustainable agriculture, and forms of development that do not exacerbate global warming). ...

Adopted by the General Board of the American Baptist Churches, November 1991
161 For, O Against, 1 Abstention
Modified by the Executive Committee of the General Board, March 2001
Modified by the Executive Committee of the General Board, September 2007
(General Board Reference # - 8189:6/91)

Unitarian Universalist Association of Congregations

*Threat of Global Warming/Climate Change**

2006 Statement of Conscience

Earth is our home. We are part of this world and its destiny is our own. Life on this planet will be gravely affected unless we embrace new practices, ethics, and values to guide our lives on a warming planet. As Unitarian Universalists, how can our faith inform our actions to remedy and mitigate global warming/climate change? We declare by this Statement of Conscience that we will not acquiesce to the ongoing degradation and destruction of life that human actions are leaving to our children and grandchildren. We

---

* See http://www.uua.org/socialjustice/socialjustice/statements/8061.shtml for complete statement.

as Unitarian Universalists are called to join with others to halt practices that fuel global warming/climate change, to instigate sustainable alternatives, and to mitigate the impending effects of global warming/climate change with just and ethical responses. As a people of faith, we commit to a renewed reverence for life and respect for the interdependent web of all existence.

This statement is the first of several pages on the topic, including a call to action. The statement was last updated Thursday, June 3, 2010.

General Board of the United Methodist Church[*]

Advocacy Focus Issues: Climate Change

Not everyone agrees on how climate change takes place, but the scientific community overwhelmingly acknowledges the reality of global warming. Many companies contribute directly to global warming through greenhouse gas (GHG) emissions; however, all are susceptible to the effects. This is a concern of many corporate stakeholder groups—legislators, regulators, insurers, consumers, and investors.

Anticipating how climate change may affect a company's ability to operate in the future has financial opportunities and risks for shareholders. For example, corporate leaders are learning that competitive advantage can be achieved through attention to GHG emissions. Participants in the Environmental Protection Agency's Climate Leader program report saving tens—and sometimes hundreds—of millions of dollars through energy efficiency and emissions reduction programs. On the other hand, the lack of federal emissions standards resulted in more than 20% of states enacting their own carbon regulations. This requires corporations to achieve varying levels of compliance, which may be costly for heavy emitters.

Accordingly, the General Board calls upon companies to report on their response to issues relating to global warming and climate change.

The United Methodist Church calls for the "control of global warming" (Resolution 1001.8), the support of "strenuous efforts to conserve energy and increase energy efficiency" (Resolution 1001.1), the United States to "move beyond its dependence on high carbon fossil fuels that produce emissions leading to climate change" (Resolution 1002.1) and "measures calling for a reduction of carbon dioxide, methane, nitrogen oxides, and sulfur dioxide, which contribute to acid rain and global climate change" (Resolution 1023).

---

[*] See http://www.gbophb.org/sri_funds/issues.asp#climate.

Central Conference of American Rabbis

This is an excerpt from the Climate Change Resolution* adopted by the 116th Annual Convention of the Central Conference of American Rabbis.

> The following Jewish and secular moral principles serve as the foundation for the Conference's position on the development of agreements and policies to address climate change:
>
> Responsibilities to Future Generations: "Therefore choose life, that you and your descendants may live." (Deuteronomy 30:20) Humankind has a solemn obligation to improve the world for future generations. Minimizing climate change requires us to learn how to live within the ecological limits of the Earth, so that we will not compromise the ecological or economic security of those who come after us.
>
> Integrity of Creation: "The human being was placed in the Garden of Eden to till it and to tend it." (Genesis 2:15) Humankind has a solemn obligation to protect the integrity of ecological systems, so that their diverse constituent species, including humans, can thrive.
>
> Equitable Distribution of Responsibility: Nations' responsibilities for reducing greenhouse gas emissions should correlate to their contribution to the problem. The United States has built an economy highly dependent upon fossil fuel use that has affected the entire globe, and must therefore reduce greenhouse gas emissions in a manner that corresponds to its share of the problem.
>
> Protection of the Vulnerable: "When one loves righteousness and justice, the earth is full of the loving-kindness of the Eternal." (Psalm 33:5) The requirements and implementation procedures to address climate change must protect those most vulnerable to climate change both here in the United States and around the globe: poor people, those living in coastal areas, those who rely on subsistence agriculture.
>
> Sustainable Development: The Earth cannot sustain the levels of resource exploitation currently maintained by the developed world. As we work towards global economic development, the developed world should promote the use of renewable energy sources and new technologies, so that developing nations do not face the same environmental challenges that we face today because of industrialization.
>
> Strong action to reduce greenhouse gas emissions is consistent with a number of long-standing public policy priorities, including: improving air quality, increasing mass transit, development of non-polluting alternative energy sources, energy efficiency, and energy conservation.

---

* See http://data.ccarnet.org/cgi-bin/resodisp.pl?file=climate&year=2005.

Together, the people of the world can, and must, use our God-given gifts to develop innovative strategies to meet the needs of all who currently dwell on this planet, without compromising the ability of future generations to meet their own needs.

Other Faith-Based Statements

Many other faith-based statements are available at http://www.iccr.org/issues/globalwarm/Faithbased070507.doc.

Appendix B: Statistical Inference

Statistical inference is a tool for analysis and discussion of options, alternatives, and actions. There are two types of errors:

- Type 1 is when you accept a statement as fact (the hypothesis) and take action and it turns out that the statement (the hypothesis) is false.
- Type 2 is when you reject a hypothesis and take no action and it turns out that the hypothesis is true.

The base assumption or statement or *null hypothesis* is: *humans are causing dangerous global warming.*[*] In statistical inference, the base assumption usually is phrased that things are unsafe until proven safe, which is the basis for the specific wording. A Type 1 error often occurs when data are scarce and scientists and decision makers are concerned about misleading society into action, then being blamed for undue alarm or needless expenditures or restraints if the adverse event does not occur.

An example is the decisions faced by the Centers for Disease Control (CDC). If they have data that suggest a particular flu strain will be prevalent in the coming season, they are faced with a decision—possibly making a Type 1 error and strongly urging the population to get a flu shot that includes the strain, and then it turns out the strain was not as virulent as originally expected. Or do they do nothing and make a Type 2 error and the strain is exceptionally virulent and kills thousands of people? This second kind of error is a false negative. In the case of the climate hypothesis, if it is decided to do little or nothing until much of the perceived uncertainty is resolved, then it would be discovered that serious climate change "ensues unabated with much more damage than if precautionary policies had been undertaken to adapt to and mitigate the effects."[†]

---

[*] This assumption is proposed by John Cook of SkepticalScience.com in a brief essay on his blog titled "How We Know Recent Global Warming Is Not Natural," February 6, 2011.

[†] Steven Schneider. Confidence, consensus and the uncertainty cops: Tackling risk management in climate change. *Seeing Further, the Story of Science, Discovery & Genius of the Royal Society*, The Royal Society and Harper Collins, London, 2010. pp. 24–443.

In medicine also, for example, a drug company must show a drug is safe; it cannot just assume that a new drug is safe with the burden of proof on the users to prove it unsafe. The null hypothesis is that the drug is unsafe. The testing is performed to illustrate that the drug is safe. If there is a relatively small amount of statistically significant evidence that a drug is unsafe, the null hypothesis that the drug in unsafe stands and the drug is not marketed. You need a large amount of evidence to satisfy the Food and Drug Administration (FDA) that a drug is safe or that the null hypothesis of unsafe is incorrect.

There is a very large amount of evidence that humans are causing global warming and very little, if any, to the contrary. Therefore, the hypothesis that *humans are causing dangerous global warming* would not be rejected and action should be taken. In fact, there are no peer-reviewed, credible studies that show humans are *not* causing dangerous global warming. This is out of tens of thousands of scientific studies performed over the past decade. In the case of the climate, many policymakers are ignoring basic principles of statistical inference.

The few errors in scientific studies or the few studies that do not support the hypothesis out of the thousands that do are often highlighted as if they were sufficient to cause rejection of the hypothesis that humans are causing dangerous global warming[*]. If this logic were used in medicine, only one or two adverse reactions out of thousands of successful treatments would keep a drug off the market.

Two things are obvious: First, a Type 1 error is preferable to a Type 2 error. The latter is inviting disaster. Second, while it is obvious from a risk management perspective that you should take measures recognizing the validity of the hypothesis, this is not the way the current political system works.

Paul Lewandowsky, discussing this same issue, pointed out the illogic of avoiding action because there might be some "uncertainty" in climate science. His analogy was eliminating uncertainty about what happens when you drive toward a brick wall at 50 mph. Yes, there is uncertainty regarding getting killed, but no one in their right mind would drive into a brick wall because the outcome is "uncertain." Similarly, no one in their

---

[*] A rough estimate comes out that less than 0.1% of peer-reviewed papers may challenge the anthropomorphic global warming alarm. See Rob Honeycutt, http://www.skepticalscience.com/meet-the-denominator.html (accessed February 12, 2011) for the calculation. There are close to 1 million scholarly climate change articles.

right mind should delay action on climate change because we don't know exactly how bad it is going to be.[*]

Appendix A addresses the "uncertainty" issue regarding the threat of climate change due to global warming caused by humans. It clearly illustrates the overwhelming support of the scientific community worldwide.

A future-oriented decision maker should be focused on avoiding a Type 2 error. But it appears at this time that the majority of the governmental decision makers are opposed to the actions necessary to avoid a Type 2 error since the really adverse outcomes will likely occur in the future when the current decision makers are no longer in office and are not likely to be held accountable. The short-term incentives are to delay action or do nothing and pass the risks and the recriminations on to the next generation. System theory indicates that delays in feedback loops will lead to instability.

But it is probable that program and portfolio managers and their senior manager peers will still be in their positions or at least at the same company 10+ years from now when the serious impacts of the relentless climb of CO_2 and related temperatures become apparent as to cause and effect—even more than today. It is difficult to currently attribute, at a high probability, a specific serious weather event to climate change, even though the number of annual serious events has been climbing regularly in concert with temperature increases. So program and portfolio managers need to use the classic principles of risk management and avoid making a Type 2 error by hedging the hypothesis: *humans are causing dangerous global warming.*

As Dr. Jim Hansen addresses in his book, *Storms of My Grandchildren,* he believes we need to recognize that we have already made a Type 2 error and need to restore the planet's energy balance by immediately reducing emissions significantly. Specifically, we must reverse the climb of CO_2 emissions and revert back to 350 ppm from the current 390 ppm.[†] His concern is his young grandchildren growing up and living in the middle of the twenty-first century in a world significantly less friendly than our current one.

In the discussions of whether or not action should be taken, the recognition that humans are causing dangerous global warming will eventually provide the basis for actions.

---

[*] Guest post by Stephan Lewandowsky, *Long Term Certainty,* www.skepticalScience.com (accessed February 6, 2011).

[†] James Hansen, *Storms of My Grandchildren* (New York: Bloomsbury), 166.

Appendix C: Risk Management[*]

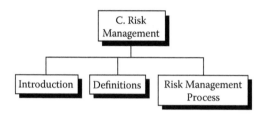

Appendix C outline.

INTRODUCTION

Risk management activities are designed to assist the project manager and team members in understanding project risks and the probability and consequences of failure, and to plan appropriate responses. In recent years, risk management has moved up in importance as project managers realize the benefits to be attained by an aggressive risk management program. Risks can be either internal or external to the project, and risk analysis addresses both good and bad (opportunities and risks).

Risk management is an ongoing iterative process that follows the life cycle. Risk planning is performed at a high level during the initial phases and at increasing levels of detail as the planning phase is implemented. Budgets and schedules are created considering risk mitigation, and project risk management techniques are used in the implementation phases of project. The results and effectiveness of the risk management activities are included in the final documentation of lessons learned.

Risk management activities include determining what is necessary to mitigate and control the risks. Risk planning consists of the up-front activities necessary to execute a successful risk management program. It is

[*] Haugan, Gregory T., *Work Breakdown Structures for Projects, Programs and Enterprises* (Vienna, VA: Management Concepts, 2008).

an integral part of normal program planning and management and is an ongoing activity that is performed throughout the project life cycle.

The nature of the implementation of a risk management program within a project depends on the size of the project and the level of the organization's maturity. Sophisticated schedule and cost risk software using Monte Carlo simulation and other tools is available. These tools operate as add-ons to the normal project management software. Like all tools, they follow and support the process.

DEFINITIONS

Risk is a measure of the inability to achieve overall program objectives within defined cost, schedule, and technical constraints. Risk has two components: (1) the probability of failing to achieve a particular outcome and (2) the consequences or impacts of failing to achieve that outcome. Or stated a simpler way: (1) the probability that the risk item will happen, and (2) the resulting impact on the overall project objectives.

Risk items are those events within the project that, if they go wrong, could result in problems in meeting the project's objectives. Risk items are defined to the degree that the risk and causes are understandable and can be assessed in terms of probability/likelihood and consequence/impact to establish the level of risk.

Technical risk is the risk associated with the evolution of the project work affecting the level of performance necessary to meet the specified requirements of the deliverable items or the operational requirements. In projects without explicit specifications, technical risk and quality risk are synonymous and refer to the risk associated with the ability to meet the customer's or sponsor's expectations or other quality criteria.

Cost risk is normally associated with the program's ability to achieve its life-cycle cost objectives. Two risk areas bearing on this definition of cost are: (1) the risk that the cost estimates and objectives are accurate and reasonable and (2) the risk that program execution will not meet the cost objectives as a result of a failure to handle cost, schedule, and performance risks.

Schedule risks are those associated with the adequacy of the time estimated and allocated for the project duration and delivery of required end items. Two risk areas bearing on schedule risk are: (1) the risk that the schedule estimates and objectives are realistic and not reasonable and (2) the risk that program execution will fall short of the schedule objectives as a result of failure to handle cost, schedule, or performance risks.

RISK MANAGEMENT PROCESS

Risk management process section outline.

The generic process for risk analysis is illustrated in Figure C.1. For simplicity, this book focuses on the four core steps in a risk management program. (Obviously, the first step is to plan your work and plan the risk program.) The Project Management Body of Knowledge (PMBOK®) guide includes a discussion of six processes, leading off with risk management planning and separating qualitative risk analysis from quantitative risk analysis. Other authors identify five processes.

RISK MANAGEMENT

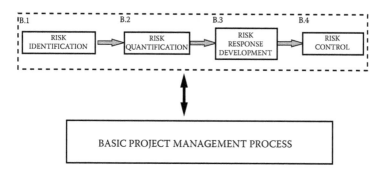

FIGURE C.1
Risk management process.

> *B.1 Risk Identification* consists of determining sources of risk and risk events that may be expected to affect the project.
>
> *B.2 Risk Quantification* involves determining which risk events warrant response.

The combination of these first two steps is a classic strengths, weaknesses, opportunities, and threats (SWOT) analysis that includes evaluation of internal and external factors in a performance audit. The internal performance audit examines the project's current performance in terms of meeting cost, schedule, and performance objectives, and projecting and forecasting likely future performance. It also involves identifying specific sources of potential degradation of the ability to meet project objectives.

Risk analysis and performance audits also include consideration of forces and conditions outside the project that may affect success in reaching project goals.

> *B.3 Risk Response Development* is the process of determining the specific actions to be taken as a result of the first two steps. This includes *avoidance*—eliminating a particular threat; *mitigation*—reducing the impact of the threat; or *retention*—accepting the consequences if they occur. Risk response development also may be positive, where opportunities, in addition to threats, are pursued.
>
> *B.4 Risk Control* is the process of initiating corrective action, such as implementing a contingency plan and constantly updating the risk management plan as the project is implemented and anticipated risk events occur or fail to occur.

One feature of the project management methodology that is the core of project management is the definition of critical control points (CCPs) during the Establish Checkpoints and Performance Measures* step. At each one of these CCPs, a risk analysis should be performed. In addition, risk analyses of varying comprehensiveness are performed as part of the activity at each of the other major steps.

Risk analyses are either quantitative or qualitative. Quantitative analysis is based on the use of the logic network, modeling, and probability analysis, and qualitative analysis is based on the knowledge, experience, and intuition of the project team members and stakeholders. The quantitative approach appears to be most useful on the larger projects where the value of

---

* Haugan, *Work Breakdown*. 97.

the output is consistent with the analysis effort required. Software is available to incorporate both types of analyses into a risk management program.

The types of risk fall into two general categories: scope risk and resource risk. *Scope risk* is the risk that the team will not be able to physically produce the project's deliverables that meet the performance requirements. *Resource risk* is the risk that the team won't be able to produce the deliverables on time, or within the staffing or spending limits specified by the sponsor. Projects with scope risk problems usually have resource risk problems as well.

The key to any risk management program is the ability to identify and evaluate risks. The two most difficult aspects to risk management are: (1) identifying the risks and (2) establishing priorities. This assumes, of course, that the project manager has the discipline to implement a risk management process.

Risk Identification

Risk identification deserves special attention. Common sense is involved, and the experience of the project team and other stakeholders is important in the identification process. The difficulty is that often there are too many choices. All of the activities on the schedule occur in the future, so there is some risk regarding schedule completion of every activity. No matter how the cost estimate was determined or the resource requirements estimated, there is some risk regarding the accuracy of the estimate—at every level.

If a work breakdown structure (WBS) was not used to define the scope, some important work may not have been priced. Each WBS element, work package, and activity has some risk. Many assumptions are always made in planning the project—for example, availability of funding or availability of key personnel or facilities—that add some element of risk.

Over 25 years ago an article in *Fortune* magazine featured a discussion with a senior manager from Lockheed regarding cost overruns on aerospace projects and why they occurred. The response was essentially, "It is not the unknowns that are the problem, but the unknown unknowns." This concept was also expressed by Defense Secretary Rumsfeld.* This is a

---

* On December 2, 2003, U.S. Secretary of Defense Donald Rumsfeld won the United Kingdom's Plain English Campaign's annual "Foot in Mouth" award for the most baffling statement by a public figure. Mr. Rumsfeld said in a press briefing, "Reports that say that something hasn't happened are always interesting to me, because as we know, there are known knowns; there are things we know we know. We also know there are known unknowns; that is to say we know there are some things we do not know. But there are also unknown unknowns—the ones we don't know we don't know." See "Rum Remark Wins Rumsfeld an Award" *BBC News*, http://news.bbc.co.uk/2/hi/3254852.stm (accessed May 14, 2010).

difficulty with risk analysis—that you identify all the major risks and the appropriate response and a totally unanticipated element arises. These are the *unknown unknowns*—the ones we don't know that we don't know, and your project is all of a sudden in trouble. It is important to recognize that this might occur; it also is important to have a risk management program so that those risks that are identified are effectively addressed.

Each project is unique and at the same time is similar to other projects, especially in the same organization. So this is where experience comes into play.

The intent of the risk identification step in the risk management process is to come up with a list of all the sources of risk and risk events that may be expected to affect the project significantly. This can be accomplished in many ways. Some items may come from the "lessons learned" document prepared at the completion of other projects in the organization. The preferred approach is to use the project team and as many other experienced persons and stakeholders as possible in the process.

Each risk item has two factors associated with it: (1) the probability that the risk event will occur and a stated requirement is not met and (2) the severity of the impact of the risk event on the project objectives.

Risk identification is accomplished by an organized and comprehensive survey of all project areas that could engender risk to the project. To encompass the entire project, project key elements are reviewed.

In these meetings, the typical documents and plans to be reviewed include:

- Statements of work and delivery requirements
- Contract requirements
- Performance specifications
- Work breakdown structure
- Test and evaluation plans
- Master schedules
- Management plans
- Production and facility plans
- Experience from similar projects
- Lessons learned documents

Risk Assessment

Risk assessment is a process by which potential problems and identified risks are analyzed and quantified to classify the risks according to their potential severity. This step can get very complex and sophisticated;

however, a simple exercise can be used to identify and establish priorities for risk items on small to medium projects:

1. Assemble the project team and others. Assign a facilitator.
2. Use the WBS as a framework and brainstorm a list of possible risk elements. Do not be restricted to the WBS, but use it as a place to start discussion. Use other documents as well.
3. List the potential risk items on a flipchart. The order is not important at this step.
4. For each risk item on the list, assign a probability number of the likelihood of it happening.
5. For each risk item, assign a number from 1 to 5 to indicate the degree of the impact on the project should the risk occur. The higher the number, the higher the impact.
6. For each risk item, multiply the risk probability by the risk impact factor to arrive at a risk index.
7. Rank the items by the risk index. The higher number would be the most risky.
8. Discuss and identify reasonable responses to reduce the threat posed by each risk.

This is a "poor man's" approach to risk identification, quantification, and response development—the first three steps in the risk management process of Figure C.3. One of the most valuable outputs of this exercise is the focus of the project team, at least for a short time, on where the risks are and it provides a rough basis for ranking. This is important input to the project manager and also starts the process of continuous risk evaluation.

You can use these steps for assessing risk for any type of project—simple or complex, small or large. Leading the team through the steps builds understanding of what the potential problems might be and agreement about how the team will prevent them from occurring.

This is the approach used to develop the risk matrix presented at the end of each "Threat" section of the SWOT analysis for each chapter power source in Part 3, "Energy Overlay." Table C.1 presents the template.

Developing a Risk Response

After the program's risks have been identified, assessed, and ranked, the approach to handling each significant risk must be developed (Step 8 in

TABLE C.1

Risk Matrix Template

Item Number	Risk Event	P1	P2	Px
1				
2				
3				
4				
Etc.				

Note: P1 = likelihood of risk event occurring; P2 = probable impact on the industry if P1 occurred; Px = risk index (product of P1 and P2, used to assign ranking)

the exercise). There are essentially four techniques or options for handling risks: avoidance, control, transfer, and assumption. For all identified risks, the various handling techniques should be evaluated in terms of feasibility, expected effectiveness, cost and schedule implications, and the effect on the objectives of the project.

For the items classified as high risk, as well as selected medium-risk items, a solution is prepared and documented. A comprehensive solution for a major potential problem could include the following: what must be done, the level of effort and materials required, the estimated cost to implement the plan, a proposed alternative schedule showing the proposed start date, the time phasing of significant risk-reduction activities, the completion date, recommended metrics for tracking the action, a list of all assumptions, and the person responsible for implementing and tracking the selected option. Making sure that someone is responsible for the action, and that the person is aware that he or she is responsible, is an important step.

Risk Control

Assigning individual responsibility for each risk item is crucial to effective risk monitoring. Project team members are the "front line" for obtaining indications that risk-handling efforts are achieving their desired effects. Each person is responsible for monitoring and reporting the effectiveness of the handling actions for the risks assigned.

Risk will be made an agenda item at each project review, providing an opportunity for all concerned to offer suggestions for the best approach to managing it. Communicating risk increases the program's credibility and allows early actions to minimize adverse consequences or impacts.

TABLE C.2

Risk Item Watch List Template

Item Number	Risk Item	Risk Reduction Actions	Responsible Person	Due Date	Date Complete	Notes
1.						
2.						
Etc.						

A *watch list* should be prepared that includes all the identified risks, risk-reduction actions, responsible person, and current status. Table C.2 presents a sample format. The column widths of course need to be adjusted to the contents.

Appendix D: Geology and Climate Change

The Geological Society of London (http://www.geolsoc.org.uk) is a learned society and professional body. It is the oldest national geological society in the world and arguably the first single-science discipline society. It was formed on 13 November 1807 and currently has 10,500 members (Fellows), 2000 of whom live overseas. It is a publisher of geoscientific content (see Lyell collection, http://www.geolsoc.org.uk/gsl/publications/lyellcollection) and runs scientific discussion meetings. For more information, see http://www.geolsoc.org.uk/index.html.

It has prepared a position statement on climate change, focusing specifically on summarizing the geological evidence.[*]

GEOLOGY SOCIETY OF LONDON POSITION STATEMENT

The geological record contains abundant evidence on the ways Earth's climate has changed in the past and provides important clues on how it may change in the future. Their statement is based on geological evidence, not on recent temperature or satellite data or climate model projections and is summarized below.

The Earth's temperature changes naturally over time scales ranging from decades, to hundreds of thousands, to millions of years. In some cases these changes are gradual and in others abrupt. Evidence for climate change is preserved in a wide range of geological settings, including marine and lake sediments, ice sheets, fossil corals, stalagmites, and fossil tree rings. Cores drilled through the ice sheets yield a record of polar temperatures and atmospheric composition ranging back 120,000 years in Greenland and 800,000 years in Antarctica. Oceanic sediments preserve a record reaching back tens of millions of years, and older sedimentary rocks extend the record to hundreds of millions of years.

---

[*] Policy Statement from the Geological Society of London, http://www.geolsoc.org.uk/gsl/views/policy_statements/climatechange (accessed November 4, 2010).

Evidence from the geological record is consistent with the physics that shows that adding large amounts of carbon dioxide to the atmosphere warms the world and may lead to higher sea levels, greatly changed patterns of rainfall, increased acidity of the oceans, and decreased oxygen levels in seawater. Life on Earth has survived large climate changes in the past, but extinctions and major redistribution of species have been associated with many of them. When the human population was small and nomadic, a rise in sea level of a few meters would have had very little effect. With the current and growing global population, much of which is concentrated in coastal cities, such a rise in sea level would have a drastic effect on our complex society, especially if the climate were to change as suddenly as it has at times in the past.

Sudden climate change has occurred before. About 55 million years ago, at the end of the Paleocene, there was a sudden warming event in which temperatures rose by about 6°C globally and by 10–20°C at the poles.[*] This warming event, called the Paleocene-Eocene Thermal Maximum or PETM, was accompanied by a major release of 1,500 to 2,000 billion tons or more of carbon into the ocean and atmosphere. This injection of carbon may have come mainly from the breakdown of methane hydrates beneath the deep sea floor, perhaps triggered by volcanic activity superimposed on an underlying gradual global warming trend that peaked some 50 million years ago in the early Eocene.

CO_2 levels were already high at the time, but the additional CO_2 injected into the atmosphere and ocean made the ocean even warmer, less well oxygenated and more acidic, and was accompanied by the extinction of many species on the deep sea floor. It took the Earth's climate around 100,000 years or more to recover, showing that a CO_2 release of such magnitude may affect the Earth's climate for that length of time.

The most recent estimates suggest that between 5.2 and 2.6 million years ago, the carbon dioxide concentrations in the atmosphere reached between 330 and 400 ppm, equivalent to today's levels. During those periods, global temperatures were 2 to 3°C higher than now, and sea levels were higher than now by 30 to 75 feet, implying that global ice volume was much less than today. The Arctic Ocean may have been seasonally free of sea ice.

Human activities have emitted over 500 billion tons of carbon to the atmosphere since around 1750. In the coming centuries, continued emissions of carbon could increase the total to 1500 to 2000 billion tons—close

---

[*] Multiply by 1.8 to convert centigrade to Fahrenheit.

to the amounts added during the 55 million year warming event. The geological evidence from the 55 million year event and from earlier warming episodes suggests that such an addition is likely to raise average global temperatures by at least 5 to 6° C, and possibly more. Recovery of the Earth's climate in the absence of any mitigation measures could take 100,000 years or more. In the light of the geological evidence presented it is reasonable to conclude that emitting further large amounts of CO_2 into the atmosphere over time is likely to be unwise, uncomfortable though that fact may be.

The theory on which the truth of this position depends appears to me so extremely clear that I feel at a loss to conjecture what part of it can be denied.*

---

* Malthus, *An Essay*, Chapter 2, 12.

Acronyms and Abbreviations

ABWR: advanced breeder water reactor
AFC: alkaline fuel cell
ANWR: Arctic National Wildlife Refuge
BAU: business as usual
BPA: Biomass Power Association
BtCO$_2$: billion tons of carbon dioxide
BTL: biomass-to-liquids
BTO: Biotechnology Industry Organization
BWR: breeder water reactor
CAA: Clean Air Act
CAFÉ: Corporate Average Fuel Economy
CAIR: Clean Air Interstate Rule
CBO: Congressional Budget Office
CCGT: combined cycle gas turbine
CCP: critical control points
CCS: carbon capture and storage
CH$_4$: methane
CHP: combined heat and power
CHP: cogenerator heat and power
CNG: compressed natural gas
CO$_2$: carbon dioxide
CRS: Congressional Research Service
CTL: coal to liquids
CWA: Clean Water Act
DBT: design basis threat
DMFC: direct-methanol fuel cell
DOE: Department of Energy
DRB: demonstrated reserve base (Coal)
E10: Fuel containing 10% ethanol and 90% gasoline by volume
E85: Fuel containing a blend of 70% to 85% ethanol and 15% to 30% gasoline by volume
EGS: engineered (enhanced) geothermal systems
EGS: enhanced geothermal systems
EIA: U.S. Energy Information Administration
EOR: enhanced oil recovery

EPA: U.S. Environmental Protection Agency
EPIA: European Photovoltaic Industry Association
EU: European Union
FCV: fuel cell vehicles
FEMP: Federal Energy Management Program
FERC: Federal Energy Regulatory Commission
FFV: flex-fuel vehicle
FGD: flue gas desulfurization
GDP: gross domestic product
GHG: greenhouse gas
GIF: Generation IV International Forum (Nuclear Energy)
gigaton: billion tons
GRACE: Gravity Recovery and Climate Experiment (German and NASA Satellite)
GRI: Gas Research Institute (Illinois Institute of Technology)
GTL: gas-to-liquids
HDNGV: heavy-duty natural gas vehicle
HEV: hybrid electric vehicle
IAEA: International Atomic Energy Agency
IFR: integral fast reactor
IGCC: integrated gasification combined cycle
INPRO: International Project on Innovative Nuclear Reactors and Fuel Cycles
IPCC: Intergovernmental Panel on Climate Change
ITC: investment tax credit
K: Kelvin (temperature scale that has absolute zero as the base, centigrade degrees)
kW: kilowatt, 1000 watts
kWh: kilowatt-hour
LCFS: low-carbon fuel standard
LED: light-emitting diode
LEU: low-enriched uranium
LNG: liquefied natural gas
LPG: liquid petroleum gas
LWR: light water reactor
m: meter
MBD: million barrels per day
MCFC: molten-carbonate fuel cell
MHEV: micro-hybrid electric vehicle

mpg: miles per gallon
MW: megawatts
MWe: megawatts, electric power
N₂O: nitrous oxide
NAFTA: North American Free Trade Agreement
NAS: National Academy of Sciences
NEA: Nuclear Energy Association
NEMS: National Energy Modeling System (EIA)
NGL: natural gas liquids
NGPL: natural gas plant liquids
NIMBY: not in my backyard
NPP: nuclear power plants
NRC: Nuclear Regulatory Commission
OECD: Organization for Economic Cooperation and Development
OPEC: Organization of the Petroleum Exporting Countries
PAFC: phosphoric acid fuel cell
PBMR: pebble bed modular reactor
PEMFC: polymer exchange membrane fuel cell
PHEV: plug-in hybrid electric vehicle
PV: photovoltaic (solar)
RES: Renewable Energy Standards
RFG: reformulated gasoline
RFS: Renewable Fuel Standards
RPS: Renewable Portfolio Standard
RTF: Royalty Trust Fund
SAE: Society for Automotive Engineers
SCR: selective catalytic control equipment
SF₆: sulfur hexafluoride
SO₂: sulfur dioxide
SOFC: solid oxide fuel cell
SUV: sport utility vehicle
TAPS: Trans Alaska Pipeline System
TSI: Total Solar Irradiance
TV: television
TWh: trillion watt-hours
USGS: U.S. Geological Survey
VMT: vehicle miles traveled
W: watt
WNA: World Nuclear Association

Glossary

aerosol: A gaseous suspension of fine particles or liquids.

albedo: The fraction of the sun's radiation reflected from the surface of the Earth.

Btu Content:

Physical Unit	Btu Equivalent
Barrel (42 gallons) of crude oil	5,800,000 Btu
Gallon of gasoline	124,000
Gallon of diesel fuel	139,000
Gallon of heating oil	139,000
Barrel of residual fuel oil	6,287,000
Cubic foot of natural gas	1,028
Gallon of propane	91,000
Short ton of coal	19,988,000
Kilowatt-hour of electricity	3,412

electricity: Electricity production and consumption are most commonly measured in kilowatt-hours (kWh). A kilowatt-hour means 1 kilowatt (1,000 watts) of electricity produced or consumed for 1 hour. One 50-watt light bulb left on for 20 hours consumes 1 kilowatt-hour of electricity (50 watts × 20 hours = 1,000 watt-hours = 1 kilowatt-hour). The average American household consumes about 10,000 kWh annually. Most readers of this book use approximately twice that figure.

energy conversion ratio: The amount of output of a solar panel divided by the solar input from the sun. Input is measured in watts per square meter.

gigaton: one billion tons

gigawatt: A unit of electric-generating capacity, equal to 1 billion watts. One gigawatt of generating capacity is enough to power about 800,000 average American households.

insolation: Amount of sunshine or solar radiation that reaches the Earth.

irradiance: The sending forth of radiant light; sunshine.

joule: A measure of the quantity of energy; a unit of electrical energy equal to the work done when a current of 1 ampere is passed through a resistance of 1 ohm for 1 second; or a unit of energy equal to the work done when a force of 1 newton acts through a distance of 1 meter.

Kelvin: A temperature scale where zero degrees K equals absolute zero. One Kelvin degree equals one Celsius degree. Water freezes at 273.15 K and it boils at 373.15 K. Absolute zero is therefore –273.15 Celsius.

metric ton: 1,000 kilograms = 2,205 pounds

OECD member countries: United States, Canada, Mexico, Austria, Belgium, Chile, Czech Republic, Denmark, Finland, France, Germany, Greece, Hungary, Iceland, Ireland, Italy, Luxembourg, the Netherlands, Norway, Poland, Portugal, Slovakia, Spain, Sweden, Switzerland, Turkey, the United Kingdom, Japan, South Korea, Australia, and New Zealand.

OPEC: Organization of the Petroleum Exporting Countries (OPEC): Algeria, Angola, Ecuador, Iran, Iraq, Kuwait, Libya, Nigeria, Qatar, Saudi Arabia, the United Arab Emirates, and Venezuela.

short ton: 2,000 pounds

tropopause: The boundary between the troposphere and the stratosphere, varying in altitude from approximately 5 miles at the poles to approximately 11 miles at the equator.

troposphere: The lowest region of the atmosphere below the tropopause. It is characterized by decreasing temperature with altitude.

turbidity: The amount of pollution, smoke, or fog that exists.

watt: An International System unit of power equal to 1 joule per second. In simpler terms, the amount of power put out by a 1-watt light bulb.

watts per square meter (W/sq M): The amount of power falling on an area of 1 square meter (or 1550 square inches).

Bibliography

Allison, I., N. L. Bindoff, R. A. Bindschadler, et al. *The Copenhagen Diagnosis*. Elsevier: Burlington, MA, 2009.

Updating the World on the Latest Climate Science. Sidney, Australia: University of New South Wales Climate Change Research Centre, 2009.

Archer, David. *The Long Thaw*. Princeton, NJ: Princeton University Press, 2009.

Bowen, Mark. *Thin Ice: Unlocking the Secrets of Climate in the World's Highest Mountains*. New York: Henry Holt and Company, 2005.

Bryson, Bill, ed. *Seeing Further: The Story of Science, Discovery & the Genius of the Royal Society*. London: The Royal Society and Harper Collins, 2010.

Campbell, Colin J. *The Coming Oil Crisis*. Brentwood, Essex UK: Multiscience Publishing Company, 1997.

Cohen, Joel E. *How Many People Can the Earth Support?* New York: W. W. Norton and Company, 1995.

Craven, Greg. *What's the Worst That Could Happen? A Rational Response to the Climate Change Debate*. New York: Penguin Group, 2009.

Cribb, Julian. *The Coming Famine: The Global Food Crisis and What We Can Do to Avoid It*. Berkeley CA: University of California Press, 2010.

Deffeyes, Kenneth S. *Hubberts's Peak: The Impending World Oil Shortage*. Princeton, NJ: Princeton University Press, 2009.

Diamond, Jared. *Collapse: How Societies Choose to Fail or Succeed*. New York: Penguin Books, 2005.

Downey, Ken. "Executive Summary." In *Fueling North America's Energy Future: The Unconventional Natural Gas Revolution and the Carbon Agenda*. Cambridge, MA: HIS-Cambridge Energy Research Associates, 2010.

Flannery, Tim. *The Weather Makers: How Man Is Changing the Climate and What It Means for Life on Earth*. New York: Atlantic Monthly Press, 2005.

Friedman, Thomas L. *Hot, Flat, and Crowded: Why We Need a Green Revolution and How It Can Renew America*. New York: Farrar, Straus and Giraux, 2008.

Froggatt, Antony, and Glada, Lahn. "Lloyd's 360 Risk Insight." In *Sustainable Energy Security, Strategic Risks and Opportunities for Business*. London, UK: Chatham House White Paper, 2010.

General Accounting Office. *Crude Oil: Uncertainty About Future Oil Supply Makes It Important to Develop a Strategy for Addressing a Peak and Decline in Oil Production*, Report GAO-07-293, Washington, DC: U.S. Government Printing Office, February 2007.

Gore, Al. *Our Choice: A Plan to Solve the Climate Crisis*. Emmaus, PA: Rodale Press, 2009.

Grant, Lindsey. *Too Many People*. Santa Ana, CA: Seven Locks Press, 2000.

Hansen, James. *Storms of My Grandchildren*. New York: Bloomsbury, 2009.

Haugan, Gregory T. *Work Breakdown Structures for Projects, Programs and Enterprises*. Vienna, VA: Management Concepts, 2008.

Haugan, Gregory T. *Project Management Fundamentals: Key Concepts and Methodology*, 2nd ed. Vienna, VA: Management Concepts, 2011.

Heinberg, Richard. *Power Down*. Gabriola Island, BC, Canada: New Society Publishers, 2004.

Helm, Dieter, and Cameron Hepburn, eds. *The Economics and Politics of Climate Change.* New York: Oxford University Press, 2009.

Henson, Robert. *The Rough Guide to Climate Change*, 2nd ed. Strand, London: Penguin Books, 2008.

Hoggan, James. *Climate Cover-Up: The Crusade to Deny Global Warming.* Vancouver, BC, Canada: Greystone Press, 2009.

Holland, Heinrich, and Petersen, Ulrich. Living dangerously: The Earth, its resources, and the environment. New Jersey: Princeton University Press, 1995.

Hulme, Mike. *Why We Disagree About Climate Change: Understanding Controversy, Inaction and Opportunity.* New York: Cambridge Press, 2009.

Intergovernmental Panel on Climate Change (IPCC). Contribution of Working Group I to the Fourth Assessment Report of the Intergovernmental Panel on Climate Change (IPCC4). In *Climate Change 2007: The Physical Science Basis.* Edited by S. Solomon, D. Qin, M. Manning, Z. Chen, M. Marquis, K. B. Averyt, M. Tignor, and H. L. Miller. New York: Cambridge University Press, 2007.

Intergovernmental Panel on Climate Change (IPCC). Contribution of Working Group II to the Fourth Assessment Report of the IPCC (IPCC4), Martin Parry and Osvaldo Canziani, co-chairs. In *Climate Change 2007, Impacts, Adaptation and Vulnerability.* New York: Cambridge University Press, 2007.

Klugman, Jeni. *The Real Wealth of Nations: Pathways to Human Development. Human Development Report 2010.* New York: United Nations Development Program and Palgave Macmillan, 2010.

Kotkin, Joel. *The Next Hundred Million: America in 2050.* New York: Penguin Press, 2010.

Krupp, Fred, and Miriam Horn. *Earth: The Sequel.* New York: W. W. Norton & Company, 2008.

Kunstler, James Howard. *The Long Emergency.* New York: Atlantic Monthly Press, 2005.

Lynas, Mark. *Six Degrees: Our Future on a Hotter Planet.* Washington, DC: National Geographic Society, Harper Collins, 2008.

Malthus, Thomas Robert. *An Essay on the Principle of Population, 1798.* Lexington, Kentucky: Maestro Reprints, 2010.

Mann, Michael. *The hockey stick and the climate wars.* New York: Columbia University Press, 2012.

Mann, Michael E., and Lee R. Kump. *Dire Predictions: Understanding Global Warming.* New York: DK Publishing, 2008.

Mastrandrea, Michael D., and Stephen H. Schneider. *Preparing for Climate Change.* Cambridge, MA: MIT Press, 2010.

McEwan, Ian. *Solar.* New York: Nan A. Talese/Doubleday, 2010.

Mitchell, Alanna. *Sea Sick: The Global Ocean in Crisis.* Toronto, Ontario: McClelland and Stewart, 2009.

Moniz, Ernest J., Henry D. Jacoby, Anthony J. M. Meggs, Co-Chairs, *MIT Study on the Future of Natural Gas, Interim Report.* Cambridge, MA: MIT Energy Initiative, 2010.

National Research Council. *Informing an Effective Response to Climate Change.* Washington, DC: National Academies Press, 2010.

National Research Council. *Limiting the Magnitude of Future Climate Change.* Washington, DC: National Academies Press, 2010.

Oreskes, Naomi, and Erik M. Conway. *Merchants of Doubt: How a Handful of Scientists Obscured the Truth on Issues from Tobacco Smoke to Global Warming.* New York: Bloomsbury Press, 2010.

Orr, David. *Fundamentals of Applied Statistics and Surveys.* New York: Chapman and Hall, 1995.

Pearce, Fred. *When the Rivers Run Dry.* Boston: Beacon Press, 2006.

Pearce, Fred. *With Speed and Violence*. Boston: Beacon Press, 2007.

Pearce, Fred. *The Coming Population Crash and Our Planet's Surprising Future*. Boston: Beacon Press, 2010.

REN21. 2010. *Renewables 2010 Global Status Report*. Paris: REN21 Secretariat, 2010.

Roberts, Paul. *The End of Oil*. New York: Houghton Mifflin Co., 2005.

Rodhe, Henning, and Robert Charlson. eds. *The Legacy of Svante Arrhenius: Understanding the Greenhouse Effect*. Stockholm, Sweden: Royal Swedish Academy of Sciences, 1997.

Sandford, John. *Heat Lightning* (fiction). New York: G. P. Putnam's Sons, 2008.

Smith, Laurence C. *The World in 2050: Four Forces Shaping Civilization's Northern Future*. New York: Dutton, Penguin Group, 2010.

Spencer, Roy W. *Climate Confusion: How Global Warming Hysteria Leads to Bad Science, Pandering Politicians and Misguided Policies that Hurt the Poor*. New York: Encounter Books, 2008.

Steiner, Christopher. *$20 per Gallon: How the Inevitable Rise in the Price of Gasoline Will Change Our Lives for the Better*. New York: Grand Central Publications, 2009.

Ward, Bud, National Science Foundation. *Communicating on Climate Change: An Essential Resource for Journalists, Scientists, and Educators*. Narragansett, RI: Metcalf Institute for Marine & Environmental Reporting, 2008, http://www.metcalfinstitute.org.

Washington, Haydn, and John Cook. *Climate Change Denial: Heads in the Sand*. London: Earthscan Publishing, 2011.

Weart, Spencer R. *The Discovery of Global Warming*. Cambridge, MA: Harvard University Press, 2008.

Weeks, John R. *Population: An Introduction to Concepts and Issues, Tenth Edition*. Belmont, CA: Wadsworth Cengage Learning, 2008.

Worth, Kenneth D. *Peak Oil and the Second Great Depression (2010–2030)*. LaVergne, TN: The Outskirts Press, 2010.

Yaukey, David, Douglas L. Anderton, and Jennifer Hickes Lundquist. *Demography: The Study of Human Population, Third Edition*. Long Grove, IL: Waveland Press, Inc., 2007.

Index

For Product Safety Concerns and Information please contact our EU
representative GPSR@taylorandfrancis.com
Taylor & Francis Verlag GmbH, Kaufingerstraße 24, 80331 München, Germany